T0267841

Spinning Spells
Weaving Wonders
Modern Magic for
Everyday Life

About the Author

Patricia Telesco has been a part of the Neo-Pagan community for over 30 years. During her speaking engagements across the U.S., Trish met many wise people working behind the scenes who blessed her with down-to-earth perspectives for going forward with books and life. Along the way, cooking at festivals led to writing more about culinary topics. The result has been very happy bellies for family and friends alike.

Food is love; food is hospitality. Food changes life, and life changes food.

Spinning Spells
Weaving Wonders

Modern Magic for
Everyday Life

Over
300
Spells

Patricia Telesco

Chicago, Illinois

Paperback ISBN: 978-1-959883-52-4
Library of Congress Control Number on file.

Disclaimer: Crossed Crow Books, LLC does not participate in, endorse, or have any authority or responsibility concerning private business transactions between our authors and the public. Any internet references contained in this work were found to be valid during the time of publication, however, the publisher cannot guarantee that a specific reference will continue to be maintained. This book's material is not intended to diagnose, treat, cure, or prevent any disease, disorder, ailment, or any physical or psychological condition. The author, publisher, and its associates shall not be held liable for the reader's choices when approaching this book's material. The views and opinions expressed within this book are those of the author alone and do not necessarily reflect the views and opinions of the publisher.

Typesetting by Gianna Rini.
Editing by Cole Brown.

Published by:
Crossed Crow Books, LLC
6934 N Glenwood Ave, Suite C
Chicago, IL 60626
www.crossedcrowbooks.com

Printed in the United States of America.
IBI

DEDICATED TO:

Religious freedom; that we might weave our spells, sing magical songs in the light of day, and say, "Never again, the burning," with conviction.

ACKNOWLEDGMENTS
FROM THE FIRST EDITION, 1996

As I WRITE THIS, another year has passed, and spring is in the air. In recent months, I have been fortunate to travel a little more and meet many wonderful magical people, each of whom has reminded me of the greatest gift of metaphysical traditions—harmonic diversity!

First, an enormous amount of appreciation goes to MayRose and David. Both people's patient, sensitive, and detail-oriented editing gave form and focus to these pages. Similarly, I am very grateful to Elaine and Linda for believing in me and in what this material represents.

Next, to Dorothy, Diana, Mindy, Colleen, Endora, Majel, and Katherine—thank you for becoming a part of my long-distance family. Your letters always bring a much-needed smile to my face and a brief respite from hectic days.

To Vinney and the gang at Spellbound Books, I have but one word to sum up my weekend with you: You! Thank you again for such lavish hospitality. I anxiously await my return visit. Oh, and by the way, Scorpios might sting, but Pisceans can swim upstream!

I owe thanks to my son, Karl, who has an innate ability to teach me more about magic than he realizes with his simple, trusting ways. Also, a special welcome to Samantha Elizabeth, born in April 1994. You are already a very special part of these pages, just for your carefree, loving smiles.

Finally, to those readers who have not been timid about asking questions regarding the art of spellcraft. Your reflective letters inspired many of the examples found in these pages. In this way, your search reached beyond your own hearth. What greater wonder can spiritual living offer than this opportunity to serve one another? Bravo!

Contents

APPENDIX A
COMPONENTS, SYMBOLS, AND
COMMON MAGICAL ASSOCIATIONS • 201

APPENDIX B
GODS, GODDESSES, SPIRITS,
AND HEROES FOR SPELLCRAFT • 216

APPENDIX C
HANDCRAFTING MAGICAL COMPOUNDS • 223

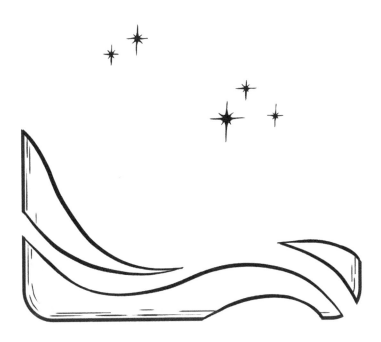

Introduction

*There need not be in religion, or music, or art, or love, or
goodness anything that is against reason; but never while the
sun shines will we get great religion, or music, or art, or love,
or goodness without going beyond reason.*
—Harry Emerson Fosdick

SPELLCRAFT IS NEARLY AS OLD AS HUMANKIND. Throughout
history, commoners and monarchs alike have looked to magic
for assistance in controlling the mysteries of the universe. When
someone known for magical skill could not be found, individuals
were left to design their own rudimentary rituals and spells,
using ingenuity and keen observation to guide them. Though
techniques varied greatly, depending on the originating culture
or individual, one universal theme came through mastering one's
destiny through supernatural means.

Common sense and sharp scrutiny of the natural world were the
integral elements that made early magical procedures truly potent.
Down through time, spells enacted by the majority of the populace
were usually not fancy, but they were meaningful. They were tied
to the moon, the seasons, natural cycles, and lessons learned from
the Earth. The chosen components were items readily available and
symbolic to the spell caster. With these empowered unions of mind
and soul, everyday life and people's spiritual nature stood hand in
hand, working for the betterment of the practitioner.

Modern magical traditions have not lost sight of this goal. Spell work is still a mainstay for Wicca and Paganism, two of the most predominant modern forms of magic practiced. Within spellcraft, however, there are many techniques to potentially apply, ranging from the intensive rituals of High Magic to the simple spells originating with folk magic.

Spinning Spells, Weaving Wonders presents spellcraft that has grown specifically out of the folk magic tradition, as it speaks to our world today—specifically our desire for creative, practical magic that meets everyday needs. Folk magic originated with sensible country dwellers who kept their spells unadorned out of necessity. Busy with farms and families, they had little time for lengthy, detailed ritual gatherings. Instead, their magic found a haven in everyday activities. Their deeply respectful attitudes made every spell and ritual, no matter how uncomplicated, an act of worship. This recognition of and appreciation for the sacred in everything is essential for enhancing our spiritual lives, too.

The contemporary preoccupation with elaborate procedures and trappings can sometimes impede results in spiritual realms. We need to free ourselves from the notion that fancy means better. It is not the packaging that determines the success or failure of any magical procedure; it is our intention and conviction. Keeping magic uncomplicated provides more time to focus on our goals instead of on the procedures used. By so doing, we reclaim the freedom to get inspired and empowered by the simplest things. Our hearts become the helms for our lives and our paths, and our environments become the stimuli for originality.

This approach generates wonderful, resourceful differences in our spell weaving. By using pragmatic folk magic as a substructure, spells become personal recipes to nourish our spirits. These recipes blend distinctive components from our own hearths into harmonious, potent magic.

The best spell recipes, however, are frequently those that we tinker with to suit the moment. There are many circumstances in our modern world that make it necessary to change a spell or to create a unique magical approach. Many enchantments handed down to us, while important to our understanding of history, no longer reflect the contemporary hearth and home. Their language, procedures, or ingredients may not be appropriate to our times. The words are often unnatural to our way of communicating; the movements may prove too awkward or precise to keep our minds focused on a goal; the components may not be safe, Earth-friendly, or available.

This means that moving magical traditions into the future requires innovative development and modification. The beauty of practicing a living faith is that our methods can and do change to reflect the transformations around us. One means to that end is to study the ingenious approaches of our ancestors and adapt them accordingly. In this way, our spells become a creative process motivated by tangible reality, our own discernment, and our current needs.

Intangibles also have a role in spellcraft. Some people may choose to call on divine entities or a universal power for aid. Others may call upon elemental or devic beings to assist the magic. No matter the approach, the visible and invisible worlds dance together throughout contemporary folk practices.

Many people who write to me worry that spellcraft is perhaps better left in the hands of magical practitioners with many years of experience to guide them. Consequently, they are hesitant to alter a given procedure or to design original spell materials. While their caution is sensible, it can hinder inventiveness that responds to the moment.

I wrote *Spinning Spells, Weaving Wonders* for these individuals and for others seeking good foundations upon which to build magical formulas. This material provides examples of solidly constructed spells that may be modified to more personal goals. Experimentation and adaptation are important aspects of ecstatic, Earth-centered beliefs that focus on personal vision over rote litany.

Additionally, these pages emphasize spellcraft as our birthright. Organized religions have clouded the true potency, longevity, usefulness, and charm of magical traditions. It is time to reclaim this treasure trove.

But how do we adapt old spells or invent totally new ones? What tools and symbols should be used? What timing is best? It is from this groundwork that this information begins.

Part One is a spellcraft primer, with information made available to immerse you in the basics. You'll discover material that provides a glimpse into the historical foundations for spellcraft, explores the nature of magic and spellcraft, and defines the basic tools and components for creating spells. There's also information that in Part Two provides step-by-step instructions on how to construct spells from scratch and how to personalize the spells.

Part Two is, in essence, a spell book in virtual form, alphabetized by topics that address a broad range of daily needs common to the human experience. I chose these topics by culling from my mail the questions that appeared most often and by asking friends around the country about what they'd like to see in a modern grimoire. The spells themselves derive from both ancient and modern resources and from a little experimentation. While these charms, spells, and amulets are complete as presented, they allow for considerable modification to suit your specific circumstances. I encourage you to personalize them to obtain the most meaningful results.

Finally, the material here includes three corresponding lists that will help with the personalization process. The first is a listing of potential spell components found readily in or around your home, along with their associated magical correspondences. The second is a topical list of gods/goddesses, spirits, and heroic figures you may wish to call upon to bless your spellcraft. Lastly, there are patterns and instructions for craft-related items through which your spells can find physical expression.

Spinning spells in the modern world requires taking our traditions in hand, getting resourceful, and making magic that is sensible here and now. Weaving wonders means finding ways to bless our reality twenty-four hours a day. Reading the information shared here represents the first step toward achieving both. Bright blessings on this tremendous adventure!

PART ONE

A SPELLCRAFT PRIMER

The most beautiful thing we can experience is the mysterious.... To know that what is impenetrable to us really exists, manifesting itself as the highest wisdom and most radiant beauty which our dull faculties can comprehend only in their most primitive forms—this knowledge, this feeling, is the center of true religiousness.

—Albert Einstein

Chapter One

THE NATURE OF MAGIC
AND SPELLCRAFT

The soul of music slumbers in the shell,
Till waked and kindled by the master's spell....
—Samuel Rogers

THE CURRENT PUBLIC INTEREST IN MYSTICAL ARTS and perceptions is not something new to our world. The desire to comprehend more than what one's senses can assimilate traverses time, possibly to the beginning of consciousness. During our evolution, all manner of objects and experiences must have made an impression on humankind. Everything from the color of the sky to a delicate aroma affected human feelings and demeanor.

Given our capacity to reason, our forebears found themselves with the difficult task of making sense of this information, assimilated from their own reactions to the world around them. To these early, curious minds, nature was truly alive. Thus, early people attributed spirits to the wind, the trees, and other aspects of their environment. This laid the groundwork for all religious belief systems to follow, especially magical ones, which are abundantly noticeable in animistic faiths.

Prehistoric cave paintings illustrate this, having been devised to bring success in the hunt. In the metaphysical sense, these paintings were a type of imitative spell used by an entire tribe, who gathered for one common goal: to bring these vivid portraits into reality. The belief portrayed by such actions is that like produces like. Therefore, painting a successful hunt sends out a sympathetic energy supporting that intention.

Animal costumes and masks common to early cultures prevailed for much the same reason. As noted by James Frazer in *The Golden Bough*, people used attire as a vehicle for magical mimicry. If one dresses as an ancestral god, it is a way of invoking that god. Or, if the tribe required an improved harvest, a shaman priest might have dressed in leaves and danced around the fields, jumping high into the air, hoping that the crops would follow that example by growing tall and full.

Each time a ritual technique was followed by a positive outcome—for example, the hunt was successful or the harvest plentiful—it became part of that tribe's traditions. These customs subsequently were handed down until they became an almost instinctive part of that culture's awareness. Exactly how that awareness manifested itself varied according to the time, the place, and the prevalent state of human evolution. In contemporary times, for instance, the notion of affirmative thought and action and the idea of "doing unto others" both illustrate elements of magical sympathy, neatly concealed in psychological or religious jargon, respectively.

Alongside the belief in living, willful nature spirits, early humans developed the concept of sacrifices and offerings. They hoped to discover ways to appease these powerful beings so that their clans could live in greater safety under that spirit's protection. In addition, other techniques were employed to attract positive attention from spirits. Three excellent examples of such techniques that still endure today are going to temple (i.e., sacrificing personal time for worship), dancing around sacred objects such as a fire or cauldron at Witchcraft gatherings (i.e., sanctifying the dancer or object, and raising power), and repeating specific words or sounds, as in chanting (i.e., to focus one's mind as in prayer). These approaches reconnect the seeker with universal powers (or God) and help channel positive energy.

With the emergence of great literate civilizations in Egypt (3000–30 BCE), Greece (800–300 BCE), and Rome (31 BCE–476 CE) came hundreds of books on dream lore, magical techniques, and a medley of folk wisdom, including spellcraft. Cultural expansion through commerce and exploration resulted in this written knowledge being carried around the world, adding to earlier oral traditions.

Historical Foundations for Spellcraft

From the chronicles of these long-forgotten times, the first foundations for modern magic were established and then built upon by philosophers, mages, and commoners. While a comprehensive history of spellcraft is beyond the scope of the information shared here, I do want to offer a few snapshots from spellcraft's rich history. This brief portfolio is intended to provide some insights into where specific ideas and techniques originated and how they continue to shape modern versions of spellcraft:

- The rod of Moses commanded the element of Water and conjured plagues on the house of Ramses. For the modern spell-weaver, this account equates with using a wand to direct and focus energies or a dousing rod for locating energies.

- When written language developed, the Egyptians called their hieroglyphs "the speech of the gods." The Greeks also respected writing to the point of veneration. In both cultures, anyone with the power to "capture" sacred words on paper was thought equally capable of brandishing them for formidable magical results. Oral and written components are still common elements in modern spellcraft.

- The Egyptians gave form to the first poppets (representative cloth dolls), which were marked precisely with a series of power words (the spell) for specific effects. For example, a poppet made from the clothes of a sickly friend, filled with protective herbs, and marked with an ankh (for "life") was a type of spell invoking wellness for that person. Poppets are still frequently employed by contemporary spell casters as props or focals.

- The Greek mathematician and philosopher Pythagoras lived from 582 to 507 BCE in southern Italy. Pythagoras utilized music as a spell component to render cures, foresee the future, and command the elements. This concept has been rekindled in New Age methods for improving one's focus during meditation and for enhancing vibrational energies.

- In ancient Rome, a spell designed to help Roman citizens preserve their peace accords required the public summoning of Jupiter while the priest or priestess struck a pig. The implication was that Jupiter would smite any Roman who dared to break their oath. This pantomime mirrors some modern spells wherein a physical change in components reflects the goal of the magic: for example, breaking a cigarette to "break" one's habit.

- Arabic peoples developed a unique approach to spellcraft: working with knots. This ancient method characterized spells as a web or network, with literal expression through string. The magician tied a strand or cord multiple times, sometimes with objects inside the knot, while speaking an incantation several times. If left bound, the knot kept energy trapped within. If loosened, the power was released toward its goal.

    This example illustrates two notable aspects of spell weaving that still endure. First is the use of common items for magic. Fishermen's nets and ropes were customary tools for early peoples. Since such tools were readily available, they were used for magic, too. Today,

Kitchen Witches and folk magicians utilize household paraphernalia similarly.

The second facet of spellcraft illuminated here is that of reiteration. Numbers have specific magical symbolism from which the spellcrafter draws more power. In knot magic, a specific count was always important, as was the repetition of power words. Contemporarily, a Witch's ladder exemplifies this tradition's endurance. This is a circle of string with forty beads and knots, contrived to aid one's concentration for spells. The practitioner repeats a spell, incantation, mantra, or other verbal element while tying a symbolic number of knots. The continuous echo of sacred words induces a semi-meditative state in which the spirit is free to commune with the divine and direct the ensuing energy beneficially.

- The potent characteristics of animals found their way into charms, amulets, and spells of the Renaissance (although they appeared much earlier, too). In Celtic regions, for example, hair from a woolly beast was added as a spell component in incense intended to reverse baldness. In contemporary magic, we still hear the term "familiar" regularly, which in some way continues this tradition and that of our animistic ancestors.

No matter the time or place, through periods of peace and persecution, magic and spellcraft have endured as a means of helping people take back the reins of their lives. Consequently, I believe that contemporary metaphysical techniques can be sustained and augmented by allowing the best lessons from the past to act as signposts today.

As spiritual seekers standing at the threshold of a new millennium, we, like our forebears, want to find prototypes for spellcraft that fit the changing face of our world and our own needs. Therefore, when time permits, I heartily encourage you to read more about the history of magic and spellcraft as you learn to create your own traditions.

What is Magic?

"It's a kind of magic." Someone said those words to me a long time ago when describing a folk spell. "It's really very simple and works almost every time," she exclaimed with excitement. Despite my respect for this individual, I couldn't fathom how a few words, a piece of paper, and some water could work together for my benefit.

I suspect almost everyone getting a first taste of magical procedures feels similarly. For logical, "sky is blue, trees are green" people, it is difficult to reconcile simple faith with the desire for verifiable proof. Yet, without belief in something, very little can be achieved in religious realms.

True conviction comes first from trusting yourself, second from an awareness of your spiritual nature and abilities, and third from an acknowledgment of the life force that is part of all things. Yes, it sounds simple. Inherent, intuitive things should be uncomplicated. There need not be any hocus-pocus about it.

Dictionaries define magic as the use of charms and spells to control events or forces, producing extraordinary results. To achieve this, some type of power source is necessary. Just as a battery makes a flashlight work, the energy of life around us makes magic work, and the universe is full of potency.

We know from basic physics and the law of conservation of energy that energy cannot be created or destroyed. It simply changes shape. Metaphysical techniques fashion this ambient life power and then direct it toward a specified objective. The exact methodology used depends on the path chosen by an individual, coupled with their own inventive approaches. Wording, movement, and tools vary from tradition to tradition.

Scientists in many disciplines agree that humans regularly use only a small fragment of the brain's potential. Our main disadvantage is not knowing how to mobilize those unused portions. Magic—and spellcraft in particular—provides one means for doing just that. In so doing, we open ourselves to universal energy, allowing it to flow in ways that help govern our present and future.

Consequently, magic makes each individual the principal partner in their own destiny. Teachers in all positive metaphysical traditions stress responsible, constructive use of knowledge and abilities. While the divine is available for guidance and direction in all matters, we manifest positive change in our lives by also calling on common sense and practical wisdom. Our greatest tools are two willing hands, a loving heart, and an open mind. Finally, but perhaps most importantly, magic allows us to set aside the tangibles for a moment and reach beyond into unseen realms. These spheres are not just within ourselves, but they span the universe and dimensions. Within the magical circle, a sacred space, we achieve a higher awareness of mind and soul and create a connection to the higher self, collective unconscious, or sacred energies. With this connection, a truly amazing understanding is achieved: we are divine, we have the power to control our destiny, and we are the magic!

IS MAGIC A RELIGION?

It is for some. A religion is any specific system of belief and worship, often including ethical codes. While some New Age systems base their ideas on soft sciences, a certain element of faith in a power outside our normal perceptions remains essential.

One may believe in a universal power without worshiping it. One can also attempt to use that power without embracing any specific laws of conduct. For this individual, magic would not be a religion.

Conversely, Wicca and other forms of Paganism are sacred belief systems that include the practice of magic. This does not necessarily make magic the religion, but it does give it a religious setting. Put aside the traditional views of religion for just a moment. Do not see lofty cathedrals, rows of pews, and Sunday morning services. Do not think of ministers preaching at the pulpit. Instead, look to your home and heart as God's residence.

Next, abandon the notion that magic is anything like what you have seen in Saturday matinees. True spirituality is not flashy lights and fancy words. It is the piece of starlight gathered by a trusting child, help given in selflessness, and those periodic wonders born from conviction. Magic is but one plow in a great field of sacred belief systems, and individual vision and expression steer it.

Knowing that you carry a divine spark in your soul, that your spirit is immortal, and that the world is a classroom for eternal lessons—this is the substance of magic. This knowledge cannot be quantified; it simply exists like an anchor to all spiritual endeavors. In this respect, magic within religion (or as a religion) is not secluded away in one corner of your life. It gives form and meaning to every moment of living.

Wicca and Paganism can be regarded as both religions and philosophies. Philosophically, we seek to relate to the universe through a system of ethics. Our religion provides those ethics. So, the questions remain: what constitutes magic as a religion, and how does someone express that principle in their life?

These are difficult to answer because New Age traditions are fundamentally devoted to harmonious diversity. We believe that each person's religious experience is unique. In effect, there could be as many versions of magic and spellcraft as there are people practicing this art.

Positive magical practitioners tend to follow three simple rules: never manipulate another's will, take care so that your magic doesn't harm yourself or others, and be aware that whatever you send out returns to you threefold (also called the Threefold Law). Almost every major world religion mirrors these precepts; the only difference is in the phrasing.

Additionally, modern magical creeds reflect a living, vital system of belief that grows with you. They confront both personal and world transformation with appropriate change throughout the practicing community. For example, animal sacrifice was sanctioned and common in many religious settings, including those of Mesopotamia, Egypt, Greece, and Druidical Circles. Yet no part of the creature would be squandered since wastefulness insulted the divine visage.

Today, however, many modern practitioners regard any use of animals (including eating meat) as distasteful. Why? Because greed eventually overcame the frugal, respectful methods and abused nature's resources. In response to the Earth's needs, the ethical guidelines of magic as a religion constrain us to fight for and protect those resources.

So, in essence, magic as a religion (or in a religious setting) strives to do what all religions hope to do: make us better people. It challenges us to be aware, to get involved, and to make a difference. Spellcraft's goal should be comparable: that of guiding the energy in and around our lives toward positive, fulfilling objectives.

SPELLCRAFT AND RESPONSIBLE MAGIC

What is a spell? Every person you ask this question will give you a slightly different definition. A spell is a will-driven mechanism through which a desired goal is achieved. The material world, however, plays very little part in attainment. Instead, the spell weaver combines words, symbols, and tools into ritualized forms to represent their purpose. The power raised by this procedure is then carefully directed either outward to the universe or to a divine entity to generate change.

When calling on a deity, verbally or mentally, to aid a spell, I recommend using the phrase "By your power, through my will" (or something similar) at some point. This phrase respectfully acknowledges a chosen divine visage for the potency they can bring. It also shows that you accept that the translation of energy is an act of free will, aided by a petition to the God or Goddess to manifest that will. This approach is one I use, having had positive results in my experiences. However, since the most important factor in magic is personalization, this strategy may not be appropriate for you.

Intuition also plays an integral role in the magical process, as does our subconscious (or perhaps "superconscious" is a better word for metaphysical matters—e.g., "going beyond"). Even so, using reason to formulate spells can be very helpful. The rational mind weighs our unique circumstances and then determines a functional construct for those circumstances.

The most productive and responsible spell weaving requires that we understand what we are doing and why we are doing it. This criterion necessitates us to mold spells into forms with substantive meaning in both our path and day-to-day reality. For example, if you have no discernment of runes and no emotional connection to them, you would not want to use a rune as a spell component. This would only confuse or derail your efforts.

Another example comes when we participate in group or public rituals. When you gather with people, each group will have its own way of enacting a spell. However, this doesn't mean you have to follow their lead. If others' actions or words make no sense to you, or if you are uninformed about the particular situation, quietly meditate and extend positive energy in the group's direction. This way, you do not have to compromise personal approaches or principles and can still aid others' efforts.

Along with comprehension, another important factor in spell-craft, and all magic, is personal culpability. The general rule is never to devise a spell that could potentially harm yourself or someone else. This means taking care not to exploit another's free will. It also suggests blending in a healthy portion of balanced judgment and sagacity for good measure.

There are very few scenarios in life where we can know all the external or internal factors at work. If we presume such knowledge, the magic created could produce all the wrong results. For this reason, keep the phrase "For the greatest good, and it harm none" (or something similar) as part of your working metaphysical maxims. This way, even if you have originated a spell that bungles the real point of need, your final words permit universal powers to step in with guidance.

Personal accountability also brings to bear the Threefold Law mentioned earlier. Like the Christian motto "do unto others," the Threefold Law warns that anything we send out will return to you thrice—if not now, then in our next incarnation. This admonition is not a slap on the wrist but a reflection of Universal Law demonstrating just how self-destructive the Left-Hand Path (Black Magic) can be. The Threefold Law encourages us to take care with our use of natural energies and again reminds us of the liability for our actions (or lack thereof).

Because external influences exist, not all spells will provide the results you expect. Sometimes, they outwardly appear to give anything but what you asked for. In one scenario, someone doing prosperity magic might suddenly find that instead of working less, more projects have appeared upon their desk. Once those projects are undertaken, however, they bring improved financial flow by way of a raise. This is one way that the universe keeps us honest, by requiring us to remain active participants in our own well-being instead of relinquishing our fate to some unknown source (and thereby abdicating real responsibility).

Last but not least, there are some guidelines for choosing spells prudently. This list of cautions is good to keep in mind not only throughout the examination of the material here but any time you read directions for a spell you might like to try:

- Never work in foreign languages if you don't have a fluent grasp of their meanings in untranslated form. Subtle changes in inflection and tone, let alone mispronunciation, can alter the meaning of a spell.

- Never execute a spell whose components or wordings make you uneasy or those that go directly against personal taboos.

- Never perform a spell that seems to manipulate or control another person's free will by its outcome.

- If any book says you must enact a spell in a specific way or promises that a spell will be one hundred percent effective, this should trigger a warning bell in your mind. No trustworthy writer makes such a broad-based claim without a reasonable explanation. For example, ritual magic generally requires more precision than folk magic. Writers in this field must be exacting in their instructions to present responsible material. Still, even ritual magicians sometimes adjust standard procedures so that they are more individually satisfying.

  Furthermore, while some spells prove useful to many individuals and other spells work better when rendered under precise circumstances, this is only a tendency. Knowing a spell has been successful for others can help us decide if we want to follow that same route. That doesn't mean we can't take personally meaningful detours along the way.

- Always review the construction of a spell to see if personalization is desired or needed.

The Human Factor:
Enabling the Energy

Folk magicians, sometimes called "Kitchen Witches," regard objects, symbols, and tools as handy, but not always necessary, props for Spellcraft. In spinning spells for everyday life, all the devices normally equated with magical procedures act as a support for our training. They lend character, ambiance, and feeling, but without the human factor, their potential lies inactive.

We become the enablers for latent natural energies when we choose the right components for the right job (see "Finding and Using Spell Components" below). If the prescribed props aren't available, however, that doesn't mean planned procedures come to a screeching halt. Instead, the enterprising magician applies creative elbow grease and finds an alternative approach!

Remember, it is not the complexity of a spell that makes it effective. Some people get trapped in the misconception that elegant words or intricate accouterments will determine the outcome of their magic. Nothing could be further from the truth.

In this respect, the term "folk magic" or "folk spells," meaning spells directed to daily concerns, can be misleading. It gives the impression that homespun techniques lack potency or are too simplified to work. The effect is the opposite. Because you devise such spells according to your personal vision, the results improve. Individually formulated magics focus their attention on relevant daily matters and can literally become the foundation for your entire faith.

What provides positive results in spell casting are your ability to concentrate, perseverance, and confidence. Other metaphysical procedures then augment these abilities. For example, meditation and visualization are two popular techniques that provide improved focus; they also settle your mind and spirit before attempting magical procedures. Another simple and commonly endorsed method of changing one's level of perception is breathing work, as oxygen carries vitality to every cell in our bodies. This, aided by image work, soothes the nerves and enriches our awareness.

Before beginning any spell work, start by getting comfortable. Next, envision the air around you as a color—something you find tranquil but also filled with restorative energy. Sparkling blue tones are a good choice. Close your eyes and picture that color swirling all around. Each time you inhale, the colored air transports cleansing energy throughout your entire being. Continue until serenity replaces tension.

Once you've achieved this calm resolve, set about the task of considering your spell. If possible, consult friends who can provide fresh perspectives. Look around your home with a creative eye to discover items that immediately remind you of your goal. These can become part of your spell as components, props, or tools.

Finding and Using Spell Components

Spell components are the ingredients that balance out your recipes for magic. These ingredients give flavor, form, and focus to your efforts and bring your intuitive abilities to the forefront. Magic, while sensible in its formation, works through the instinctive faculties rather than the logical mind. These same instincts will let you know when a spell has been rendered correctly. Like the still, small voice within, an assurance resonates in your mind and heart when magic activates.

Before moving onward to review some of the major constituents of folk magic, I think it is important to stress that you need very little for spells to work well. If you have the will and the concentration necessary, spells can be woven almost anytime, anywhere. This means that the most important ingredient in spellcraft is you!

Spell Focals

Something that keeps our mind on magic and adjusts all our attention toward a specific goal is a focal. One recognizable example is a crystal ball used for divination. Here, the surface of the ball becomes an area where the scryer fixes their eyes while concentrating on questions and eventually receives visions as symbolic or literal answers.

Sometimes, a focal is used in the preparation for spellcraft, and other times, it becomes a tool for directing energy. For example, a wand with a crystal affixed is an excellent implement to secure our concentration beforehand. However, it also can be wielded to assign and direct the spell, acting like a pointer on the chalkboard of the universe.

The latter approach holds tremendous merit if the object chosen is symbolic of your purpose. For example, you may choose to use your hand as a focus in energy for healing or support. For this, direct your energy into the hand itself, feeling it grow warm as it's empowered. Next, stretch your hand out toward the recipient (a photograph or personal item may substitute) to direct the power. This way, from settling your mind to the final act of releasing the magic, you have maintained a congruity of meaning. You also won't have to be distracted by stopping to pick up other tools.

Exactly what the focal will be for each person or each spell will vary. I would love to say that there are concrete rules to reference, but this is simply not the case. One person may find that candlelight improves concentration. Another might ascertain that darkness is bothersome and prefer natural lighting from outdoors. Neither individual is incorrect; they are using media appropriate to their way of thinking and reacting.

Sometimes, the nature of a spell itself will dictate the atmosphere in which to work, possibly requiring conditions that make your routinely exercised focus inappropriate. For instance, if you use thematic music to underscore the intention of your spells, there are still cases where silence would be a better choice, such as when preparing a charm to quiet gossip. Thus, it is good to practice with several types of focals, each chosen to coincide with your intention. Some examples follow.

Candles

Candles equate to the element of Fire. Inspiration, energy, purification, and change may be found in their flames. They also act as good meditative aids.

For this, observe the flame of a candle. Make it the center of your attention. Watch as it dances and twists while moving your breathing to a slow, steady pace. Eventually, your vision will blur; don't make an effort to clear it. Continue to keep the intentions of your spell in your mind. If you want to close your eyes at some point, follow that instinct.

To accentuate your intentions further, match the color of your candle to the goal, carve the wax with fitting symbols, and/or anoint it with a scented oil. For example, when enacting a spell to change negative habits, choose a black candle for banishing. Carve the rune of the warrior (Tyr for strength and determination) into the wax near the top and anoint that region with clove oil for power and transformation.

Next, extend your hands toward the taper while you visualize the habit leaving you and being burnt away in the fire. The candle will begin to smoke (from the oil) and eventually burn itself down past the carving. Your spell is now complete, and there is enough wax remaining for another banishing effort.

Music

A quiet instrumental piece is advantageous for centering. Consider the title, theme, and prevalent feeling of the music. You can keep this music playing throughout spellcasting.

For musicians, creating and playing music can become a spell unto itself. Many of the medieval bards, particularly Taliesin, created tremendous magic woven from the beauty of song or instrument. In this case, tuning and practice become the means to prepare yourself. Then, the final canticle blesses everyone who hears the enchanted energy floating on each note.

Consistently use the same music each time you render a spell of similar subject matter. Your subconscious will learn to recognize that musical pattern and immediately equate it with a particular type of energy. This will prompt a smoother shift in awareness.

Dances

There are many historical precedents for dance and sacred movement as a focus for spellcraft. In *The Sacred Dance* by W. O. E. Oesterly, the author explains, "*...but associate yourself with it [God], and already you are in an indefinable way in communion with it; you have in some sense made friends with it...*" (Oesterly 17). In other words, dance in a ritualized setting engendered a sense of oneness with the Great Spirit.

Since magic seeks to open the doorway to higher realms, dance and movement both offer ways to find the right key. The Sufi whirling dervishes, for example, turn themselves around in circular dances to achieve ecstatic states. Choose your own steps and movements, so they likewise engender a deeper meditative attitude where your mind can focus solely on your magical goals.

Art/Pictures

Images depicted through sculpture, photography, painting, and printing can become powerful focal points for magic. Like music, visual art is useful for composing yourself and/or as a magical channel. For best results, the artistic design needs to be personally meaningful and somehow representative.

Individuals who are able can use the creation process to formulate each step of their spell, helping manifest their will with the finished portrait, even as the ancient cave dwellers did with their art. For example, in ancient Egypt, someone working a prosperity spell may have added a money pouch to their figurine. A modern painter might instead depict "pennies from heaven" on canvas.

Objects

Any item in your home can become a focus for magic. Cultivating this imaginative eye is an essential part of becoming an adept folk magician. Everyday items are handy, comfortable, and already filled with personal energy from regular use. Good examples include the telephone for communication spells and an alarm clock for organization or alertness. Other functional examples can be found in the "Props" section.

Aromas

Incense, perfume, potpourri, fresh flowers, and open windows all offer fragrances that can heighten awareness. As with music, repeated use of a particular aroma in incongruous settings associates that scent with specific functions. When I do an auric cleansing, I always use homemade frankincense and myrrh oil on my hands. These oils are aligned with purification and are permeated with energy during their preparation. The fragrances immediately sets my spiritual tone and purpose.

To determine exactly which bouquet is best, look to a listing of herbs, flowers, and magical correspondences. Consider associated folklore or personal meanings to increase your options. For instance, a serenity spell for a loved one who has passed over might incorporate some of that person's favorite cologne. This way, the winds carry the scent of your magic as manifestations of activated energy.

Verbal and Written Elements

Once you have brought your mind, body, and spirit into harmony with your intentions and found symbols to portray those intentions, the next step is to give verbal or written form to your thoughts. Generally, it is good to conceive phrases before you begin establishing sacred space so your incantation articulates comfortably.

Historically, oral and written constituents united repetition, rhyme, and meter into a catalyst to expedite the magic's success. The lyrical component encourages a receptive state and improves the flow of unfettered energy.

Rhyme

Free-form poetry is a relatively new contrivance that didn't become popular until literacy increased. Before this, people heard epic stories in poetic form and memorized them. The rhyming words helped them retain the tale and then share it with others.

Rhyme, along with meter (discussed shortly), were exceptionally important to maintaining the integrity of oral history. Much of the Old Testament, for example, was originally preserved through oral tradition. Today, the work of temple cantors is a beautiful remnant of that heritage.

You can still find contemporary teachers using rhyme to help young children with memorization. Since this learning style has been with us since our youth, it is also very serviceable in a magical environment. If you don't have to read from a piece of paper, you are free to concentrate more fully. Also, have you ever noticed how rhyming jingles on TV tend to stay with you? This also will happen with your rhymed verbal components. Each time the ditty comes to mind, you are helping to reinforce the magic.

Your poems don't have to be literary masterpieces to function well. If you have trouble thinking of a good rhyme, look at children's poems and songs for a starting point. Use their basic construction, then substitute phrases that have comparable scanning (the same number of syllables in the same order).

Let's try this once with the nursery rhyme, *"See a penny, pick it up, all the day you'll have good luck."* This works just as it stands, especially if you use the penny as the focus for good fortune. If you wanted to be more specific or had a different purpose in mind, here are sample rewrites:

For Health:
See a penny in my hand,
now I plant it in the land.
Buried now, my cold to stay,
don't come back another day.

For Prosperity:
See a coin upon the ground,
surely more will come around.
To my pocket, it will fly,
so my money multiplies.

Meter

Meter has the same function as rhyme for improving memory, with one small difference. Certain meters have connotations to embellish your magical goals. One example is iambic pentameter (just read Shakespeare's sonnets). This poetry has a repeated series of five punctuated sections in a sentence, each section containing one short and one long accent. These syllables (and sometimes whole words) carry the verse from one stanza to the next like a wave.

From a magical viewpoint, the number two equates to partnership and balance, while five is versatility, awareness, and the points of the pentagram. So, if you were creating a spell to bring improved understanding in your relationship, a verbal component in iambic pentameter would be a perfect choice.

To determine the mystical implications of your meter, just count as you would through a musical score. A four-four beat is good for elemental magics and success, while a waltz rhythm (three-four) equates to the triune nature and symmetry.

Meter also has another function. In *The Sacred Dance*, the author discusses the importance of meter in sacred dancing (Oesterly 128). In the ecstatic dances of Arabia and Assyria, rhythm provided growing momentum through which people achieved an altered state of awareness. Drums, cymbals, clapping, and other percussive sounds can improve our trance states in the magical circle as well. For this, the cadence should move slowly at first and slowly increase as the energy builds. At the height of a spell, the sounds will be vibrant, giving life to the magic. When the power is released, silence should fall once again on the group.

Repetition

Mantras and chants dramatically portray the spiritual energies created by repetition. Both allow the potency of words to enfold us until the surrounding air vibrates with power. Each time we utter a spell, the words echo through our minds and strengthen our internal resolution. The combination of two senses—speech and hearing—continues giving guidance to the energies you create.

As with meter, the number of repetitions can be symbolic and harmonious with your magical aspirations. For example, try repeating the verbal component for love or partnership magic twice or a charm relating to prophetic vision seven times, and note the feelings you get. If a number has a different meaning for you (as with birth dates), please use that as your primary source of interpretation.

Visual Form

The most time-honored visual spell is "Abracadabra." Written on paper in a descending cone (see illustration), this charm gets tossed into running water so sickness will wane. Other phrases for banishing or diminishing use analogous construction systems. To the contrary, drawings for growth or strength spells are upright.

```
a  b  r  a  c  a  d  a  b  r  a
   b  r  a  c  a  d  a  b  r  a
      r  a  c  a  d  a  b  r  a
         a  c  a  d  a  b  r  a
            c  a  d  a  b  r  a
               a  d  a  b  r  a
                  d  a  b  r  a
                     a  b  r  a
                        b  r  a
                           r  a
                              a
```

Penned spellcraft has several predominant geometric figures, including squares, circles, and hexagrams. If you decide to use a shape, choose one that reflects your goals. For conception, a circle with a dot in the center, surrounded by the names of maternal goddesses, is an option worth considering. Or, if you prefer, use other meaningful emblems around the dot instead. Visual spells do not have to include words to be effective.

People throughout history and in many different lands carried the visual charms made for them by a priest or mage (or themselves) for protection and blessing. Alternatively, charms might be burned, buried, thrown to the winds, given away, or hurled into water. Each action had a symbolic purpose that varied depending on the mage's school of thought. Burying in earth equated to keeping something secure, hiding it from sight, or encouraging growth. Healers used soil, too, probably with the thought that sickness could filter through the Earth as easily as rain does. Burning the words made a problem visually disappear, the smoke relinquishing the supplication to the gods. Fire was also an emblem of drastic purification. Water equated to health, fertility, cleansing, and movement, while Air was activity, release, or lifting. Exactly how you decide to use any of these symbols is purely a personal choice.

Please note that many seals or talismans can be purchased inexpensively online and at many magical bookstores. I highly suggest, however, if possible, that you purchase such items in person so that you can get a "feel" for their energy and make certain the item is right for you.

Expressing Time Frames

The dictionary also defines the word "spell" as a span of time or activity. While not all magic works exactly as you specify, it is prudent to mention when the spell should begin taking effect, how long it should last, and when you need results.

If the spell doesn't manifest successfully when originally anticipated, there can be various reasons why. First, the magic may be subtle in its workings. This gives the outward appearance of nothing happening when change is really occurring. Second, your sense of "necessary" timing may not have been in your best interest. Love, for example, cannot be rushed or pressured if you want to achieve lasting results. Third, you may have expected too much too soon. Many things in life require gestation. Since magic works within natural laws, it is to those guidelines that spells must adhere to maintain equilibrium.

Calling on Divine Visages

A final ingredient of the verbal recipes for spells is that of divine names. As mentioned earlier, I reviewed the use of sacred names to empower a spell or as a supplication to aid your magic. You can also use them for setting your spell.

Setting in this context means putting the spell ingredients together and then using the name of a god or goddess to position them properly. For this, a phrase similar to *"By _____'s (insert appropriate god or goddess) hand I seal this spell"* can be used. This invites the power of a god or goddess to secure, sanctify, and protect your effort.

Empowering a spell is similar to setting. In fertility charms, I use the names of goddesses associated with maternal qualities. Since it is their domain to watch over mothers and children, the writing is an appeal for action. Your faith then supports that request.

In supplication, you are petitioning a specific god or goddess for their direct intervention in a cause. To this behest, you add the energy of your will and other components, trusting that your efforts will be answered.

Please note that divine visages should always be approached with an appropriately respectful demeanor. Honor their presences in your sacred space and upon your altar. Prepare small libations or offerings for them, appropriate to their characteristics, and always thank them when you've finished your work (and when you see manifestation).

Thought Forms

Awkward circumstances sometimes require silent spellcraft. Maybe paper and pen aren't handy; maybe you're in a public place where reciting an incantation is inappropriate. No matter the situation, remember that thoughts have power. Allow them to become your verbal elements by repeating a phrase over and over in your mind, like affirmations. Add to this process a productive visualization and a supportive spell later in private, and the outcomes can be just as dramatic as spells cast with all the extras, such as props and focals.

Props

Props have several different functions in spells, at least one of which, focals, has already been covered. Like focals, props can serve more than one purpose in a spell. Let's use a protective spell for a depiction. Suppose a candle is used to aid centering during a white-light visualization. The same protective energy generated by the visualization can be directed back into the candle at the same time. From now on, each time that particular candle is ignited, the taper will radiate safety and security. Essentially, the candle has become both a focal and prop thanks to the energy you stored there.

Props provide visual, auditory, and other sensory clarifications for your spell. They are the emblems of everything you hope to achieve. So, any changes you anticipate from the magic should also occur to your prop during casting.

The easiest way to characterize this is through a banishing spell. Here, you want an entity, habit, or negative energy source to withdraw. When you disengage your magic to work, remove the prop you have been using from your sight. This can be accomplished by covering, burying, burning, placing it in a box, or having a partner hide the item for you. In all cases, the object has literally disappeared, visually emphasizing the attainment of your purpose.

Almost anything can become a functional prop. The beauty of folk magic is that it neglects no opportunity to discover spiritual potential in the most mundane actions or objects. Thus, there is no limit to your range of choices other than what makes sense in terms of your intentions. Listed below are a few samples.

Colors

It is almost impossible to read metaphysical material without finding references to color symbolism. Colors act like subtle underscoring that delineates meaning to our subconscious mind. Just consider how different hues of paint make you feel. The range of emotions each elicits shows the extensive role color can conceivably play in spell creation.

Besides visualization, everything, including tablecloths, decorations, and lights, can be selected for their coloration. Also, items can be dyed during spell casting to portray a change in state. For instance, to bring tranquility to your life, add blue food coloring to chamomile tea and drink it to internalize the magic. Or you can color a piece of paper totally black, pouring all your negative emotions into it, and then burn the paper to stimulate the transformation in attitude.

Costumes

The old Dutch saying, "Clothes make the man," has an important bearing on magical procedures. What we wear influences how we feel about ourselves. It would be difficult to act in a businesslike manner at a work function if one wore jeans and a sweatshirt. Similarly, it can be difficult to enact magical rites in "normal" attire. Everyday clothing reminds us of mundane tasks instead of spiritual realities.

There are four ways this discomfort can be relieved: the use of robes or special clothing, donning jewelry, going skyclad (i.e., without clothing), and wearing masks. Simple robes can be spiced up a bit by painting or embroidery, and jewelry can be chosen according to its significance. A skyclad person effectively sheds the material world with their clothing. Finally, masks are helpful with imitative magic.

In this last instance, a mask mimics the spell's topic. When seeking out a familiar, a generic animal mask can be made. When performing a spell for rain, a cloud with blue teardrops might be designed. The idea is to become wholly unified with your purpose in action and appearance. This creates a sympathy that attracts similar sacred energy to achieve that purpose.

Herbs

Almost every natural object has been classified for its metaphysical characteristics. This is especially true for herbs, flowers, vegetables, and trees. From Hippocrates and Plato to Wordsworth and Yeats, many well-known thinkers and writers regarded nature as the perfect representation of divine and universal truths. Consequently, each living thing was itemized according to its sphere of influence, ruling planet, divine energies, and resulting uses. To the contemporary practitioner, this data is invaluable for creating anointing oils, incense, and other accents to their art.

Say you're adding an enchantment for kinship to a meal for special friends. You might choose to bake an apple-nutmeg bread (for love and commitment), served on a bed of lettuce (for peace). While you knead the bread and bake it, you can chant or sing an incantation. Then, when the bread is sliced, it will release the magic from within!

Knots

If you are adapting knots for magic, remember to keep in mind the symbolism of binding and releasing. Consider also numerical and color significance before you begin tying. Once you've tied the knots, leave them in sunlight or moonbeams to absorb energy. That allows the inherent characteristics of that light (the sun equates to the masculine, strength, and victory while the moon equates to the feminine, healing, intuitive senses) to saturate your prop.

The best part about rope spells is their longevity and durability. When you need to manifest that specific force, simply take the knotted rope from its resting place and untie one knot while focusing your will (possibly repeating a verbal component). Once you release the knot, your spell's energy takes flight.

Personal Items

For spells intimate to yourself or to someone else, it helps to have a personal token as either a prop or a focus. An alternative to this is a photograph. In both cases, the idea is to create a resonance between the natural energy of that person and the magic. That way, you can direct your spell specifically and accurately.

Paper

When the Egyptians started making paper out of papyrus, it was immediately used for charms, especially those for health or to protect the dead. For written components to function properly, the magician pens exact drawings of the sacred words or symbols while concentrating on specific intentions. Exactly what happens to the paper at this point depends on the intention of the spell. For more specifics, see "Visual Forms."

Paper is a very serviceable prop because it is recyclable and easily disposed of. Additionally, paper may be colored, folded (as in origami), mashed, shaped, dried, burned, or scented to accentuate the intentions of your magic. If possible, I suggest using post-consumer, recycled, or tree-free paper to honor the Earth.

Pointers

The assignment and direction of energy is an influential part of spell casting. Having an implement to guide your gaze and the energy you create toward your goal is a terrific asset. Lots of common household tools work for this, including wooden spoons, pencils, pot handles, or closed umbrellas. Other options consist of a wand, an athame, your finger, an arrow, or perhaps the hands of a clock. This last item would be exceptionally useful in conducting magic pertaining to duration, fate, or cycles.

Timing

Some magical traditions regard the exact timing of a spell as a necessity. To my thinking, however, if you can't get up at 2 a.m. to perform a spell suggested for that hour, then execute it whenever you can. As with other aids, timing reinforces your magic but will not solely determine its success or failure.

Daytime hours accentuate the cognitive nature, God and Fire magic, vitality, energy, logic, and leadership. Evening hours are for the intuitive, nurturing, healing, and Goddess aspects.

In addition to these choices, each sign of the zodiac, each hour of the day, and each day of the week can be considered for their potential influence. Again, use only those associations that make sense to you and that are logistically possible, considering your time constraints.

Yourself

It's easy to forget that the positioning or movements of your body can be useful in spellcraft. This particular approach returns to the idea of imitation and mimicry for its foundation. For example, in Great Britain, men started carrying women over the threshold as a protective spell. They believed the Ankou, or death spirit, waits for an unsuspecting soul beneath the doorway of all new homes. By physically lifting his bride from the ground, a man symbolically kept his loved one from harm.

A more modern illustration of this can be seen when a coven completes the building of a cone of power, and the priest or priestess raises their hands sharply. This brisk movement indicates what the priest or priestess and group wish to do: release the energy and direct it on its way. Afterward, those gathered may lower themselves to the Earth, quite literally grounding any excess power and returning to normal perceptions.

So, if no other props are available, consider what you might do with the prop that's always with you. For love, mime a hug during your spell. For overcoming problems, visualize the difficulty below your feet and stomp it out.

Etcetera

Just a few more ideas to tickle your creative spirit here. Stones, crystals, and metals hold and transport spells like a battery might. Quartz and copper are two good choices for this since both have the capacity to conduct energy.

Use poppets to represent the person (or animal) to whom your spell is directed. Feathers can be included in enchantments for laughter or movement, or your favorite pillow can become a focal to bring sweet sleep. All these things, and many more around your home, can add wonderful dimensions to the spellbound art.

Always remember that creativity, resourcefulness, and fortitude are an integral part of our spiritual heritage. Begin meeting the changes in your life with humor in one hand and magic in the other—just give your inner child and inventive nature a little leeway. In the process of creating distinctive personal spells to transform your life, you not only reclaim an honored ancestry but reignite a spark of the God or Goddess at your own hearth.

Chapter Two

CREATING MODERN FOLK SPELLS

I consulted with my two brothers, Dr. Reason and
Dr. Experience, and took a voyage to visit my mother
Nature, by whose advice, together with the help of
Dr. Diligence, I at last obtained my desire....
—Nicholas Culpeper

REASON KEEPS OUR PASSIONS from overwhelming us. Experience dictates which methods are most successful. Nature guides us with subtle clues to the inner workings of the universe, and diligence keeps us from giving up hope. Each virtue, when developed, becomes a substructure to magic and to every portion of living. From this starting point, we can move into the actual working of spells with greater assurance and stability.

SPELL PERSONALIZATION

Not every enchantment you find will suit your discretion, requirements, or magical ideals. For example, a Hungarian love charm calls for blood to be rubbed into an intended's hair to bind the spell and that person's affection. If that doesn't sound appealing, try adapting the idea using a little creative substitution.

In this scenario, two people who wish to increase their love could place snippets of their hair in a bowl, cauldron, or other container and then mix in beet juice, catsup, tomato sauce, or another red substance as a blood surrogate. This substitution preserves the congruity of meaning through color and, thus, the potency of the magic. The mixture could then become part of two matching amulets for the couple to carry.

As seen above, substitution is an important factor in personalizing spells. This particular technique also can be applied to the spell's wording, focals, timing, etc. Always feel free to change any phrases you find uncomfortable. Find a proxy for unavailable or undesirable ingredients by using color, number, and other meaningful emblems. If you like the basic construction of a spell and would like to use that format for another purpose, adjust each element accordingly. For example, people in the Middle Ages used an herb bundle known as a *pomander* as a magical charm to ward off sickness. If you want to make something similar that will draw love, then change the herbs and verbal components to match that goal. In this example, I suggest rose petals, lavender, orange powder, or other romantic aromatics.

What's most important about any folk spell is not how much you change from the original source but how meaningful the final design is to you. True empowerment for magic comes from its significance in our reality. The best verification then comes through testing, which is well worth the effort. In the end, you will have a totally intimate construct through which your magic can flow.

Ten Steps to Create Personal Spells

Creating spells from scratch is, in many ways, no different than baking a cake. You have to go step-by-step through the recipe. When you understand how it works, you'll be ready to adapt it for personal taste by choosing flavors, ingredients, baking pans, and toppings. Magically, this equates to the following steps.

1. Consider Your Purpose, Choose Symbols, and State Your Goal

Shaping your thoughts for a specific purpose is not always as easy as it seems. Spells move through the astral plane and have an impact on things outside our awareness. Magical energy is rarely linear; usually, it grows like a web. The central strand represents your spell, whose outcome affects everything and everyone involved. Therefore, a precise understanding of your aims is important, as is having some ability to anticipate possible side effects. This means taking a little extra time deliberating upon the motivation for, and final development of, our spell(s) so that the universe does not misconstrue our intentions.

Decide exactly what your spell is for. Choose symbols that either reflect your goals or help define them. Finally, create the verbal components with phrases that specifically state that goal. If you're uncomfortable with saying spells out loud, write them or recite them in your mind. Alternatively, use a combination for stronger emphasis.

Here is a healing spell to illustrate. First, decide exactly what the malady is, then distill that concept into one word or a short phrase. For symbolism, write the name of the malady backward on paper and in descending form, as was done with *Abracadabra*. This illustrates your desire for the sickness to shrink into nothingness. Keep a nearby fire source ready with healthful herbs like apple peels and allspice. Burn the paper in the fire while chanting, *"God/ Goddess, bless my sacred goal, make my body well and whole."* Finally, add the ashes to your garden or an indoor potted plant, thereby enriching the soil so positive energy can grow.

In this example, both written and spoken recipes indicate to the universe and your higher self exactly what is needed to prevail. The other props—the visual form on paper, incense, and the garden— stress that goal.

2. Find Components to Express Intentions

This step equates to choosing spell focals and/or props. The process of choosing emblems is educational and beneficial since it allows you to consider your goal and any of its connotations as they directly pertain to your magical path and preferred techniques. While deciding among components, your determined concentration increases the energy available. This can be used later when casting the spell or to charge the object.

In step one of the health spell, the traditional form of diminution (as with Abracadabra) was the starting point. From here, I selected each component (including actions) for the spell so they specifically reflected the purpose of the magic. For example, having a Fire component visually negates the disease by burning the paper.

Adding another component, that of timing, could accentuate this effort even further. In this case, performing the spell during a waning moon or when the moon is in Aries would provide proper support.

Nonmagical books often include material to consider for components or symbols. Herbals are a good illustration, having tremendous potential for magical applications. For example, English healers sometimes recommend a tea of raspberry, clove, and honey for a cough. You could prepare the recipe as it stands, stirring it counterclockwise to banish sickness, and then add an incantation. Or you could use raspberry leaves and powdered cloves in incense for the Eastern point of your altar to relate breath (cough) to the element Air.

Collections of folklore and superstition offer choices for creative spellwork, too. Take the superstitions surrounding vampires as a case in point. Stories from Eastern Europe (specifically Slavic regions) tell us how to safeguard ourselves from these malevolent creatures: wearing garlic, sprinkling salt across your doorway, and staying on holy ground. The symbolism here is flexible enough to be used in spells for protection. For example, one might mix salt and garlic buds along with apple peels in a cache to safeguard vitality.

The examples above take common ideas and modify them into potent, meaningful symbols that represent magical desires. Again, please remember that folk magic's success depends on the final construction of your spell making sense to you. Otherwise, you are just "going through the motions" without an emotional or mental connection to those actions. Spells are not a rote litany to recite nonchalantly. They are potent tools that mobilize magical energy. Like any good tool, if you understand how they work and use proper precautions, spells will be more effective in your magical workshop.

3. Cleanse, Bless, and Charge Props, Focals, and Tools

This is a very important step that shouldn't be skipped. You wouldn't want to cook meals for your family in rusty, dirty pots. Similarly, magic should have a psychically clean region from which to originate. Tools common to your living space tend to absorb random energy. Cleansing eliminates the spiritual static and leaves a utensil through which power can flow unhindered.

Purification can be accomplished in several ways. If the item is washable, old-fashioned soap and water combined with white-light visualization is perfectly apt. An aspersion with mineral water can substitute if the object cannot be immersed. Alternatively, move the tool through cleansing incense vapors such as frankincense, myrrh, or sage. There are many other ways of cleansing tools, but these three are pretty standard and easily done at home. While you work, add a prayer, chant, song, or another environmental factor that will inspire you even more.

Blessing the components for a spell means setting them apart for a specific function and asking your chosen divine visage to sanctify that function. The form a blessing takes is somewhat of a personal matter. Many people find that holding the item or placing their hands upon it while petitioning the divine works well. The words need not be intricate to convey your heartfelt desire. One example is: *"Lady/Lord, see this tool that is pure and prepared to help in my magic. Bless it now to become an implement of _____."* (Fill in the blank with your intentions.)

Finally, charging an item is like plugging it into an electrical outlet. To increase their potency as much as possible, place the objects either on your altar during appropriate astrological periods or beneath the light of the sun or moon.

4. Settle Your Mind and Spirit

Before moving forward to create a safe haven for your magic (Step 5), it's important to be calm, centered, and attuned to what's about to take place. Your working area will soon become the nucleus of your magical energy. You, yourself, will be a channel for that power. Therefore, for best results, approach this time with a positive attitude, a fresh spirit, and good motivations. Spell focals are one excellent aid for this, as is meditation.

Additionally, it is unwise to weave magic when you're ill, angry, or out of sorts. Negativity can change magical output in unexpected, and sometimes unpleasant, ways. Think of it like putting an electrical plug into an incorrectly wired socket; usually, sparks result. In these moments, unless urgency is a factor, consider waiting until your body, mind, and spirit are all up to the task.

5. Prepare Sacred Space

From the perspective of clean, controlled energy, developing an enhanced region for spell casting is a good idea. The magical circle acts as a barrier between external influences and the sacred power you are building. Like placing a plug in a sink full of water, this sphere contains the magic until properly devised and directed toward your goal.

The busy nature of our lives does not always afford time to create a full, formal circle (see the discussion later in this section). Fortunately, many simple enchantments that deal with common needs do not demand extensive preparations. A great example is parking magic. When I go into a filled parking lot, I repeatedly whisper the phrase, *"Great squat, I need a spot"* as a verbal component. Nothing else is added except intense observation. While humorous in construction, I never forget this ditty, and the spell always seems to work. I think almost everyone who drives uses this type of magic, but I sincerely doubt that they stop to set up a formal circle first.

So, let your inner voice guide you. If you are not in a position where a circle is plausible, then envision yourself surrounded by a white-light sphere instead. This takes very little time and encloses your magic until you're ready to release it.

When time and circumstances allow you to create a sacred space, do so! The more often you make a haven in your magical niche, the more it will be permeated with shielding energy. Two techniques for circle casting, one casual and one formal, follow.

Informal Circles

In preparing your sacred space, clear away anything that distracts you even innocently. Put the pets in another room, turn off the phone, play some favorite music, and remove any clutter that generates thoughts of the mundane. If it is impossible to eliminate distracting influences (such as permanent fixtures), turn your back to that area before beginning your spell.

For a casual circle, a time-saving technique is to find objects associated with the four elements (Earth, Air, Fire, Water) to adorn your working area. Each item should be blessed with a brief prayer indicating its purpose in your sacred space. A potted plant for Earth could be sanctified by saying something like, *"Great Spirit, bless this living bit of the world to represent the element of Earth in my sanctuary."* Other good possibilities for elemental objects include:

Air: An open window in the East, a paper or electric fan, feathers, bells hung in the East, a leaf, pictures of clouds, birds, or windy places.

Earth: Salt, flour, a jar of corn or grain, corn, indoor grown herbs, a globe or ball, pictures of natural settings to be placed in the North.

Fire: Matches, incense burners, candles, fireplaces, stoves, anything red or orange, representations of the sun, dragons, or other Fiery animals/emblems to be placed in the South.

Water: Sink, cup, or bowl; bud vase; any items with blue or green hues; seashells, sand, or coral; depictions of whales or fish to be placed in the West.

After blessing all four, place them in the appropriate location. Then, in a small way, you have set up a permanent sacred space. To mobilize the latent energy, add an invocation. One of my favorite poems to this end is very brief and effective:

> *Air and Fire, Sea and Land*
> *Before your presence, I (we) would to stand!*
> *Come, protect this sacred space*
> *While I (we) work magic in this place.*

An invocation like this allows the inherent magic of your blessed objects to be triggered. As you name the elements, point to them, and visualize a searing white light connecting each to each. Once completed, you should sense a sphere of energy around you, just on the edge of your awareness. It feels a bit like static electricity to some people. Others smell a change in the air or hear significantly less noise. Check all your senses to see which way you perceive spiritual changes best.

Finally, when you've completed your work, simply thank the elemental powers for their assistance and bid them farewell.

Formal Circles

In instances of greater need, or when time allows, folk magicians may want the extra sanctity that a formal circle offers. Potency and atmosphere define the distinction between this and a more casual setting. Formal circles create a stronger division between the mundane world and space "between the worlds." There is a serious, reflective ambiance to this setting, kind of like the tonal difference between a youth group meeting and the old Latin Mass of Catholicism.

The change in atmosphere creates a similar transition in the way you approach magic here. This doesn't imply donning drab clothing or losing your joy, but a truly sacred space is holy. In it, you share your magical time with the great powers of the universe. Thus, a respectful demeanor is fitting.

To begin setting this tone, follow the first step in the informal circle: straighten and clean your working area if it needs it. A tidy region is less distracting, and removing dust or clutter also removes bits of stray energy deposited with daily tensions.

Next, invoke each elemental point around the circle. As you do this, always move clockwise, beginning in the East with the rising sun and ending in the North. You may wish to light a candle at every point while speaking the invocation. The candle is a visible, active emblem of the elemental presence. Choose its color according to what it represents. Green, brown, and black are best for Earth. Use red, yellow, and orange for Fire, blue and sea green for Water, and pale yellow or white for Air. Here is a sample invocation:

East, Air: *Hail Guardians of the East,*
               Dancing spirits of the Air and
               Protectors of the rising sun and the setting moon.
               I (we) call and welcome you.
               Let fresh winds blow to inspire creativity
               In this sacred space.
               Keep me (us) safe from negativity
               coming from the East
               And abide with me (us) here until the circle closes.

South, Fire:
Hail Guardians of the South,
Joyous salamanders of Fire,
Sparks of light that banish all shadows.
I (we) call and welcome you.
Let your fires burn evenly in my (our) hearts
to empower my (our) magic.
Keep me (us) safe from negativity
coming from the South
And abide with me (us) here until the circle closes.

West, Water:
Hail Guardians of the West,
Flowing waters of intuition and healing
Waves that roll from the beginning of time.
I (we) call and welcome you.
Let your rich drops fall upon this sacred space
to fill the well of my (our) soul(s)
Keep me (us) safe from negativity
coming from the West
And abide with me (us) here until the circle closes.

North, Earth:
Hail Guardians of the North,
Soil of foundations, rich with nourishment
Earth within which the roots of my (our)
magic grow.
I (we) call and welcome you.
Let your fertile loam produce flourishing power
balanced with perfect love.
Keep me (us) safe from negativity
coming from the North
And abide with me (us) here until the circle closes.

Center, Ether:
Hail Lord and Lady of Light,
Goddess of the Moon, God of the Sun;
Grandfather of Time, Grandmother of Fate.
Join with the elements, waltz in their sphere,
and bless my (our) time.
I (we) open this sacred space to your presence.
So be it.

As with the casual circle, remember to envision rays of light connecting each part of the circle until they encase your entire working area with a glowing ball of protective energy. Once the circle is completed, a small libation and an offering to the God or Goddess should follow. This is one way to thank the Great Spirit for aid and providence before enacting your spell.

Libations may take the form of wine, juice, or water poured to the Earth (or, if indoors, another bowl left on the altar). Make offerings in whatever form with which you're comfortable. Good quality incense, grains, fruits, and coins are all options. Share leftover grain and fruit with the birds after your ritual. Coins should be donated to a charitable cause. This way, nothing offered to the divine goes to waste but continues to bless others.

The next step is enacting your spell (Step 6). Once finished, you can remain in this sacred space to study, meditate, pray, or commune as desired. When you are ready to depart, reverse the order of your invocation to release the sacred sphere, blowing out the candles as you go. Some practitioners follow the order below, and others first say goodbye to the Center.

North: *Guardians of the North, thank you for your foundation and protection. I (we) release you now with (a) grateful heart(s).*

West: *Guardians of the West, thank you for your inspiration and protection. I (we) release you now with (a) peaceful heart(s).*

South: *Guardians of the South, thank you for your energy and protection. I (we) release you now with (a) renewed heart(s).*

East: *Guardians of the East, thank you for your fresh perspectives and protection. I (we) release you now with (a) transformed heart(s).*

Center: *May the Lady and Lord watch between me and thee while*
(Groups) *we are apart from each other. Merry meet, merry part, and merry meet again.*

Center: *Lady and Lord, thank you for your presence here. Watch*
(Solitary) *over me daily and speak to my heart until I can share this*
            space with you again. So mote it be.

6. Cast the Spell

Linguistically, the word "cast" is an interesting term. For metals, it means to shape or mold. It also can mean to emit or direct, such as a vote, to assign or allocate as occurs when casting a play, or to hurl outward as in fishing. Putting all this into magical vernacular, to cast a spell means *shaping our thoughts to transmit and direct energy toward a specific assignment, then releasing the energy to that goal.* Each of these steps is vital to the attainment of your goals.

Shaping your thoughts means training your mind on one thing for the duration of the spell, namely your purpose. Your verbal components, along with any chosen props and focals, help with this. Make sure the image is kept at the forefront of your thoughts and is clear and as multidimensional as possible.

Suppose you feel the need to bring fruitfulness into your life. Some of your well-loved projects are going nowhere, and your job isn't as fulfilling as it could be. You hope to settle these problems by drawing in more constructive energy. If you assemble a chanted jingle like *"Goddess, hear my words and bless, bring to me lush fruitfulness,"* without any other components to guide it, you might end up with a thriving garden instead of professional productivity and success. Why? Because the particulars of your spell were indefinite. Be as specific as possible by adding imagery, wording, and other components.

In our next step, we must consider projection and guidance. Visualization helps tremendously with these. By using our imagination, we can depict the purpose of the spell clearly in our mind's eye. This shows our superconscious exactly what we hope to attain.

To understand this interaction, think of listening to a conversation without any frame of reference. It is easy to misinterpret the context when you don't see the whole picture. When a context (secondary perception) is added, the picture becomes clearer, and this enhances the minute features of your magical goal.

Therefore, if you can incorporate all your senses into the act of spell casting, your magic should respond with greater detail.

Assignment works hand in hand with direction, which releases the spell and gives it a designation in which to lodge itself. I once knew a woman who wove a fertility spell with the help of a friend. She later wrote me to say her companion got pregnant at an inopportune time and that she, herself, was having no luck. Apparently, the magical energy housed itself in the wrong participant. Sure enough, a few months later, the same woman wrote back. She told me that she reworked the formulation to be very personal, enacted alone, and directed inward. The difference in the approach manifested itself in conception.

The basic considerations for the assignment of energy are *who, what, where, when, and how*. When we cast spells for a job, for example, the questions need to be answered promptly to assure financial well-being. In this case, the "who" is ourselves. The where becomes important because a job offer halfway across the country probably won't help unless relocation is an option. The "what" is the employment itself, but you should delineate the types of jobs you will enjoy.

While exactly how you find a job isn't critical in this spell, there are situations where that question needs to be answered. You would not want to get someone fired unfairly, for example. Another good illustration is a personal one of mine. In my occupation as an author, a little extra notoriety can help sales tremendously. However, I would not like that attention to come through an automobile accident. Without stipulating the "how," the spell's energy is left to its own devices.

7. Build the Energy through Word or Deed

This works hand in hand with casting. If you have ever been in a circle where the dancing starts out slowly and then grows faster, you have probably experienced the feeling of cresting energy. Basically, we use media such as rhythm, music, or chanting to fashion, guide, and increase magical power. These actions either coincide with the casting of our spell or follow it, depending on your components.

Obviously, it is difficult to sing and dance while writing on paper, lighting candles, etc. In instances like these, cast the spell and hold it securely in your sacred space like a bubble of energy. Then, move clockwise around your space with rattles, repeated incantations, drumming, or other props to build the energy until you feel ready to burst. At this point, that inner well of focused power should be directed into the spell sphere before taking the final step.

8. Release the Magic

Magic will do little good if you don't release it. You have to let the energy disengage for anything to happen. For this, the visualization of cutting a line of energy from yourself works very well.

This line of energy can appear like an umbilical cord emanating from your center of gravity (near the navel), connecting to your spell bubble like the string on a balloon. Visualize also an opening in your magical sphere that is shaped like a megaphone with the pointed end directed toward your goal. Then, untie or cut the cord and channel the balloon through the opening so the energy can leave the sacred space.

Dramatic movements or loud words also can release spells. That is why you sometimes see the priest or priestess of a circle shout "now" while raising their hands upward. The sudden change in vocal tone acts like scissors on the energy. Then, the physical motion speeds it on its way.

If this imagery doesn't work well for you, try others. Try visualizing an arrow finding its mark, for example, or imagining your magic as a key that first unlocks a door in the sacred space and then moves outward.

Don't be afraid to experiment and try new approaches. Generally, you will know whether you have chosen all aspects of a spell correctly. You might find that certain words stick in your mouth or that the choreographed motions feel awkward. Such occurrences mean you need to refine the spell a little more and then try it again. The most potent enchantments roll almost effortlessly from your heart and leave a subtle tingle in the room.

9. Ground Yourself

Grounding is the final step in spell casting that brings you back to Earth. Magic can leave you lightheaded and weary. You need time after spell casting to recover your mundane thought patterns and a normal level of awareness.

Sit on the floor and take a few cleansing breaths. Have some raw vegetables handy and nibble a bit. Hard candy also works. Visualize small roots growing out of your feet and legs to anchor you to the Earth. Stay put until you feel completely back to your old self. Then, leave the gathering with the assurance that your magic has begun.

10. Repeat the Spells

Repeat a spell any time you feel the need until it manifests. Each time you focus your mind toward that goal, you reinforce the original working. Executing the spell again also gives you greater peace of mind. Generally, humans are an impatient lot, and waiting for results can be nerve-racking. Repeating our spells provides us with an opportunity to do something constructive while we wait: empower our magic.

Similarly, don't forget to do everything you can to support your magic on a mundane level. If you're looking for a job, get those blessed resumes sent and scan job listings faithfully. If you're trying to return to health, make sure to get plenty of rest and follow your physician's advice. Trusting in our magic doesn't mean relinquishing common sense. Instead, blend your best sensibilities with spiritual techniques for balanced, bountiful results.

PART TWO

SPELLS BY TOPIC

Whosoever readeth the spells daily over himself, he is whole upon the earth, he escapes from death, and never doth anything evil meet him.
—Egyptian Book of the Dead

METAPHYSICAL IDEOLOGY ENCOURAGES US to look at our mundane schedules and responsibilities in a not-so-normal way. Each morning is a new opportunity to weave a little special energy into our lives and the lives of those people we care about. The type of spell whipped up with our breakfast, energized by the light of the morning sun, or motivated by our vehicle's movement depends directly on one's needs and goals for that day. Consequently, the spells presented herein are set up topically according to prevalent, common human needs, hopes, and desires.

Most of the spells require only a little time out of your already busy day, but it is time well spent. The sacred power you call upon during spellcraft becomes a spark that can energize and shape every moment. Exactly how you do this is purely personal, but, just like exercise, the more you add spellcraft to your daily routine, the more magical life will become.

How to Use Part Two

The word *craft* implies adeptness, competence, and artfulness. Allow your magical training, insight, and creative spirit to guide you through the spells shared in the remainder of the material shared here. Each charm has been devised either by updating an old source, through conversations with magical friends, or by generative experimentation.

The whole idea was to come up with spells that are easy to execute or adapt and whose ingredients are available in your sacred space of home! Each spell or charm in this section includes the following information:

- Possible times to work
- Alternative intentions to which the spell might be applied or modified
- Secondary listings for related sections of this material
- Optional props and focals
- Simplified verbal components that can be altered with more relevant, personalized wording

This way, you can carefully select and match components to better suit your personal needs and your path. You also can combine these spells with material from Appendices A and B to accentuate goals. This individualizes the magic even further.

As with any metaphysical collection, the materials shared herein are only suggestions. Just as a good seamstress must adjust finely tailored fabric for a fitting, not every folk spell encountered will fit your sacred ideals or sense of reality. Instead, this information provides basic patterns from which your vision of magic can be shaped, assembled, and woven together. From there, individuals are free to enjoy the results of their own design.

Hints for Success

Success in spellcrafting, as with any art, comes from practice and patience. Medieval monks didn't learn to brew world-renowned beverages overnight, nor did da Vinci create a masterpiece without making some mistakes. So, be patient with yourself in honing your magical arts and follow these suggestions to help get over the rough spots:

- Bring as many of your senses into the magical procedure as possible to clarify and delineate its purpose(s).
- Always visualize your intentions in detail while you work.
- Repeat spells whenever you feel the need. Each reiteration provides supportive energy for manifestation.
- Phrase the verbal components to be geared toward your specific intentions.
- If you are uncomfortable with vocalizing spells, you can mentally recite them just as effectively. Remember, thoughts are words uttered inwardly.
- Eliminate, substitute, or augment any prop/focal you desire. Be certain to maintain the congruity of meaning.
- Use the timing as a guideline, not as an edict. Any time is the right time for magic!
- Make notes of your successes and failures. These memos will prove immensely helpful in the future.

- If you're unfamiliar with the construction of any of the craft items suggested, look to correspondence lists for alternatives.
- Not all the props and focals listed under a topic are used in the sample spells that follow. The additional ones offer alternative possibilities.
- It is not necessary to use all the props and focals listed when devising your spell. In fact, trying to do so would probably make the spell unmanageable (unless you have three hands). Choose only those items that intimately symbolize your goals and that you feel are necessary for the spell's construction.
- In some instances, you will see that a prop or focal has a specific attribute given in parenthesis. This has been done to specify further the usefulness of that item in the spell. As always, allow your inner voice to guide you. If the voice tells you that a prop or focal has a different meaning, use that as a guide.
- Have fun, relax, and be creative! The right approach for you is the one that works!

Abundance

General Uses: Improving finances. Increasing ideas or creativity. Spiritual growth. Flourishing magical gardens.

Timing: Generally, during the waxing to full moon. During moon signs of Taurus, Cancer, Virgo, or Pisces. Spring (specifically April and May).

Props/Focals: The number twelve. Shades of green, especially vibrant emeralds or lush, leafy hues. Silver coins and found pennies. Baby plants and alfalfa sprouts. Rich scents, including cinnamon, ginger, and sandalwood. Costly herbs such as saffron and vanilla bean. Sunshine for active "golden" energy to encourage development.

Secondary Listings: Prosperity, Money, Magic, Knowledge.

Sample Spells:

To make a useful balm, blend a small jar of moisturizer with the following: 2 drops of green food coloring, 2 teaspoons rose water, 1 teaspoon almond extract, ¼ teaspoon powdered clove, 1 teaspoon mint extract, and 1 tablespoon of honey. Beat the ingredients until well incorporated, always stirring clockwise for growing, positive energy. Chant while you stir, *"I leave my life no more to chance, I evoke the power of abundance."* Visualize your needs being met. Make a label for the preparation that states its purpose: "Bounteous Balm," for example. Use this cream on pulse points or areas of dry skin to bring revitalization physically, spiritually, and financially. If you can't find rose water, substitute dried, powdered rose petals or scented oil.

Take a small green cloth (approximately four inches by four inches) of natural fabric such as cotton or linen for a sachet. In the center, place twelve shards of cinnamon, twelve dried alfalfa sprouts, twelve strands of saffron, candied ginger, and any real silver item that will fit. Tie the cloth together like a sachet using green ribbon or thread. As you bind the cloth, repeat twelve times, *"God/Goddess, hear my urgent plea, bring to me prosperity."* Leave this in the light of the sun for twelve days from the new moon to the full moon, then carry it regularly.

This spell uses the Threefold Law for symbolism. It is especially nice since it anonymously blesses another individual.

Send a dollar bill (or other denomination you're comfortable with) wrapped in green paper to someone who needs extra cash. As you prepare the envelope, burn a green candle anointed with patchouli oil. Employ a small prayer, something like: *"Even as I bless others, so may I receive blessings."* Mail the envelope on the twelfth of the month and watch to see what returns to you!

ADAPTATION

General Uses: Smooth adjustments, familiarization, changes, and revisions. The powers of versatility and flexibility.

Timing: When the moon is in Sagittarius or Aries. Saturday. During October (for personal transformation). Midnight and noon, New Year celebrations, or astrological cusps.

Props/Focals: Change is a function of the conscious mind, so consider your props accordingly. Apple and rosemary (for cognitive functions). Red or yellow hues. The numbers seven and ten. Any liquid (which always adapts to the shape of its container). Also, items that can be turned or bent without being broken.

Secondary Listings: Virtue, Transformation, Conscious Mind, Judgment, Quick-Mindedness, Versatility.

Sample Spells:

On the seventh day of the month, during the lunch hour, go outside with an unshaped piece of modeling clay. Sit somewhere you will be undisturbed. Begin to fashion an image of what you wish to accommodate in literal or symbolic form. For example, if moving to a new residence is the issue, shape a house.

As you form the clay, pour as much love into it as possible. Think in short, positive affirmations (out loud or to yourself) that mirror your hopes and intentions. For this illustration, fitting phrases include "happy home" or "trouble-free move." Place this token where you can see it regularly. It will emit the positive energy it has absorbed and remind you of the positive magic engendered for adjustment.

If you have trouble coping with rapid change, this visualization spell can help. Get comfortable and have a glass of pure water nearby. Visualize yourself as you are right now but with your body fashioned from a liquid, which is held together by a transparent shell that moves and shifts with each breath you take.

Now, change your focus slightly. Envision the situation where you're having trouble changing or adjusting. Using your writing hand, open the transparent shell that contains your essence and allow the fluid-being to move toward that new scenario. In your mind's eye, see yourself filling that whole situation perfectly like water fills your glass. Begin to whisper a phrase similar to *"Magic is to bend and change; I am the magic!"* Let your voice naturally grow stronger with conviction. Repeat this phrase at least ten times or until the scene completely develops in your imagination (it should be almost three-dimensional). Then take your glass of water, saying: *"Magic is to bend and change; as this water courses into me, so too I will flow!"* Finally, drink the water to internalize the spell.

Each time you enjoy a glass of water from this day forward, repeat your power phrase as you feel the need. This regularly encourages adaptability in your life.

Just before midnight, gather seven pieces of dried apple, ten rosemary leaves, a red four-by-four-inch cloth, and a yellow ribbon for a sachet. Place the rosemary and apple in the center of the cloth and keep the ribbon handy. As the clock strikes twelve, begin tying the cloth together while repeating words like these: *"Even as night turns always today, so too I will find my way. Like eventide with light now wrapped, so my magic will adapt!"* Carry the sachet into situations requiring flexibility, or keep it somewhere in your home to help with everyday changes.

Anger

General Uses: Dispersing negative tempers, restoring calm and equilibrium, forgiveness.

Timing: Waning moons, dawn. Moon in Gemini or Aries. The months of February and August. Monday (healing) or Tuesday (to encourage logic).

Props/Focals: The numbers one and thirteen. The color white. A white flag, a picture of a dove, and peace offerings. Items to represent the focus of your anger (usually destroyed during spell casting. Breakables or tearables are best). Fires that can be extinguished.

Secondary Listings: Peace, Forgiveness, Communication, Harmony, Understanding.

Sample Spells:

This spell uses the principle of sympathy for its foundation. During the Renaissance, Sir Kenelm Digby, a period herbalist, illustrated something similar with a recipe for the Powder of Sympathy. Healers placed this powder on a blade that caused a wound. By administering the balm to the instrument of injury, people believed the wound would heal faster.

Find an object that symbolizes the issue central to your anger. The item should be something that you don't mind leaving covered with ointment. Also, go to your medicine cabinet and find some first aid ointment or any salve that heals wounds. Light a white candle (for peace) and place both the cream or ointment and the token in front of you. Slowly consider all the reasons for your anger. Let that energy pour outward into the chosen symbol until, in your mind's eye, it radiates a red light from your fury. By this point, you should feel calmer, too.

Next, take enough cream or ointment in both palms to cover the emblem. As you apply it to the emblem, say: *"As balm to this figure, so also to my heart. Where animosity has grown, healing now impart."* Repeat this thirteen times while massaging the ointment into the object. Place this in a safe place so peace may grow undisturbed.

Use this spell to inspire restitution between two people. Both individuals should begin privately by making a knotted cord. Each knot represents a specific problem area that is engendering pain or ire—for example, nagging or lateness. Name them as you work, pouring all your negative feelings into each knot.

Next, meet during a waning moon in a neutral location. Meditate briefly together to calm your feelings. One at a time, untie a knot while speaking its name to the other person. When finished, exchange cords and burn them as a sign of release, forgiveness, and the end of hard feelings.

Bury the ashes with the seed of any hardy plant, saying together, *"As this plant grows, so friendship flows. Forever goodwill stays, anger is burned away."* Make a concerted effort never to discuss those problems again.

Sometimes, the only way to rid yourself of anger is by physically disengaging it from yourself. Begin by naming a red cord or thread after your fury. Tie this around your chest (near the heart). Focus all your anger into that cord. Next, start snipping it off in thirteen sections while repeating, *"Anger, released; hostility, ceased."* Keep a piece from the thirteenth cut as a memento of your resolve. Alternatively, destroy the cord to symbolize the destruction of anger.

ART

General Uses: Creativity, the Muse, originality, innovation, removing artistic blocks.

Timing: In the moonlight, especially waxing to full. On your favorite artist's birthday. When the moon is in Aries, Taurus, or Cancer. The season of spring. Monday or Wednesday.

Props/Focals: The tools of your art (such as a brush, pen, or clay). An artistically inspiring decoration or an image of a god or goddess. The color yellow. A blue ribbon or statue to symbolize excellence. The numbers five, seven, ten, and twelve. Angelica, nutmeg, lunar herbs, and foods.

Secondary Listings: Imagination, Inspiration, New Endeavors.

Sample Spells:

For any spell involving your artistic medium, have the necessary production tools available nearby so you can reach them promptly after enacting the spell or as inspiration dictates.

Layout a yellow cloth, napkin, or piece of paper on a flat surface. Place a yellow candle in the center along with a bud vase containing an unopened yellow rosebud (or other flaxen flower). Make a cup of warm nutmeg and apple tea and sit before the candle.

As you light the flame, say: *"As this candle burns, so too is my inspiration ignited; for what my heart yearns, let it now be sighted!"* Drink the tea. Repeat this procedure before working on your art for a period of five or seven days until the rosebud opens. By the end of this period, you should experience expanded creative energies. This spell is especially effective for people trying new styles or media.

Take out a piece of your handicraft of which you are particularly proud. Set it somewhere noticeable and tie a blue ribbon around it. As you do this, say: *"Perfection is here, but drawn from my heart. Let the spirit of excellence live in my art."* Leave this item out for a period of twelve days (or possibly twelve weeks), repeating the incantation each time you see it.

When you have finished this cycle, go to your artistic vehicle and close your eyes. Take a deep breath and repeat the power phrase once more before beginning a new effort. Create wonders!

BALANCE

General Uses: Steadiness, equilibrium, symmetry, congruity.

Timing: Midnight and noon (the in-between hours). New Year, Samhain, and times of seasonal change. When the moon is in Libra and during the month of August.

Props/Focals: A triangle of equally distributed primary colors. An hourglass, a scale, stilts, or a balance beam. The number two. The Two of Pentacles (tarot), the yin-yang symbol, and mirror images.

Secondary Listings: Justice, Harmony, Negotiation, Viewpoints.

Sample Spells:

Take a brick and a piece of wood that is long enough to act like a balance beam. Place the brick, large surface down over a hand-drawn yin-yang symbol (preferably on a carpeted floor for safety) and put the wood across it. Step up onto the miniature beam and allow yourself to wobble.

Next, close your eyes while keeping your arms outstretched for safety. Visualize concentric images of the yin-yang below your feet, moving up toward the center of your being. Allow these figures to settle there, two by two, until you can physically sense that spot. It may tingle slightly or feel warm. All the while, chant a phrase like, *"Left and right, up and down; balance abides all around. Two by two, part of me, my life is brought to symmetry."* Afterward, keep the paper containing the yin-yang symbol with you or place it somewhere noticeable as reinforcement.

Please note that for your protection, you should not attempt this exercise when you have a cold, ear infection, or any other malady that disrupts physical balance or ability to stand. For accessibility reasons, if you are unable to stand or balance, feel free to sit in the center of the yin-yang symbol instead.

Turn an egg timer and allow half of it to flow into the other end, then turn it on its side so the distribution is maintained. Place it in your sacred space (on the altar if you have one). Take some time to study how the glass appears in this position until you can see it clearly with your eyes closed.

Come the noon or midnight hour on the same day, visualize this image inside of you, near your navel. Feel the steadiness of the weight, the harmony of energy. State these words, or similar ones, twice: *"Tides flow in and out, sands shift within their sway; so, balance comes about, as night gives way to day."* In the future, when you feel out of center, envision the glass again and chant the power phrase in sets of two while taking slow, steady breaths. Continue until equilibrium returns.

Banishing

General Uses: Expelling negative energies or spirits. Turning malevolent magic. Ridding oneself of obsessions, addictions, and phobias.

Timing: The light of day, specifically dawn. The months of January, July, and October. When the moon is in Aries, Gemini, or Sagittarius. During a blue moon. On your birthday or dates with special meaning.

Props/Focals: The colors of red, white, silver, or black. The numbers six and eight. Purifying scents and herbs such as clove, pine, lemon, sage, myrrh, and frankincense. Soap and water, soil, and items that can be reversed or turned inside out. Counterclockwise movement.

Secondary Listings: Cleansing, Habits, Ghosts, Overcoming, Protection, Victory.

Sample Spells:

To make a portable tool for expelling negativity, begin by dabbing your pulse points and chakras with a mixture of powdered cloves and diluted lemon oil. This opens the avenue for spiritual purification. Next, take a small, square black cloth and a slightly larger white cloth. Hold the black cloth with both hands. Visualize the habit you are trying to banish as black sludge coming out of your pores and being absorbed by the cloth.

Once you feel the negativity has been discharged, take the white cloth in hand, saying six times, *"This is the light of protection, of purity. As it covers the darkness, so it brings safety to me."* As you speak these words, imagine a blinding white light pouring into the cloth. Lay out the black swatch, place some pine needles and frankincense bits on it, and then put the white one over it. Carefully bundle the two together so that no portion of the black can be seen. Carry the token with you to expel negativity wherever you are.

To rid your home of a troublesome spirit, begin by dabbing a bit of cinnamon and fennel (oil or powder) over all your window edges, door tops, heating ducts, or anything else that represents an opening. Trace the oils in the form of a banishing pentagram, saying: *"No darkness may enter this sacred space; unless welcome by me, spirits leave this place."* Repeat any time you sense an unwanted presence in your home.

Make this charm to turn negative energy away from you. First, gather any combination of the following: eight dried white beans, eight pieces of grain, six peach pits, eight dried chrysanthemum petals, some dill, and a small bit of any reflective substance, such as a mirror. Place these in a white sachet with a little oil of pennyroyal or cedar. Anoint the pouch while saying: *"Turn, turn, turn, any evil, back to its source, thrice returned."* Keep this with you or in an area that needs protection.

BEAUTY

General Uses: Internalizing the spirit of beauty. Grace under pressure. Poise and presence. Self-confidence.

Timing: May Day. Beneath a full moon. When the moon is in Leo or Virgo. Fridays, especially during November.

Props/Focals: The numbers three and twenty-one. Pastel colors and soft lines. Classical artwork. A mirror. Avocado pit or dried cucumber peels, ginseng, and catnip. Any items such as makeup that are applied to help improve appearances. Herkimer diamonds. Swan figurines.

Secondary Listings: Passion, Transformation, Viewpoints.

Sample Spells:

One of the time-honored methods of improving physical beauty in Scotland and England was to gather morning dew on May Day and apply it to the skin. To adapt this idea using a more spiritual tone, try mixing a little catnip tea with this dew. Anoint yourself thrice over the heart with it, saying: *"Loveliness within, loveliness without, let beauty shine, remove all doubt."*

If May Day dew is not available, use rain or dew drops collected on the third or twenty-first day of any month. To gather dew, drape a fine linen or cotton cloth over a few plants at nightfall. Just after dawn the next day, wring out the fabric into a clean container. Refrigerate this; otherwise, the water will quickly become stagnant and unusable for magic.

Prepare a portable charm for yourself consisting of one avocado pit (for the self), two dried cucumber peels (for others who will see the shine of your inner beauty), a picture of a swan, and some ginseng (check the tea section of your grocery store). Tie all of these in a piece of cloth that you find very attractive. Hold the charm in your hands with your eyes closed, visualizing the most exquisite concept of loveliness you can, and say: *"As the ugly duckling became a swan, soon my doubts will all be gone. Poise and grace to guide my way, bringing confidence all the day."* This charm may be carried or left near the mirror you use most frequently.

Blessing

General Uses: Sanctification, consecration, dedication. Encouraging divine favor and bounty.

Timing: During a full moon. When the moon is in Virgo or Pisces. The month of November. Your birthday or anniversary. The day a child is born.

Props/Focals: The human hand. Anointing oil. The number two. Warm colors. Water and other elemental symbols. Halos and golden-colored light (use tinted light bulbs, the rays of the sun, or candles). Elder leaves and berries. Flower petals or seeds thrown to the winds.

Secondary Listings: Dedication, Harmony, Joy, Peace.

Sample Spells:

In many religious traditions, including Judaism and Christianity, a way to invoke blessings is the laying on of hands. Here, the palm transmits divine energy for a specific purpose. To these ends, I suggest anointing your hands with appropriate oils. For example, use lavender to encourage serenity or ginger to sanctify a power focus.

Next, lay your hands directly on the object or person. If oil will harm the surface of the item, put your hand in close proximity to it. Visualize a pure white, sparkling light pouring down from the heavens and through your hands. When they begin to tingle slightly, invoke the blessing of your god or goddess in words comfortable to you and remain in contact until that presence withdraws.

On a bright, sunny day, take a handful of fruit-bearing seeds to an area with rich soil. Hold the seeds tightly near your heart, repeating twice, *"As these seeds multiply and grow, so too blessings will be sown. For _____ (insert name of person), I release them to the wind so the magic can begin!"* At the final word of the second repetition, release your seeds, scattering them as you turn clockwise. If possible, take a rake to sow them properly into the soil so the magic germinates.

In magic circles, a familiar custom for blessing babies is to introduce the child to each element in a ritualized manner. This rite can take the form of a spell by weaving the words a little differently.

First, place the child's hand upon rich soil as an introduction to the element Earth. Then, bring the hand into contact with Air and Fire by using a feather to fan the smoke of burning sage or other cleansing incense. After this, the hand can be dipped into a chalice of water. This can be followed by a simple incantation such as: *"In fertile soil, may you ever grow; with divine flames may you ever glow; let the winds of change gently blow; with the waters of blessing may you ever flow."* As a final gesture, save the soil and feather to present to the child at their rite of passage into adulthood. Alternatively, release the soil to a nearby water source to carry the blessing.

CHOICES

General Uses: Decision making, finding alternatives, sound deductions.

Timing: When the moon is in Cancer, Libra, or Sagittarius. The month of December. Tuesday and Thursday.

Props/Focals: A pendulum, a penny or other coin, and straws of various lengths. Lots made from colored beans, pieces of paper, or stones. Scents that encourage awareness and perception, such as apple, vanilla, and nutmeg. The number ten. The colors gray, black, or white.

Secondary Listings: Adaptation, Discernment, Doubt, Intuition, Judgment, Movement, Quick-Mindedness.

Sample Spells:

The drawing of lots to aid decisions is a venerable tradition and was used in places like the Oracle at Delphi in ancient Greece. Here is an example:

Place ten black beans and ten white beans of roughly the same size in a bowl. Close your eyes and concentrate on your question. Add an incantation such as *"I put my hand into this dish to guide my choice is what I wish."*

Instead of choosing one bean, keep your eyes closed and choose three. If they all come out white, the answer is positive. If two are white, your decision is a good one, but possibly not the best you could make. If only one is white, this is probably a bad decision with minor positive aspects to it. Finally, an all-black response is negative.

A slightly different method is to indicate your range of options by color. You need as many different colored stones, beans, etc., to draw from as there are options to represent. The number of each colored token needs to equal the others and should be similar in shape and size to keep the drawing random. Read this as you would the previous example, but remember that instead of a yes-no response, you have been shown the best path given the present circumstances.

Additionally, you may interpret this second method through numerology. For example, if your question pertained to love and you drew four red beans, this is a positive omen because four portends success.

To divine a choice from alternatives, use an herbal or crystal pendulum. Choose the herb or crystal according to the topic of your question. Queries about love, for example, could employ a rosebud, willow branch, or any purplish-red stone attached to a string. The length of the string should be equal to your palm-to-elbow measurement, with a little extra for tying.

As you secure the herb or crystal, add an incantation that applies to the matter at hand. In choosing between two mates, for example, the verse could be *"Two I love, but one to hold; show me what my future holds. A choice to make, and make once right; bring my answer into light."*

After reciting your incantation, place the elbow of your strong hand firmly on a table with the cord and emblem dangling just above the surface. Steady the item completely with your other hand, then close your eyes and concentrate on the question. Front-to-back movements indicate a positive response, left-to-right a negative response, and circles indicate uncertainty.

If your question focuses on two distinct options, you can use another method. Pick out four items to symbolize the choices (two each). Place two corresponding tokens at North and South, and the other two at East and West. Carefully steady your elbow outside the circle, halting any movement in the pendulum and focusing again on your question. The direction of the movement indicates your best choice. Circular movements show equal potentialities.

CLEANSING

General Uses: Purification, refinement, purging.

Timing: The months of January and February. Waning moons. When the moon is in Aries. Before quests and other matters of deep spiritual significance.

Props/Focals: Herbs such as pine, lemon, hyssop, cinnamon, clove, and sandalwood. The numbers two, eight, and forty. Agate or chrysolite. Soap and washcloth, bath or shower, washing machine, kitchen sink.

Secondary Listings: Banishing, Liberation, Overcoming.

Sample Spells:

For Objects:

If the item can be sprinkled by or immersed in water, prepare a solution of 1 teaspoon of lemon juice, ¼ teaspoon of cinnamon, and seven whole cloves in warm water. Place the object in a container and pour the solution over it (or asperse it), saying: "*Unwanted energy is commanded to flee; with Water cleansed, grant purity.*" If the item can be soaked, leave it in the water for three hours beneath sunlight, then again beneath moonbeams to negate residual energy on all levels.

If water would prove damaging, instead, prepare an incense from sandalwood chips, pine needles, and dried lemon rind. Pass the object through the smoke and modify the incantation to something like "*What Fire cleanses, the smoke conveys, all negativity blown away. Bless this _____ with divine rays; forever, now, the magic stays.*"

For People:

Many faiths have some form of a cleansing bath, notably baptism in Christianity and the sanitary strictures of Judaism. It was considered unseemly to go before the gods with any blemish, physical or spiritual. For our purposes, a purification bath washes away vice or negative feelings that inhibit the flow of magical energy.

To prepare a cleansing bath, gather any of the herbs listed in "Props/Focals" and bundle them in several layers of cheesecloth or in a tea ball. Once they are gathered, charge the herbs with a spell, like: *"My spell, now woven, will not be broken; away from me all negativity. On these herbs bestow a purified glow. With water unbind, cleansing is mine."* Place the bundle in hot water to activate the energy while you prepare for your bath. For a more relaxing atmosphere, affix a candle to the tub, burn incense, and play quiet music.

As you wash, name different regions of your body after things you want to cleanse. One spot might be anger, another, a tendency to gossip, and so on. When you are finished, towel off and go straight to your magical tasks.

If you don't have a tub, a shower will work effectively, too. Hold the cheesecloth bundle under the water and squeeze the aromatic juice over your body. Or hang the tea ball from the shower head. Alternatively, purchase some appropriately scented soap.

COMMUNICATION

General Uses: Positive discourse. Opening lines of conversation. Messages.

Timing: Wednesday and Friday. When the moon is in Aries. Other timings change according to the topic of conversation. Magical subjects, for example, should be deliberated under the full moon, whereas sunlight enhances analytical discussions.

Props/Focals: Lilac flowers or oil (harmony or mental acuity). The color pink. The number two. Live basil plants or the dried herb. Amethyst, beryl (legal matters), carnelian (for powerful communications), or hematite (to bring out leadership qualities). Your phone, stationery, pencils, pens, keyboards, or computers. The rune of communication.

Secondary Listings: Friendship, Negotiation, Openings, Relationships, Speech, Web Weaving.

Sample Spells:

Find a small, flat item (a piece of cloth, an old card, etc.) belonging to a person with whom you hope to improve communication. If one is not available, find a swatch of paper or cloth in their favorite color. On a piece of nice stationery (not personalized), write their name and the area where communication needs improvement. Inscribe the rune in a circle around the edge of the paper. Place the token for that individual inside the runic circle, then fold the stationery around it twice (top to bottom, right to left). Hold the folded paper tightly and visualize that person calling or writing to you.

Next, place the paper in an envelope addressed to yourself, but mail it from a different location, so it will take a few days to arrive. On each day of your wait, reinforce your visualization. When the letter arrives at your home, bring it into the house and place it near where you keep your phone to keep your end of communications open. When the individual finally calls or writes, open the letter to symbolically open the discussion desired.

To make a portable amulet that will improve your own ability to communicate, take a pink cloth (four inches by four inches) and place in the center two sprigs of basil, two pieces of carnelian, and a depiction of the rune of communication. Wrap a white ribbon around the bundle, saying: *"My tongue untie, all doubt abate, allow me to communicate!"* Carry your charm with you for flowing dialogue. To reinforce the spell, repeat the power phrase twice before entering into conversation.

CONSCIOUS MIND

General Uses: Alertness, learning, sensibility, calculation.

Timing: Any time the sun is visible. When the moon is in Leo. The season of summer. After the spring and fall breaks from school.

Props/Focals: Warm, golden colors. The scent of rosemary. Amethyst and coral charms. Books, glasses, desks, or any item you associate with concentration. The number one.

Secondary Listings: Choices, Humor, Knowledge, Leadership, Organization, Quick-Mindedness, Teaching/Teachers, Understanding.

Sample Spells:

This is a charm for mental keenness. Gather rosemary, amethyst, and coral together in any yellow container. Allow them to sit in sunlight for a full day, soaking up that harmonic energy. At dusk, before the sun goes down, hold your hands to the right and left of the container so sunlight can still shine through. Visualize the rays being soaked up by your components. To empower the items, use an incantation like: *"As sunlight finds its way, let me see the light of day. Internal fires start to burn, help me now, my____ to learn."* Fill in the blank with the appropriate topic. Carry the container any time you need improved attention. Repeat the verbal component at moments when your mind begins wandering.

Find a yellow or gold candle the day before you need a particularly attentive mental state. Work only during daylight hours. Begin by carefully carving a single word that fully expresses the goal of your spell into the wax. Examples include "attention" or "observation." Strongly visualize your success in the present situation. With each letter carved, repeat a phrase analogous to *"In wax assigned, all*

qualms now bind; with _____ *endow my conscious mind.*" Fill in the blank according to your spell's central focus.

Rub the exterior of the candle with rosemary oil so it smells of this herb (rosemary encourages improved memory). Place the taper in an area where it can burn safely while unattended. Options for this include any sink, a pan of water, a pie tin, or a bathtub. Finally, light the candle just before going into the situation. Repeat your incantation to wrap the magic around yourself like a visor that directs and improves your attention.

Special note for diviners: If there is a question nagging at your heart, concentrate on that question as you light the candle. When you return, look at the patterns in the wax for a response!

COURAGE

General Uses: Fortitude, bravery, valor, boldness, tenacity.

Timing: When the sun is visible. The month of July. Tuesday, Thursday, or Sunday. When the moon is in Taurus or Leo. On Memorial or Veterans Day.

Props/Focals: The color red or red and gold. I number eight. Beryl or hematite as charms. Scents of cedar, musk, borage, or thyme. Swords, gloves, a Purple Heart, pens, or items associated with the honor of valor.

Secondary Listings: Fear, Judgment, Leadership, Overcoming, Protection, Tenacity, Victory.

Sample Spells:

To make a token that will enhance your own fortitude, you will need a picture or small carving of an animal associated with boldness or courage. Lions and bears are good choices. For longevity of use, check gift shops for durable stone carvings. Once you find an image, take it into sunlight. Speak directly to the likeness, saying: *"My image of boldness, straight to my heart, there abide softly, never depart. When held within a hand of mine, your courage to my heart consign."*

Once it is consecrated, get a small pouch to house your token of courage and carry it with you regularly. When you feel your nerve waning, take the figurine in hand and silently chant the power phrase eight times.

Before going into circumstances where you need inner fortitude, anoint yourself with scents of musk, cedar, or thyme. Place a drop of one or a blend of all three on pulse points. Additionally, rub some on your belly (the area which usually gets butterflies), saying: *"Fear be free, courage to me!"* Restate this phrase or something similar while you anoint yourself. Wear something red and gold to accentuate the energy.

DEDICATION

General Uses: Commitment, devotion, loyalty, duty, promises.

Timing: The month of June. When the moon is in Taurus, Aries, or Leo. Before weddings, engagements, handfastings, or the start of a new job/project. Thursday.

Props/Focals: Grapes and celery for mental strength and clarity. Vanilla for energy to follow through. Garnet to encourage constancy. The numbers six and thirteen. The color purple. Any sticky substance like flypaper. Image of a dog (faithfulness).

Secondary Listings: New Endeavors, Quests, Tenacity, Zeal.

Sample Spells:

To make a charm that will remind you of a promise to follow through, gather six small garnets, a piece of purple construction paper or cloth, and glue. Affix the stones to the paper in a circle (for completion), one at a time. If garnet isn't available, use dried red grapes or raisins. As you place each garnet, repeat an incantation, like: *"To do what I must, strongly in me, grows now the virtue of loyalty. To complete my task, a promise I make, an hour each day, I dedicate."* Keep the charm where it will remind you of your promise to follow through. Keep the charm with you. If you use the above phrasing, alter the amount of time set aside to reasonably suit your other responsibilities.

For devotion in a relationship, you and your partner, each bearing a small bundle of grapes, should come together during a full moon. Begin by feeding one grape to your partner and stating a wish you have for your relationship; for example, *"This grape represents my continuing love."* After the grapes have been used up, anoint your hearts and hands with vanilla.

Next, stand beneath the full moon, speaking words of dedication to each other. While I recommend writing a personally chosen incantation, here is a sample: *"As the moon is full, so do we give our hands and hearts to tend love to its fullness. Witness us, God/Goddess of love, and hold us to our sacred promise."* Exchange small tokens afterward as mementos of the occasion.

If you don't like grapes, try candy-covered chocolates instead. This component brings sweetness to love.

DISCERNMENT

General Uses: Insight, perception, sagacity.

Timing: Moon in Cancer or Libra. Waxing to full moon. Any time when light and shadows play against each other.

Props/Focals: Bay, mint, saffron, and peaches for wisdom and awareness. Jasmine and rose for spiritual foresight. Silver or stones aligned with lunar energy. Malachite. The color purple. The numbers seven and five. Any substance that can be cleared away, like dust or flour.

Secondary Listings: Intuition, Identifying, Judgment, Visions.

Sample Spells:

Prepare some incense by powdering dried bay, mint, and rose petals together. As you crush the herbs, visualize barriers being torn down (the image of demolished walls works well). Next, place the herbs in a fireproof container on a brick of self-lighting charcoal (which can be purchased at New Age or Witchcraft stores or smoke shops). Alternatively, any available fire source is fine.

While the herbs burn, get comfortable for a brief meditation that includes an incantation. Take a deep breath and repeat the following phrase five times: *"Five times I speak, perception I seek. Come on the count of four, insight will pour. On the charge of three, I will begin to see. By the count of two, all truth I'll view. On the mark of one, this spell is done!"*

Allow the incense to burn for a while, carrying your desires to the divine. Burn the same combination of herbs whenever your perception becomes clouded.

To begin a spell to sharpen your discernment, sprinkle a small handful of flour on a slightly damp surface. As you cover the area, keep the topic of your spell strongly in mind. Cover the surface lightly so it can be wiped clean with seven strokes of a cloth.

Next, place a little jasmine oil, rose oil, or rose water on your temples and get a cleaning cloth. Move the cloth seven times around the surface counterclockwise, saying with each circle: *"As this flour's cleaned, the truth will be seen. Turmoil erased, by insight replaced!"* For a portable charm, gather some leftover flour in a small container and dab it with the rose water or oil.

DIVINATION

General Uses: Oracles, prophesy, prediction, forecasts.

Timing: Moon in Pisces. During the full moon. Halloween, May Day (for matters of love). The month of November. Wednesday.

Props/Focals: Broom, dandelion, cherry, fig, orange, pomegranate. Rowan or hazelwood (for dousing). The color yellow. The number five. All divinatory tools.

Secondary Listings: Choices, Identifying, Love, Recovering Items.

Sample Spells:

Spells for divination are usually connected to a specific tool or reading. In this case, they act as motivating energy for the oracle itself. Here are some sample incantations to speak over your chosen implement(s):

> *"Divine powers, all great and wise, show me where my future lies. The past is known, today soon flies, bring the future to my eyes."*

> *"Runes [or cards] with vision blessed, bring discernment to my guest. Divine guidance, through these tools impart, guide me in this ancient art."*

To encourage visionary dreams, drink a small amount of dandelion tea with a slice of orange before bed. I suggest no more than a half cup, as dandelion can act as a diuretic. Additionally, place five hazel or rowan twigs in a yellow cloth beneath your pillow, empowering them with words like: *"On the wings of starlight, and pouring moonbeams, bring to me prophetic dreams."* The use of hazelwood for prophetic dreams originates in England.

Burning herbs for answers to simple questions is an old divinatory technique. For example, ancient Greeks burned laurel branches in a technique known as *daphnomancy.*

Begin by choosing a dried herb according to the topic at hand. Bless the herb, then place it on a fire. Follow with a verbal component, like: *"Herb placed to burn within the fire, heed my question, reveal my desire."* If the herb is silent, your answer is no. If it pops and spits, the answer is yes. If it flames up brightly, things look very positive. If it smokes and dies out, signs are negative.

To divine your future from a cup of tea, first choose some herbs that correspond to your question. For example, if your question is about love, use lemon, rose hips, orange, and/or nutmeg steeped in hot water. Let the ground herbs remain loose in your cup. Concentrate on your question while drinking until the cup is nearly empty except for the leaves and a minute bit of water.

Next, place your strong hand over the top of the cup. Swirl the remaining liquid three times clockwise. Turn the cup onto a saucer and lightly tap on the bottom five times. With each tap, repeat an incantation, like: *"One for vision, two for insight, three for wisdom, four for discernment, come five the spell is free, magic, magic…work for me!"*

Now, turn the cup back over. See if any patterns emerge in the remaining herbs stuck to the cup. Interpret the patterns according to your question. If you were asking how soon you would find a life mate, for example, and a heart shape appears near the rim of your cup (close to you), this portends someone appearing soon. Images farther away, near the bottom of the cup, indicate longer waiting periods.

You may want to place a few paper towels beneath your saucer before performing this procedure to gather up any dribbles.

One technique I use for divination is doodling. For this, have plenty of paper and a favorite pen ready. Begin by meditating for a few minutes until your mind is clear and focused on your question. Inhale deeply; then, as you exhale, begin drawing whatever images come into your mind. Try to do this with your eyes closed so the mage stays clear. If you find this difficult, go ahead and open your eyes, but don't be too picky about the portrait. Usually, the image is symbolic, meaning exact lines are not necessary for interpretation.

When you feel finished, take a few cleansing breaths. If you've worked with your eyes open, close them while you do this. Then, look at the drawings and try to find patterns or likenesses. Look these up in a good dream dictionary.

The nice part about this particular form of divination is that it draws upon your own superconscious for information as opposed to relying on an external impetus.

DOUBT

General Uses: Easing indecision. Clarifying a sense of confusion. Reservations, misgivings, skepticism.

Timing: Moon in Gemini or Capricorn. The month of August. Waning moons. On bright, sunlit days.

Props/Focals: Rose and gardenia aromas to encourage a peaceful heart. Garnet to inspire faith. Tourmaline to improve self-esteem. The number ten and bright colors. A teeter-totter or other items representing balance or stability.

Secondary Listings: Courage, Fear, Overcoming, Peace, Victory.

Sample Spells:

Gather a piece of paper, one gray crayon, one bright crayon (orange-yellow is good), matches, and a small item to represent yourself (perhaps a pebble). On the left side of the paper, write the word "doubt" in gray and draw a cloud over it. On the right side, use the bright crayon to draw a sun with the word "assurance" underneath it. Then, lay the paper before you, placing the symbol of self on the left side. Slowly, while repeating the phrase, *"From doubt to certainty, light to mark my way. Misgivings be gone, I'm seizing the day,"* move the stone across the page until it sets firmly on the word "assurance."

Next, take a deep breath and tear away the left side of the paper, releasing your breath as you finish tearing. Burn that side to literally destroy your doubt. Wrap the remaining paper around the stone or object and carry it to encourage confidence every day.

To make a poppet, take two pieces of cloth with their right sides facing each other. A bit of fabric from an old shirt or other garment is best. From them, cut an image of a person (yourself). Sew them together, leaving an opening for stuffing.

Next, take a dried rose and pull the petals off in a counterclockwise manner, repeating: *"Doubt torn away, confidence today."* Place the petals inside the poppet and sew up the hole. On the outside, paint or embroider a word or emblem that symbolizes uncertainty to you. Then, place the poppet in the light of a waning moon to reduce your reservations. After ten days, bury the poppet along with your hesitations.

Alternatively, use a symbol of assurance and place it under a waxing moon so confidence grows!

ECOLOGY

General Uses: Earth healing, connecting with nature.

Timing: Spring Equinox, Earth Day, or any celebration honoring an Earth deity such as Gaia. During the waxing moon for flourishing land or the waning moon to banish pollution. Mondays for flowing Goddess energy.

Props/Focals: The numbers nine and twelve. The color green. A globe or picture of Earth from space. Rich soil and seedlings. Natural, rustic scents like musk or dried leaves.

Secondary Listings: Elements, Nature, Weather.

Sample Spells:

Bring healing to any place you visit by gathering twelve fallen leaves on a bright, sunny day. Take them to an area that needs revitalization (almost any urban setting qualifies). Name each leaf after a month of the year, tracing that word on the leaf with your finger. Visualize a vibrant green light filling each leaf as you draw. Then, beginning with your body facing a direction equating to the twelve on a clock's face, release one leaf at a time, turning in a circle to the right to the next hour. At each point, recite an incantation, such as: *"I free these leaves with winds that blow. Month by month, the healing grows. They carry my prayer, God/Goddess, make this world whole."*

Repeat your incantation whenever you see a fresh leaf fall to bring healing to various spots you visit.

Ritualize the Earth's own healing processes by tending a seedling just starting to sprout. Use any plant you enjoy, but it is better to have one that's hardy both indoors and outdoors (so you can keep it alive during cold months). Name your seed "Earth" and place it in good soil. Visit this seedling daily. Give your miniature Earth abundant love and attention. Each time you remove weeds from its base, visualize one of the ills of this world being pulled. For a stronger association, name the weed after a harmful aspect like pollution. Example: *"I take pollution by my hand, then remove it from the land."* Chant this mini-spell while you weed, then take weeds to compost, so positive energy comes from that effort.

Similarly, when you water, see positive things being brought to the Earth. In this case, your incantation might be: *"Where water goes, healing flows."* Remember to accompany this magic with strong images of environmental improvement.

Elements

General Uses: Attunement to the four elements (Earth, Air, Fire, Water) and their associated devic entities.

Timing: Chosen according to the element. Examples include Fire awareness at noontime on Summer Solstice and Water awareness under a full moon near a lake, stream, or other water source.

Props/Focals: Combine color with imagery for best results. For example, for Fire, use a burning red candle.

Secondary Listings: Magic, Ecology, Nature, Weather.

Sample Spells:

Note: Since these spells change depending on the predominant element, I am providing an example with blanks. Fill these in according to your goal.

Find some music that reflects the element you wish to understand or commune with. Take this with some headphones to a spot that allows direct contact with that element. Also bring items whose color, texture, or appearance harmonically connect with that element. For example, if the element is Water, listen to calm, flowing music by a stream and sit on a blue-green blanket.

Settle in, taking time to set up your props within the line of sight. Breathe deeply and slowly until your perception of this setting increases. When you feel calm and centered, call on the element (or its devic energy) through incantation or prayer: *"Powers of the _____, I call to you as a friend. Come share this sacred space with me so that I might learn. Help me to know your ways of speaking to my heart."*

Once you have placed your request, sit quietly and meditate. Stay in close contact with your element. In this illustration, you could keep a hand damp with water or drink a glassful. Use all your senses to reach out to that element. If you have been successful, the element will make itself known to you on an instinctive, emotional level or through a vision. Try not to have any preconceived expectations; just open your mind. Make notes of your experiences to review later.

Faeries are elementals, each of which associates itself with a locality or type of plant life. In European and Victorian American folklore, faeries are attracted to sweet breads and fruity wines. So here, a cookie and a thimble of sangria become the components for a faerie-kinship spell.

Take these with you to the area where you want to welcome the wee folk and place the gifts in a pleasing location. A circle of flowers, toadstools or trees, or a little knoll nearby make excellent sites. While you are here, burn incense composed of any of the following to attract the fey: thyme, hazelwood (to reveal hidden things), primrose, roses, or straw.

Next, lay out your offerings, saying: *"Magic be quick, magic be free, a friend to the faeries I wish to be."* You can now either wait patiently and quietly or leave the gifts and check on them later. If they are gone, it is a sign of acceptance. You can expect some faerie-related events in the future.

Employment

General Uses: Finding work, improved prosperity, job security, and peace with one's work placement.

Timing: Moon in Virgo. Spring and summer when foliage is lush and green. Sunday afternoons. The month of April.

Props/Focals: Basil, chamomile, ginger, clove, dill, oats, peas, almond, and other herbs or foods of abundance. Tin for luck. The numbers four, six, and thirteen. Your first earned dollar bill. Job posts and business cards. Lively green hues for prosperity or orange for a successful harvest from your efforts.

Secondary Listings: Abundance, Choices, Dedication, Jobs, Money, Openings, Tenacity.

Sample Spells:

Print or write out job posts that appeal to you the most. Gather four, six, or thirteen of them, making notes to use later to contact the employers who posted them. Next, tie these together with a long string. To this bundle, attach a silver coin or piece of tin, then place it across the table from you. Burn a green candle rubbed with ginger (energy and prosperity) and visualize getting a call from a prospective employer.

As this vision becomes clear in your mind, draw the string and bundle toward you, saying: *"My goal is sure, my need is strong, help me find where I belong. To meet my needs, employment I seek; bring me success by the end of the week."* When the paper reaches your hand, keep the tin or coin to carry, then set the paper aflame. This releases the energy before inquiries begin.

Success with this spell includes getting solid leads, landing interviews, and receiving callbacks.

If sales prospects have been slow, an old European spell says that carrying kelp with you or washing floors with it draws prosperity. This is especially good for shop owners to encourage increased traffic. To these efforts, add a verbal component, such as: *"Fortune, turn your head this way, bring abundant _____ today."* Fill in the blank with a suitable term such as "clients," "leads," or "customers."

This spell also helps with job advancement. In this case, keep the kelp or something green as a component but change the incantation to match the circumstances. For example: *"God/Goddess let my talents shine, where hard work and faith combine, this promotion will be mine."*

Energy

General Uses: Power, vitality, stamina, initiative.

Timing: During the month of March. Waxing moons or noon sun. When the temperature is increasing. The seasons of spring and summer. Thursday.

Props/Focals: Gingerroot or powder or carnations. Topaz for revitalization. Bright red and orange. The numbers eight and forty. Flags, bread, incoming tides, and other items that expand or rise.

Secondary Listings: Health, Power, Zeal.

Sample Spells:

For increasing power to the conscious mind (knowledge, memory, logic, reason), gather seven pieces of red or gold string. To represent yourself, find another strand in your favorite hue. Cut the strands long enough to tie with forty knots. Carefully twirl the red or gold string together, surrounding the single piece.

Come noon, tie forty knots, repeating this phrase with each: *"With power surrounding, judgment's abounding."* Each morning for the next forty days, untie one knot. As you do, close your eyes and accept solar energy into yourself. Envision it as golden glitter pouring inward like a warm wave. As you enact this visualization, a secondary incantation can be added, such as *"The power released, my spell is complete."*

To further empower this spell, charge the knotted threads in sunlight for forty minutes, forty hours, or forty days before beginning the untying process. If time is of the essence, alter the spell so that you untie one knot per minute over forty minutes instead.

This spell is similar to the previous one but focuses on matters of spirituality and intuition. Here, use all silver or white thread (the color of the moon) around the central cord of self. Tie eight knots per evening during the three nights of a full moon, envisioning the silver rays being caught inside. Keep a strong conceptualization of your goal in mind as you work. Add a verbal component, such as: *"As on these knots the moon now shines, creative light be so entwined. When released with my life blessed, bring to me inventiveness!"*

Wait until the next full moon to untie the knots beneath the lunar disk. You don't have to undo all of them to activate the magic. For energy in love, untie two knots. To bring vigor to a special project, unfasten six.

Get a large rectangular piece of cloth that can be used to make a banner. Pastel yellow is a good color choice to represent the creative spirit. If you're working with a more cognitive goal, use bright gold, representing rational thought. Additionally, find a symbol with which to portray your goal when it is painted on the banner.

Choose the paint color according to your intentions. Use red to encourage power. Conversely, use black to banish something.

Next, depict the chosen emblem on the cloth, pouring all your energy into the work. For fortification, let the emblem dry, then recoat it eight times. Affix some rope to two corners of the rectangle and take the banner where it can be flown like a flag. Try a tree, telephone pole, lamppost, or laundry line. As you place the banner, empower it by saying: *"Enchanted power fly with each wind, so my magic can begin. As this banner dances in air, magicked energy to me bear!"* Leave the banner in place to release power with each breeze.

FEAR

General Use: Anxiety, trepidation, alarm, phobias, panic attacks.

Timing: Months of August and October. Moon in Gemini. Waning moons. When the sky is clearing of clouds. The number eight to revitalize your sense of control.

Props/Focals: Tea (especially decaffeinated), thyme, and mullein (courage). Amethyst (peace of mind) and sardonyx (to banish consternation). The colors red and silver.

Secondary Listings: Adaptation, Balance, Courage, Doubt, Ghosts, Overcoming, Understanding, Victory.

Sample Spells:

For this spell, you need some cardboard, feathers, bits of cloth, and other symbolic items that can be glued to a flat surface. From the cardboard, create a mask without eye holes. Take a moment to focus on the thing that causes you fear, and then portray that fear on the mask, literally or symbolically, using the components gathered. Allow your anxiety to pour out of your hands into the guise.

Next, tie a string to each end of the mask so that you can wear it. For a moment, imitate the thing you fear. Do this with sound, movement, or whatever feels right. Then stop and realize that fear is not your master; it does not control your actions. Feel resentment toward that fear. Let those emotions build in one hand until you must tear the fear away (remove the mask).

Finally, tear up, burn, or otherwise destroy the mask and the misgivings. To this action, add a verbal component, such as: *"Fear be gone; all fear erased, by confidence is now replaced. Fear I banish, no more in me, for now, my eyes are clear to see!"*

When you need more backbone and assurance, try drinking thyme and mullein tea from a red cup. Hold it in your hands beneath the sunlight. Repeat this incantation eight times as you hold the cup: *"Into me, into me, courage, strength, serenity."* Drink the tea to internalize your magic.

This spell may be augmented by infusing the tea beneath the sun. For this, put your ingredients in a clear, covered container. Use ½ teaspoon of each herb per cup of water. If you don't like the flavors of thyme and mullein, reduce the number of herbs to ¼ teaspoon per cup and add one regular black tea bag. Magically, black tea produces positive energy for any goal.

Place this receptacle in a window where it will receive direct sunlight. Let the herbs steep until the water is heady with their scent. Enjoy chilled over ice (to freeze fear), or drink the tea warm to engender courage.

FERTILITY

General Uses: Pregnancy, productivity, gardening.

Timing: From the waxing to the full moon. The season of spring. When the moon is in Virgo or Pisces. The month of April. Monday and Friday. During the fertile part of the menstrual cycle.

Props/Focals: The numbers seven and twelve. An easterly wind for new beginnings. Images of fish, storks, rabbits, or a pregnant goddess. Cauliflower, eggs, and cheese (for manifestation). Agate, coral, and jade (for luck). Dandelions, seedlings, hazelnuts (for men), and ash wood. The colors green (for growth) or yellow (for creativity). Knots to secure the magic.

Secondary Listings: Abundance, Art, Lust, New Endeavors, Nature, Prosperity, Relationships, Unions.

Sample Spells:

A couple wishing to conceive should come together during the most fertile part of the menstrual cycle. Coordinating this with any of the other timings listed above will improve the potential for success. Decorate the area for your spell in green and yellow. Set up an altar with the image of a pregnant person or deity in a central position to represent the Mother Goddess. Also, place a seedling from any hardy plant nearby. Make sure both participants are well rested, healthy, and calm before beginning.

Next, sit in front of the altar and light a candle together to symbolize your hope. Dedicate a moment of prayer to your household god or goddess, then begin breathing in unison and extending your senses to each other. Chant quietly in unison: *"Fertility, grow in me."* Allow this phrase to get louder as passion grows. Let nature take her course.

Finally, the couple should take the seedling somewhere to grow in rich soil that won't be disturbed so the magic can likewise begin to take root. This spell can be repeated any time you're trying to conceive. It may also be used to smooth the course of adoptions by making the appropriate changes in the verbal component. In this case, the sexual union extends loving energy to find the right child.

This spell can also be applied to unproductive areas of your life to encourage progress.

If you are having trouble carrying to term, use this spell in combination with your conception ritual. Begin by getting a sturdy piece of green rope (for growth). Tie one knot in it to represent the baby. Hold the rope gently in both hands, place it up against your heart, and say: *"Secured in my womb, a seed of love. There to grow and blossom until released by nature _____ months hence. Surrounded by safety, health, and wholeness, you shall remain until this knot is undone."* Fill in the blank with the number of months until your due date, then keep the rope bundled in a baby blanket.

When you go into labor, untie the knot at the hospital to release pain and open the birthing channel. This is similar to what many European midwives used to do. When delivering a baby, they opened every cupboard, button, and window so that labor would be swift.

In ancient Rome and China, people had special rituals to ensure fertile land. People in both cultures made circuits around the parcel while reciting prayers. In many instances, this rite took place at dawn and included a sprinkling of water to symbolize fertility.

When you wish to magically enhance your land—garden or flowerpots—you can adapt this custom by preparing this decoction. It is designed to enrich the soil and keep bugs away. Mix 1 gallon of water, 1 cup of garlic juice, 1 cup of tomato leaf tea, 1 cup of onion juice, 1 cup of cucumber peel tea, 1 cup of tansy tea, and 1 cup of marigold tea. Sprinkle this thoroughly over your soil, moving clockwise to draw positive energy. Add a song like *The Earth Is Our Mother* while you move to share nurturing energy with the land. Repeat annually before the sowing season.

To do a similar soil blessing for a large number of people, create a small amount of this infusion and add it to a cauldron full of soil. Seeds should be laid on the altar to absorb positive energy. These are later taken home by the participants, along with a scoop of the earth to bless their own land.

Note: A good proportion for decoctions is taking 2 cups of an herb or vegetable to 1 cup of water to make a strong tea. Warm over a low flame until the liquid is reduced to 1 cup, then strain it and add it to the other ingredients.

Please use this spell in moderation. If overdone, these additives can irritate earthworms and other beneficial soil microbes. If you feel you want to repeat the spell regularly, dilute the mixture to one-quarter strength and leave a good space of time before planting.

Forgiveness

General Uses: Restitution, mercy, amendments, compensation.

Timing: Moon in Aries or Libra to restore emotional balance. New moon. The month of February.

Props/Focals: Coconut, lavender, mint, and parsley. Moonstone or alexandrite. The color white. The numbers two and nine. Items that can represent the area of disagreement or discord.

Secondary Listings: Anger, Banishing, Conscious Mind, Harmony, Liberation, Negotiation, Peace, Relationships, Understanding, Viewpoints.

Sample Spells:

To make a decorative serenity talisman, saw open a whole coconut, making sure that it remains in two complete halves. Clean out the meat and set it aside to use in cooking. Next, make holes in both sides of the shell with a small nail. If desired, pattern the holes symbolically or use a specific number to enhance meaning. Set the halves aside to dry. Meanwhile, find a disposable representation of your anger. Also gather a piece of white paper or cloth, some dried mint, white ribbon, and glue.

Sit before your image of anger and pour all your feelings into it. It may help to visualize or reenact the situation that induced those feelings. Cry or shout until a sense of quiet emptiness settles over you. Then, wrap the emblem in white cloth, saying: *"I cover you with peace, harmony, and understanding. I accept peace to my own heart and extend it to _____. Where anger was born, let love replace it."*

Now, inside one half of the coconut shell lay the cloth and emblem, completely surrounding them with mint (to encircle it with calm energy). Put on the top of the shell and glue the two halves together. Finally, use the white ribbon of truce as adornment. Hang the coconut somewhere nearby so the winds can release its serene energy (and fresh scent) into your home. If the coconut ever "goes bad," bury it with your negativity.

Please note that this spell can be done alone to remove negative feelings or by two people to return peace to a relationship. If more than one person is participating, each needs to bring a small emblem of their hostility. When finished, keep the coconut in a mutually enjoyed place where you can visit together to renew the promise of peace.

Gather together the people who wish to encourage forgiveness in their interactions. Each should bring one sprig of parsley for the others, the base of which is wrapped nine times with white thread or tape. Have everyone stand in a circle.

After forming the circle, everyone, in turn, goes to the person next to them (down the entire circle), exchanging parsley tokens, saying: *"I accept peace with you into my heart."* It is good to hug at this point and to make a deliberate effort to put the past behind you. To encourage harmony, each participant then takes home the last spring received. Alternatively, bundle the pieces together as a special decoration for the group that visually signifies accord among all members.

You can make a token of settlement by first finding either a moonstone or alexandrite to represent the person with whom you are at odds. Then, get mint extract or lavender oil and mix it with first aid cream. Burn ointment is ideal since it cools the heat of Fire. You do not need much—about ½ teaspoon will suffice.

Name your stone after the person you desire to forgive or to obtain forgiveness from. Slowly anoint the surface of the stone with nine dabs of the healing salve, saying: *"As this cream smooths and soothes, so too _____'s heart. Let our bond be renewed, never again to part."* Afterward, rinse the stone to wash away any lingering negativity. Finally, give it to the other person with whom you were at odds or send it with a note of explanation.

Friendship

General Uses: Improved relationships, camaraderie, allegiance, companionship, rapport, and harmony.

Timing: Moon in Aquarius. Waxing moons. Harvest season. Spring Equinox. On your friend's birthday. The month of June.

Props/Focals: Sweet pea flowers and lemons. Jade. Shades of pink. The numbers two and twelve. Pictures of those close to you. Interlocking symbols and tokens.

Secondary Listings: Communication, Harmony, Kinship, Relationships, Unions, Web Weaving.

Sample Spells:

A fun way to celebrate friendship is through a game of cat's cradle. Play until a mutually pleasing pattern emerges. Next, carefully take the string off your fingers and lay it out on cardboard exactly as it appeared in your hands. On top, dab a bit of white glue scented with lemon so that the pattern adheres to the board.

Once the pattern has dried, both people should lay their hands on opposite sides of the board and share their feelings with one another. Then, cut the board in half. Each person takes home the half empowered by the other. This should be kept in a special place as an emblem of your connection and strong commitment to each other.

For larger magical groups, it is easier to find or to make a puzzle representative of the group. Then, each person from the assembly gets to keep a piece, adding it to the whole each time they gather.

This spell for magical unity and fellowship can include two or more people. Each participant should bring a candle to represent themselves. Place one unlit, large pink candle on the center table or altar.

To begin, have the group gather around the central area, taking time to breathe in unison and bring the individual energies into harmony. Afterward, all individual candles are lit, and each person states their name and personal contribution as part of that group; for example, *"I am _____, and I offer my song to this gathering."* In this case, you might sing a song about oneness.

This process continues until each person has spoken. (Please note that an individual's contribution can be a service, like helpfulness. No group could function well without these types of people.) Next, all participants place the flames of their candles to the central pink taper and begin a low rolling chant, something akin to: *"With perfect trust and perfect love, in spirit, we are one."* This chant should naturally rise to a peak and then fall to a whisper. In the silence, blow out the individual candles, leaving the candle of friendship to burn in your hearts.

To encourage friendship in your life, prepare a charm from a swatch of pink cloth, twelve pieces of dried lemon (or twelve sweetpea flowers), two interlocking puzzle pieces, and a bell. The charm should be prepared and blessed during a waxing moon to encourage growing companionship. Your incantation can take this form: *"Alone was I, in days gone by, but now no more to be. With this spell, I ring a bell to bring new friends to me."* Make sure to ring the bell at the appropriate moment in the incantation, then bind it up inside your sachet with the other ingredients. Carry this token into situations where you're likely to meet new people.

FOUNDATIONS

General Uses: Grounding, support, justification, establishment.

Timing: Planting season. Moon in Sagittarius. The month of May. Saturday.

Props/Focals: Lead for keeping one's feet on the ground. Earth tones. The numbers one, three, and twelve. Seedlings, rich soil, farms, trees, and roots. Anchors.

Secondary Listings: Adaptation, Grounding, New Endeavors.

Sample Spells:

Find a solid twig. To one end, affix a piece of lead. If this is not available, substitute a pencil for the twig and lead. You will also need a baby tree or tomato plant (or any plant you would normally truss to help it grow). If you live in an apartment, the latter is a better choice because you can keep the plant indoors.

Gather some good soil and a planter (or go to your garden). Take care to prepare the soil well. Name the plant after yourself, symbolically giving your spirituality good ground to grow in. Place the twig or pencil behind the vegetation, with the lead end firmly in the ground. Add your verbal component. One example is: *"With this plant that I have bound, I'll keep both feet upon the ground. My spirit with this plant to spread, yet firmly rooted with the lead."* Tend this plant lovingly, allowing it to remind you of your own growing spirit.

If, in the future, the plant becomes ill, it can mean one of two things. Symbolically, you may not be taking good care of your roots. Mundanely, indoor potting soil becomes nutrient deficient after a while. In either case, you will need to remove the lead from that ground and cultivate a new, healthy plant to represent your foundations.

This spell requires a pot big enough to put in both of your feet, potting soil, and three pieces of root from any hardy plant. Begin by placing a little soil in the bottom of the pot, then stand on it with your bare feet. Next, pour in enough additional soil to cover your feet completely.

With your strong hand, place the three roots, one at a time, in a triangle around your feet. As they are planted in the soil, say: *"By planting one, my spell's begun. With two to sow, my spirit grows. Where three are bound, I'm on solid ground."* After this, it is good to stand in the soil for a while, visualizing yourself as a strong, well-rooted tree. Enjoy your connection to the soil. Keep a little of the dirt and roots as a portable amulet. Return the remainder to the Earth by way of a blessing.

If you use comfrey roots, they will almost certainly grow when returned to the Earth. Also, store-bought carrots—even just the tops—will often sprout nearly anywhere. So, if you have a garden, consider using these two roots. In this spell, carrots grant a foundation in which your dreams and visions may grow. Comfrey symbolizes healing.

To keep yourself from daydreaming too much, find a picture or a piece of jewelry depicting an anchor. Bless this object by repeating an incantation either three or twelve times as you hold it in your strong hand. One example is: *"When my dreams fly like eagles free, my anchor be to reality."* Keep the image in your wallet, on a necklace, or someplace convenient.

GHOSTS

General Use: Conjuring and banishing. Communication with and understanding the purposes of spirits.

Timing: In-between times (noon, midnight, dusk, and dawn). Halloween. Seasons of late fall and winter. Moon in Libra. Eclipses. Wednesday.

Props/Focals: General ones include candles, items sensitive to the wind, Ouija boards, personal effects of the person being contacted, and sheets. To summon beneficent or reveal present spirits: Sweetgrass, tobacco, and wormwood; agate, lodestone, and turquoise. To protect from or banish negative spirits: Beans, chrysanthemum, dill, fennel, garlic, myrrh, sage, tobacco, and pepper; jade, jasper, and malachite.

Secondary Listings: Banishing, Cleansing, Discernment, Intuition, Protection, Wisdom.

Sample Spells:

Word of warning: Spiritual entities should not be banished or called for amusement. It is best to contact a knowledgeable, experienced psychic for advice or assistance before undertaking any of these spells.

To see spirits, old European grimoires recommend mixing together aloe, pepper, musk, vervain, and saffron and burning this in a cemetery. We can adapt this for other locations (like those in which the spirit lived) by adding a bit of sweet grass or tobacco to a specially prepared incense. Create the incense on the anniversary of the death of the individual you wish to contact. This is then burned at 11 a.m., in the safety of a magic circle that also holds symbolic items to connect you to the entity. An incantation to encourage the spirit's presence is: *"Guardians of the Spirit realm, hear and guide my plea. When the witching hour rings true, bring my friend (loved one, etc.) to me. Other souls who hear my call are not welcome in this place. Only the one known as may enter sacred space."*

Repeat the request three times, twenty minutes apart, then wait quietly for indications of a presence. Signs include the scent of flowers or a favored cologne, a cool wind, movement of curtains, and candles going out or twitching erratically. Once you feel sure the spirit is with you, do not make it tarry overly long. Take care of your business, say farewell, and thank the guardians for their assistance.

To rid your living space of an unwanted spirit, begin by putting everything in its proper place. Clean your house to perfection, open the windows, and bless all your magical implements (see "Blessing").

Next, always moving to your left (counterclockwise, or "widdershins" as it is called in magical circles), anoint the doors, windows, and all openings of your home with a mixture of water (Water), fennel (Fire), oats (Earth), pine (Air), and sage (Wisdom). These represent all elements of the magic circle. For a blend that is less bulky, place the herbs in hot water to steep, then strain and use only the aromatic tea.

As you go, visualize bright light pouring from your hands into every area that houses shadows, saying: "*Where light dwells, all darkness flee; Spirit move away from me. This home is mine; I will not fear. Your presence is not welcome here.*" Follow the entire circuit of your home, repeating the procedure in every room. When finished, go outside if possible, making one full loop around the exterior. The leftover water can be refrigerated or frozen for future use.

Finally, return inside and move clockwise through each room while burning basil, dill, and marjoram. These herbs encourage blessings and joy. Invoke the protection of your personal god or goddess in your sacred space of home. Then, close the windows, leaving any negative spiritual energies outside.

Goals

General Uses: Manifestation and aspirations. Bringing dreams into reality. Realistic targets.

Timing: Waxing to full moons. Tuesday, Thursday, and Sunday. When the moon is in Taurus, Leo, or Sagittarius. March and April.

Props/Focals: A bullseye, dart board, or other target. Arrows. Any items like step stools and ladders that allow you to stretch or reach things normally unobtainable. The number four. The colors red, orange, and brown. Daisy, clover, cinnamon, and ginger. The image of an ant (for tenacity). Agate, beryl, and jade. Southerly winds for active energy.

Secondary Listings: Choices, Dedication, Energy, Judgment, New Endeavors, Organization, Tenacity, Victory.

Sample Spells:

Step one is to get a piece of construction paper and mark it with a representation of your goal. Place this securely on a wall within your sacred space. Next, obtain some cellophane tape, a blindfold, four strips of red or orange paper, a glue stick, and a little powdered ginger. Stroke one side of each paper strip with the glue stick and fasten a circle of tape to the other side.

Sprinkle the gluey portion of the paper with ginger while saying: *"Success I claim, today I shine, soon (insert goal) will be mine."* Next, focus all your energy toward the paper. Continue to repeat the power phrase. Visualize the attainment of your goal. Then close your eyes and don the blindfold. Hold fast to your visualization and take the strips of paper in hand. Concentrate on your intentions before placing the strips on the marked construction paper on your wall. It's just like *"Pin the Tail on the Donkey,"* only with a magical purpose.

Now remove your blindfold and see how close you came. If your marks are way off, repeat the spell every few days until you hit a bullseye. Afterward, fold the target in quarters (once for each element) with the tail attached and then burn it, the entire thing, thereby releasing your hopes to the winds. The heated ginger provides added energy for manifestation.

This charm helps in obtaining goals. Gather together a red cloth, a piece of agate, four clover leaves, four small pinches of cinnamon, and any item that represents success. By the light of the waxing to full moon, empower this by saying four times: *"Bit of cloth, by string wound, let my magic be unbound. Leaf and herb within combine, soon attainment will be mine."* Carry it until you accomplish your objective.

First, set a reasonable time to obtain your goal. Divide this figure by four and round off. For example, if you need something accomplished within two months, this equals sixty days or four fifteen-day intervals. Keep the results in mind for this spell. If time is wanting, you may shorten this spell by using shorter intervals (hours or minutes).

Next, place an item signifying your aspiration in a tree, high on a wall, or in any other inconvenient location. Go to this place four times at intervals, based on the limit you set. At each visit, slowly loosen whatever bindings you have on that goal.

Each time you climb toward the emblem, use a verbal component to empower your actions. For example: "*Higher still and higher, my magic shall not tire. The first try, my goal I see. My second try, my will is free. My third try, aim is gained. My fourth try, the goal's obtained.*" On the fourth visit, loosen the object just enough so the wind will naturally finish the job, carrying the magic toward its intended target.

GOSSIP

General Uses: Halting misinformation, rumors, and slander. Getting to the truth of a matter.

Timing: November, December, and January. Waning moons. When the moon is in Libra or Virgo. Tuesday or Sunday (to illuminate untruths).

Props/Focals: The numbers four, eight, and nine. Carnelian. Worms, oranges, cloves, and grass. The element of Fire. Any binding utensils such as paper clips, staples, glue, or clothespins.

Secondary Listings: Banishing, Communication, Courage, Discernment, Identifying, Justice, Negotiation, Prejudice, Viewpoints

Sample Spells:

Across a plain piece of paper, neatly write the name of the person gossiping. On the top of the paper, attach four metal paper clips. As each is placed, say: "*I bind untruth by _____.*" Fill in the blank with Earth, Air, Fire, and Water, respectively.

Next, secure a spring-type clothespin to the top of each paper clip. Wait for a southerly wind, then put the paper out on a line and carefully ignite it. Let the winds of truth and transformation carry away any malicious energy.

Take eight orange peels and place four whole cloves lengthwise in each. String these together, four to a string, keeping them in place with a knot under each. As you secure each knot, speak purposefully: *"Gossip I bind, the truth will be mine. I gather them both with each knot that I wind."*

Hang the strands in a southern window. At this point, include a small prayer, such as: *"With the light at my sill, let all hearsay be stilled."* Add small silver bells blessed for protection to the bottom of the strings. They will warn you when gossip starts circulating again. In its finished form, the fruit strands act like a wind chime and air refresher.

GRIEF

General Uses: Acceptance of loss, easing distress. Funerals or Summerland rituals.

Timing: Waning moons. Bright sunlight. During astrological Water signs. Months of February, August, or November.

Props/Focals: Jet. Lavender, marjoram, chamomile, basil, and blueberry. The numbers one and twenty-one. Balms, feathers, and anything associated with emotional healing, relief, and lifting of heaviness. Tea for courage. Cocoa or chocolate.

Secondary Listings: Anger, Banishing, Courage, Doubt, Humor, Overcoming, Remembrance, Understanding.

Sample Spells:

To make a tea for peacefulness, prepare a quart container with 3 teaspoons each of basil, chamomile, marjoram, and black tea. Fill the container with hot water and leave the herbs steeping on a windowsill, in the light of a waning moon, for twenty-one minutes. As they saturate the water, begin reciting a verbal component, like: *"As the moon grows small, so too my pain, let joy return to my life again."* Drink in ½ cup lots every night before bed for the next twenty-one days. Take care to keep this properly refrigerated.

Cut the shape of a heart from a piece of construction paper. Apply a healing salve such as first aid cream to the image. Place this with a feather in an idea box or other easily carried container. Empower the spell with a verse, such as: *"Grief be not long, let my heart grow strong. Darkness, fly away; bring me happiness today."* Carry this charm during your mourning period to renew strength and cheer.

In the Victorian era, people carried jet when grieving for a loved one. They believed this black stone soaked up sadness and restored emotional balance. This type of amulet is still useful, especially if blessed with a prayer, incantation, or supplication to your personal god or goddess. The amulet should be carried until grief has lifted. Keep the stone with other mementos for those times when sadness returns, such as the anniversary of a death.

GROUNDING

General Uses: Foundations, support, justification, and growth. Responsible disbursement of magical energy.

Timing: Planting season. Spring months, especially May. When the moon is in Capricorn or Sagittarius. Thursday or Saturday.

Props/Focals: The numbers one (for stability), six, and twelve. The cellar or other rooms near the ground. Rich soil, trees, maple wood, root bundles, and grains or Earthy crops like potatoes and carrots. The color brown.

Secondary Listings: Balance, Foundations.

Sample Spells:

To ground energy after a spell or a particularly potent magical circle, use simple symbolism. Sit on the ground, placing your hands in direct contact with the Earth. Let the excess energy pour out of you while repeating this statement twelve or thirteen times: *"From nature shared, we reciprocate; let this energy disseminate."* Continue relaxing until you feel the buzz in the air passing and your senses return to normal. It also helps to eat some simple foods like raw vegetables.

This spell also works for people who feel the need to keep their feet on the ground. If an outdoor location is not available, go to an area close to the Earth, like a cellar or sun porch. Use the same verbal component. While reciting the incantation, see yourself as a tree or other plant with deep, strong roots.

Another function of grounding energy is to root a spell to a particular location, such as a garden. For example, take some compost or topsoil and bless it. To this base, add some dried maple leaves or wood (as a foundation). As you plant the garden, your magic will flourish with that soil. While you sow, chant: *"With love you are blessed, with love you are grown, let be reaped with each seed that's sown."* Fill in the blank with the general theme for your garden. Examples include health, love, and magic.

You can place six or twelve stones in a star-shaped pattern around the garden as guardians. This networks your magical energy.

HABITS

General Uses: Inspiring or banishing behavior patterns and customs. Changing tendencies and dispositions.

Timing: To develop positive attributes—waxing to full moon; moon in Leo or Sagittarius; Thursday or Saturday; the month of October. To rid negative attributes—waning moons; moon in Gemini, Capricorn, or Aries; Monday (for healing); the months of March and July.

Props/Focals: Representations of the habit or characterization. Items that can grow or be reduced according to your ultimate goal. Examples of this include yeast bread dough, which rises to encourage positive attributes, or soda pop left to go flat, which reduces negative energy. Pine, nutmeg, ashes, and butterflies (transformation). The colors red or green.

Secondary Listings: Adaptation, Banishing, Choices, Dedication, Liberation, Overcoming, Versatility, Victory.

Sample Spells:

To develop a good habit, defrost a loaf of frozen bread dough. Knead in some nutmeg and any other edible that represents that action. For example, add apple slices to stimulate thoughtfulness before action. Once your ingredients are prepared, follow the directions for rising and baking as given on the package. Add a verbal element either before cooking or eating. In this illustration, such an incantation accompanying baking might be: *"Bread of Earth, rise for me; with wisdom wrought my thoughts will be."* Or, upon eating, try: *"Wisdom within, wisdom without, let this magic come about."*

To give this spell an additional boost, carve a symbol of your goal into the bread before it bakes. The heat will activate your magical energy. I also heartily encourage making bread dough from scratch. Nothing beats the flavor, texture, and personal energy in homemade bread!

During a waning moon, add three drops of green food coloring to a bottle of ginger ale. Recap it securely, put the bottle beneath the lunar beams, and say: "_____ *is not a part of me. When the moon is dark, I will be freed."* Fill in the blank with the name of the negative habit being banished.

From that night until the new moon, drink a little of the ginger ale every day, focusing on your intention to change. Remember that breaking bad habits is not just a magical endeavor but also a function of your own will and honest desire.

For a portable amulet that provides extra strength in overcoming a negative habit, begin by finding a breakable representation of it. Completely crush the token beneath your feet.

As you do, shout: "_____ *has no dominion over me.*" Feel yourself stomping that pattern out of your life. Continue until you feel drained, calm, and centered.

Gather the remnants and mix them with pine needles and lemon rind. Cautiously place this blend in a portable container. Choose a sturdy container (not cloth) so you don't accidentally cut yourself. Each time you feel tempted to slip back into old tendencies, carefully sprinkle a pinch of the mixture on the ground behind you and walk firmly away. Repeat your power phrase to reactivate the magic.

HARMONY

General Uses: Peace, symmetry, compatibility, agreement, accord.

Timing: Dawn and dusk. During daylight hours when the moon is visible. New Year and Halloween. Midnight and noon. Waxing moons. Moon in Gemini, Libra, or Pisces. The month of August.

Props/Focals: The colors pale blue or white. The number two and three. Basil, rose, water, olives, coriander, and aloe. Gentle, blended music or objects in which different items come together in beauty, such as a flower arrangement or a patterned fabric. Scales.

Secondary Listings: Balance, Communication, Friendship, Kinship, Peace, Unions.

Sample Spells:

To encourage harmony in the home, an English custom is to hang a bundle of coriander near the hearth. Before you do so, accent your bundle with three braided blue ribbons. While you braid, play peaceful music and add an incantation, such as: *"Harmony, harmony, harmony, brought into my home. Peace, joy, and happiness, magic through my poem."* To accentuate this effort, add dried basil to the bundle and dab the ribbons with rose water.

If dried coriander and basil aren't available, substitute mint and chamomile, bundled in blue or white cloth. These two herbs have strong tranquilizing qualities. Both may be purchased in tea bags. Alternatively, since coriander is a member of the parsley family, use fresh sprigs of parsley.

HEALTH

General Uses: Overall well-being. Return to wholeness of body, mind, and spirit. Strength and vitality.

Props/Focals: Comfrey, rosemary, fennel, garlic, mint, apple, and ash wood. The number three. Turquoise, amber, and coral. Adhesive bandages, an ankh, or a red cross. The colors red, blue, and green. Orange juice, chicken soup, or other foods associated with feeling better.

Secondary Listings: Cleansing, Energy, Liberation, Sleep.

Sample Spells:

Note: Health spells usually pertain to one type of sickness. So, a general, all-purpose health enchantment appears below, along with examples, for common maladies. However, these should in no way take the place of modern medical care, especially for persistent symptoms. Let them act as a magical accent to conventional methods.

A spell that originated in Renaissance England to rid oneself of a toothache or mole begins with the wrapping of a red string or cloth around a piece of coal, a potato, or a stone. Carry this with you for three days, then take it to a water source that flows away from you. Throw the bundle into the water, turn away, and don't look back. The water will carry the pain or mole with it. Alternatively, bury the item where it will remain undisturbed.

To reduce any sickness, write the word *abracadabra* in descending form on a piece of paper. Make a hole in the base of a tree and spit in it, placing the paper therein. Bury the paper to bury your illness.

Another charm to banish sickness is made by placing a gold coin in a glass of red wine. Put this beneath the stars and a waning moon for three nights, and each night, drink one-third of the wine to shrink your sickness until it's gone. This originated in rural Welsh regions, with some similar spells appearing in Scotland and England.

As has been done traditionally in China and in England, to diminish a fever or cold, wrap a red flannel cloth around your neck before bedtime. Then, drink a cup of warm whiskey mixed with fennel, cinnamon, and cloves. Repeat this procedure for three days, and the cold should ease. For a nonalcoholic alternative to whiskey in this recipe, use apple cider.

To create an amulet for well-being, place a piece of coral, a bit of fresh mint, a slice of orange rind, and an apple peel in a small container. Empower the amulet, saying: *"Keep sickness at bay, bring health each day!"* Repeat the incantation three times, visualizing the bundle filling with greenish-white light. Carry it with you often. If you associate healing with a different color, adapt the visualization accordingly.

Heartbreak

General Uses: Relieving sadness, melancholy, depression, or loneliness.

Timing: The waning moon. Friday. Moon in Gemini or Capricorn. The month of October. Dawn.

Props/Focals: Chamomile, comfrey, lemon, thyme, valerian, witch hazel, morning glory, lemon balm, and violet. Carnelian and coral. Birchwood, elm, and redwood. The number eight. Tissues.

Secondary Listings: Adaptation, Courage, Forgiveness, Friendship, Joy, Kinship, Love, Overcoming, Relationships, Understanding.

Sample Spells:

Prepare a cup of warm tea with ¼ teaspoon each of comfrey, chamomile, lemon, and thyme. Add a little honey as a balm for your heart. Stir counterclockwise, repeating these words four times: *"Sadness depart, don't anchor my heart."* Then, stir clockwise, saying four times: *"Joy is growing, sadness must flee, even as I drink my tea!"* Now enjoy the beverage. Also, consider taking yourself out for a special treat afterward to encourage a more positive attitude.

Cut a red heart out of fabric and tear it into two pieces. Next, by a waxing moon, stitch together the parts using green thread (or another healing color). While you sew, add a chant that you repeat until your work is finished: *"What was ripped asunder, let magic restore; return happiness to me, even greater than before."* Keep this with you in your wallet, pocket, or near your heart to continue the flow of healing energy.

Humor

General Uses: Amusement, improved spirits, pleasant diversions, breaking a negative mood.

Timing: Waxing to full moon. Sunny days, especially in spring. April Fools' Day. Moon in Aquarius.

Props/Focals: Hawthorn wood, anise, catnip, agate, almond, zinnia, and feathers. Playful or comical animals such as kittens or otters. Gag gifts, toys, and bright colors. The Fool in tarot.

Secondary Listings: Adaptation, Communication, Joy, Virtue.

Sample Spells:

You will need a fairly large feather or a clean feather duster. Start by standing quietly and centering your thoughts. Visualize yourself looking as silly as possible. If need be, stand on one foot, pat your head, and rub your belly. Do anything that helps relieve anxiety and tension.

Next, see the aura around yourself in bright, lively colors. Over this dancing energy field, brush your feather(s) clockwise, saying: *"A little comedy for me, to lift my mood, bring youthful glee. Tickled by feathers, tickled by light, let good spirits return this night!"* Continue to do this, or perhaps watch a silly movie until you cannot help but laugh. Remember that joy is powerful magic in itself!

To make a charm that encourages a good sense of humor, first, find an amusing picture of yourself. Around the edges of this picture, attach feathers, a few agates, almond oil, catnip, and perhaps a small toy. As you affix each, add the appropriate part of this verbal component: *"Feathers for fancy, agate for smiles, oil smooths all the wrinkles, catnip for wiles. Then comes a trinket to remind me to play. Humor tomorrow, humor today!"* Keep this amulet near your clothing so that it draws light, happy energy into items you use regularly.

IDENTIFYING PERSONS AND OBJECTS

General Uses: Finding lost goods. Discovering the source of difficulty. Classification of the basic magical matrix in an object. Uncovering personal spiritual gifts.

Timing: Wednesday and Sunday. Moon in Libra or Cancer. From the second day of the new moon to the full moon. Any holidays associated with oracular attempts, such as May Day and Samhain.

Props/Focals: Clay balls (uncovering thievery, specifically), tea leaves, flour or dust, nutmeg, beer, and hazelwood. The number five and the color yellow. Any dowsing instrument.

Secondary Listings: Discernment, Divination, Intuition, Recovering Items.

Sample Spells:

To identify an area where a lost item may be found, begin by getting some yellow modeling clay. Make a small, gumball-sized sphere for each area you have visited recently. For example, if you visited a friend, went to two different stores at the mall, and stopped at a gas station, make four clay balls. Take care that the clay spheres are equal in size.

Mark each with a symbol. Here, your friend's symbol might be a house, the mall stores could be depicted by the first letter of their names, and the gas station's emblem could be a dollar sign. If there are many possibilities, make a list of what each emblem represents.

Place the spheres in an earthenware bowl in bright sunlight and have a large vessel of water handy. As you pour the water over the clay, say: *"Truth shall rise, facts before my eyes. To the surface now steer, let the resting place appear!"* Continue repeating this phrase, keeping in mind a strong image of the item you have lost until one or more of the balls bob to the surface of the water. Begin your search at the place indicated. If, after five repetitions, none of the balls comes to the surface, it may be that you are looking in the wrong places.

This spell also works to discover people who are working against you. In this case, you mark the clay with the possible candidates' names. Please note, however, that your personal feelings can dramatically affect the outcome of this spell. So please gather facts that prove your hunch before condemning anyone. One way to keep things in balance is by calling upon an appropriate god or goddess to guide the magic.

To identify the source of a problem in your life, warm some beer with loose-leaf black tea and a little nutmeg. Place ½ cup of this mixture in a yellow teacup. Sip it until only a little liquid and the herbs remain. Swirl this thrice with your strong hand and concentrate on your difficulty. Turn the cup over onto a saucer, tapping the bottom lightly five times to loosen debris. Right the cup and look at the patterns that emerge.

The answer you get will likely be symbolic. For example, if the problems in your life stem from overt romanticism, you may see a heart shape near the rim of the cup.

IMAGINATION

General Uses: Encouraging the spirit of invention and originality. The ability to dream.

Timing: Waxing moons. Spring and summer. Moon in Cancer. Wednesday. Windy April days. Weekends or days off from work.

Props/Focals: Pomegranate. The color yellow. Birds, butterflies, and other winged creatures. Clouds, the closet, kites, your third eye. Any place that brings out your inner child.

Secondary Listings: Art, Inspiration, Quick-Mindedness, Visions.

Sample Spells:

Get yourself a yellow kite in early spring. To the tail, add feathers or yellow ribbons and something more to represent your imaginative sense. This object will need to be light enough to allow the kite to fly.

Next, go to an area where you can lose the kite on a nice breezy day. When it reaches a good altitude, take a pair of scissors to the string, saying: *"Higher still and higher, creativity taking fire. Fancy reborn in me, as my magic's freed!"* Cut the string and let your imagination soar with the winds. Finally, sit and daydream for a while, remembering the joys of childlike fantasy.

For people who find themselves a little too firmly rooted in reality, a visualization performed regularly by children can help. Go outside on a day when there are fluffy clouds in the sky. Lie on the grass beneath a tree and pick out shapes in the clouds. Slowly, try to find shapes of things that seem to hold you back and imagine those problems attached to the clouds. Let the winds of change move them away from you while you spend the day merrily dreaming!

If no clouds are available, let your worries and burdens be taken to wing by bird. Once you feel your spirits lifting, try to imagine yourself flying with a robin to renew your perspective. If you spy a bluebird, that's even better, as bluebirds spell happiness.

To your imagery, add a short verse, like: "*Help me fly, just share your wings. Reborn the song my inner child sings. Teach me how to have some fun while with you soars my imagination!*" Each time you see the same type of bird, take a moment to repeat the verbal part of this spell and dare to dream!

INSPIRATION

General Uses: Revelation. Spiritually kindled flashes of insight or creativity. Motivation and encouragement.

Timing: Waxing to full moon. Moon in Cancer or Aquarius. September. Wednesday. Special days filled with good memories.

Props/Focals: The number seven. Rowan wood, figs, grapes, beer, tea, and sprouts. Bright colors, especially green and yellow. Light sources, open windows, or the representation of an open eye.

Secondary Listings: Art, Discernment, Movement, Unconscious Mind, Visions, Zeal.

Sample Spells:

Place a bundle of grapes near a light source for seven minutes. Then, gather the grapes in your hands while strongly visualizing the area of your life that needs improved creativity or insight. Continuing your thoughts, slowly pattern the grapes into the image of an eye. Lastly, eat the portrait to quite literally bring vision into yourself!

For a portable amulet that encourages inspired action and thought, cut three strips of green fabric and four of yellow. Lay the strips on top of one another, alternating colors, so they form a star with their corners. In the center of the star, put a few dried figs with dried tea and bean sprouts. If Rowan wood is available, add a tiny piece of it as well.

Tie the cache together, then go to a window, opening it wide to bless your magic. Say: "*Come into this charm, discerning winds, that my magic can begin. Inspired in thought indeed I'll be, whene'er this charm is upon me.*" Carry the charm whenever you feel a little extra motivation and encouragement will be needed.

To overcome artist's block, wrap the implements of your craft in yellow or green cloth. Put the tools in the rays of the noon sun to empower them with bright, inspiring light. Then, transport them to your work area. Hold the cools gently in your hands with your eyes closed. Feel the energy within from the sunlight and your previous artistic efforts.

Intuition

General Uses: Improving instincts and subconscious signals.

Timing: Full moon. Monday. Moon in Cancer, Pisces, or Libra. The month of November. On your birthday or during positive biorhythm cycles.

Props/Focals: Lamps; coffee, water, or other fluids; mushrooms; eggs; and keyholes. The colors silver, yellow, and green. The number five.

Secondary Listings: Adaptation, Discernment, Quick-Mindedness, Unconscious Mind, Wisdom.

Sample Spells:

One way to improve your discernment is by making a magical meal for yourself. Begin by sautéing ¼ cup of diced mushrooms until they are tender. Next, add two well-beaten eggs and a little diluted coffee (instead of water) for energy. While you stir the mixture clockwise, visualize bright yellow light pouring into the pan. Play particularly uplifting music while you work, then eat the meal to accept the energy of those foods.

To bring empathy throughout your home, anoint the windowsills and doors with weak coffee. Call on the personal god or goddess of your family for blessings at each stop or add an invocation like *"Energy for empathy, within these walls is sympathy. Let none disrupt the care here placed, blessed by magic, this sacred space."*

JOBS

General Uses: Improving employment prospects, job performance, or promotional chances.

Timing: Spring and summer. Moon in Virgo. Before interviews or reviews for raises and promotions.

Props/Focals: Any type of money, job advertisements, status symbols, and logos of companies. The number thirteen. Grains, peas, saffron, meat, gourmet food, or anything symbolic of security.

Secondary Listings: Abundance, Adaptation, Communication, Dedication, Discernment, Employment, Leadership, Openings, Tenacity, Prosperity, Victory, Zeal.

Sample Spells:

Collect thirteen dried peas, 1 teaspoon of grain cereal, and a strand of saffron. Place these in a green pouch with a silver coin or dollar bill. Sleep with the amulet for thirteen nights. As you fall asleep, visualize your needs being met. Carry the token with you while looking for work, interviewing, or being considered for promotion. When not in use, store it in a safe place to act as a prosperity charm.

Find job advertisements that interest you and for which you meet minimum qualifications. Take notes from them, then anoint the newspaper with patchouli oil. Place the paper in a heat-safe container and ignite it as you say: *"By paper known, by Fire relayed, power now waters the seeds I've laid. With this smoke, my wishes rise. Show me where prosperity lies."* Keep the ashes as a charm or bury them with a blossoming plant so the energy grows.

Take a copy of your resume and the business cards of companies where you have recently interviewed. These firms should also be ones where you would enjoy working. Fold these inside your resume using thirteen folds. Then, wrap the bundle with gold thread or ribbon, tying it with thirteen loops or knots. Say: *"My potential and desire, wrapped within a seal of gold, let an offer soon unfold."*

Keep the charm somewhere safe until you find the job you want. Afterward, untie one of the loops each time you have a performance review to help present the best aspects of yourself to management.

JOY

General Uses: Improving one's mood. Happiness, personal satisfaction, and delight.

Timing: Spring, especially April and May Day. Moon in Virgo or Aquarius. Sunday. When the sun is shining.

Props/Focals: Agate, almonds, balloons, cake, cheese, hawthorn, feathers, honey, sugar, gelatin dessert, peaches, and berries. The color blue.

Secondary Listings: Harmony, Humor, Love, Optimism, Peace, Youthful Outlook.

Sample Spells:

Prepare a box of regular gelatin dessert, following the directions, and add peaches or fresh berries. (All three items are associated with joy and good feelings.) Once the gelatin sets, eat it to transport those positive emotions into yourself.

For creative panache, form the gelatin into a smile. Use a piece of aluminum foil for a mold. Double the foil over before shaping it into a smile. Pour a little of the liquid gelatin into the aluminum foil separately from the rest of the batch and chill.

Write your wish for happiness on a small piece of paper. Tie this loosely with a blue ribbon into a tree, saying: *Joy be free, joy be free, by winds come loose, be born in me.* Do something fun while you wait for the wind to liberate the wish and carry the magic back to you. Alternatively, write the wish on a carrot or other item that can be eaten by animals.

Make a special wand just for spells and rituals centering on joy. For this, you will need a hawthorn twig. Carefully remove the bark and sand any rough edges. Decorate the nooks using agate crystals adhered with blue-tinted glue. Add a handhold secured by a leather thong. Cut the thong long enough to have extra at the ends for tied-in feathers. For best results, prepare the wand in early spring. Leave it in the light of a rising sun for three days to charge before you wield it.

JUDGMENT

General Uses: Decision-making and analysis. Opinions. Interpreting sketchy information. Conclusions.

Timing: Waxing to full moon. During times of strong sunlight. The months of July and December. Moon in Cancer or Libra. Tuesday.

Props/Focals: Amethyst, birds, apple, vanilla, beans, coffee, pansy, elder wood, hazelnut, and mushrooms. The colors gold or indigo. The number ten. A magnifying glass, a two-sided scale, or a calculator.

Secondary Listings: Balance, Choices, Discernment, Intuition, Quick-Mindedness, Viewpoints, Visions.

Sample Spells:

Find an amethyst or a piece of cloth with similar coloration. Anoint the stone or cloth with a drop of vanilla, then place it over your third eye while you meditate. Visualize that area glowing with golden light, pouring inward in concentric circles. Repeat this visualization ten times from waxing to full moon to engender wise decisions.

On a nice, bright day, sit beneath an elder tree or apple tree. Bring an apple with you. Bless it by saying: "*Fruit of Gods/Goddesses, ripe and wise, open now my sleeping eyes. Filled with health and deep insight, magic lies within each bite.*" Eat ten bites of the apple. Take the rest home, slice it thinly, then dry and store it. Nibble a small piece any time you need improved judgment.

Take any magnifying glass along with a symbol of improved deductive skills (perhaps a correctly solved crossword puzzle). Move the glass so that you can look through it toward the item and say: "*Through the looking glass, my magic shall pass. From eye to heart, discernment impart.*" Next, lay the glass securely on top of the item, leaving it in a special spot, such as an altar, until circumstances remedy themselves. Just take care that the magnifying glass is not in a direct line with sunlight lest fire result.

JUSTICE

General Uses: Equity, fairness, truth, and legal matters.

Timing: When the sun is brightest. Moon in Libra. Months of July and December. Tuesday.

Props/Focals: Two-edged items. A scale, gavel, or law books. The yin-yang symbol, a "thumbs up" sign, a triangle, or a ruler. Hematite. Vanilla and sunflowers (or seeds). The numbers one and eight. The color gold.

Secondary Listings: Balance, Communication, Discernment, Identifying, Liberation, Movement, Negotiation, Protection, Wisdom.

Sample Spells:

Note: Spells for justice will not function to erase guilt, nor should they be attempted for such ends. Instead, these spells return things to balance, so the results are fair to all concerned.

If you are facing a judgment in court, write down all possible verdicts on a piece of paper. With scissors or a knife, cut out only the desired conclusion while focusing your mind on a positive outcome. Carefully burn the unwanted portion until nothing but ash remains. Release or bury this ash so it is symbolically "lost" to you. Carry the other piece of paper into court, wrapped in gold cloth, as a protective amulet.

To foster scrupulous dealings with others, make this charm. Wrap a vanilla bean, eight small pieces of hematite, and eight sunflower seeds in gold or yellow cloth. Leave this packet in sunlight for eight hours (or eight minutes) on a cloudless day. Before you use the charm, hold your hands over it and envision those golden sun rays pouring into the item. Say, *"As sunlight chases the shadows, my magic chases away lies and dishonesty. Where this token abides, there truth will be freed."* This token may be carried or kept at home to stimulate honesty.

KINDNESS

General Uses: Benevolence, consideration, generosity, tenderness, and thoughtfulness.

Timing: Warm months. Holidays, especially Thanksgiving and Yule. Moon in Pisces. The month of November. Monday.

Props/Focals: Supple items. Things that soften or smooth, such as sandpaper, fabric softener, and skin lotion. Easily recognized symbols for charity organizations. Flowers and cookies. The color orange. The number nine.

Secondary Listings: Blessing, Communication, Forgiveness, Harmony, Relationships, Understanding.

Sample Spells:

From an old piece of pale orange clothing, make a poppet of yourself stuffed with nine sweet-smelling spices. As you place each spice within, repeat a little rhyme, like: *"With one, the spell is begun. With two, there's still much to do. With three, bring kindness to me. With four, I open the door. With five, the magic's alive. With six, the spell is affixed. With seven and eight, I banish all hate. With nine, benevolence be mine."* Wrap the token in a soft cloth so that you will always be wrapped in good feelings and keep it safe. This poppet not only brings kindness your way but develops that attribute within.

Send yourself flowers once a week for nine weeks or once a month for nine months, using a special incantation after each order. One choice might be: *"Kindness be free; come quickly to me."* This action sets up a sympathetic pattern that motivates gentle energy in and around you.

Save one petal from each flower you receive and tie each separately to a piece of orange string. Repeat your power phrase again. Then, when you need extra sympathy, untie one of the knots and release the dried petal to the winds. Again, the original verbal component will release and direct the magic.

KINSHIP

General Uses: Family lines, associations, close bonds, and affinity.

Timing: Waxing moon or full moon. Moon in Aries, Gemini, or Aquarius. The month of June. Warm days.

Props/Focals: An interlocking web or chain. Spider webs, trees, or roses. A coat of arms, a broom, knots, and bread. Jade. The color pink. The numbers one (unity), nine, and twelve. Warm, cozy items. Picnic tables or barbecues. Cardamom and rosemary.

Secondary Listings: Communication, Friendship, Harmony, Love, Relationships, Understanding, Web Weaving, Unions.

Sample Spells:

For kinship in a group, first form a circle. Then, gather pink ribbons (one for each person) and affix them securely to a spot in the center. Have each member of the circle tie a pink rose into one ribbon and state a wish for the group as a whole. Once everyone has done this, weave the ribbon by passing the flowers clockwise over a ribbon and then under the following one (as with a Maypole dance). Continue once around the circle. The leader of the group keeps the braided flowers and brings them to each gathering. In this form, the decoration releases harmonious energy and symbolizes unity among the members.

To strengthen the ties between yourself and any group of people, use pink ink or crayon to draw a spider web. At random junctures, like in a family tree, place the names of the individuals to whom you wish to remain close. While you draw and write, quietly chant, *"Unity, oneness, accord."* Allow this chant to rise naturally, then quiet down as you finish. Frame the paper or keep it where it cannot be torn or stained.

If this group ever needs to part, the process can be reversed. Each person tears out their name and takes it. Any remnants should be buried with a healthy tree so the good things the association brought will continue to flourish.

A couple wishing to link their destinies, encourage fertility, and show their oneness may do so by drinking from one common cup of wine spiced with cardamom and rosemary (an ancient tradition among Pagans, Romans, Celts, and Romani). Then, the couple should jump over a broomstick or sword (a rural European practice). This makes a fun addition to marriage and handfasting rites.

Knowledge

General Uses: Intelligence, learning, awareness, realization, aptitude, improved concentration, and keen wit.

Timing: Waxing moons. In bright sunlight. Months of May, July, and October. Moon in Leo, Taurus, Scorpio, and Sagittarius. Moon in any Air sign. Tuesday and Sunday.

Props/Focals: Books, glasses, a library or school room, desks, notepads, light bulbs, sharp items, and computers. The colors yellow and gold. Sunflower, vanilla, walnut, coffee, and rosemary. The numbers three, four, six, and ten.

Secondary Listings: Conscious Mind, Judgment, Organization, Quick-Mindedness, Teachers teaching, Wisdom.

Sample Spells:

Drink a cup of blessed vanilla coffee to which three sprigs of rosemary have been added. Enjoy this just before studying. Refill as desired.

Purchase a yellow light bulb at the supermarket or hardware store. Place this in a lamp near your work area. Anoint the bulb with a dab of walnut oil, rosemary oil, or vanilla extract. As you turn on the light, release your verbal component to begin its work: *"In the light of reason, I wish to grow and learn. Retain this knowledge in my heart each time this bulb is burned. Now is not the time for sleep nor a time for fun. Teachers of the astral realm, grant me concentration!"* Repeat the last phrase each time you feel your thoughts wandering.

Cover all your educational texts with gold or yellow paper. In the center of each cover, depict an emblem for learning and understanding. Bless your work in any manner you see fit. Possibly, dab the cover with rosemary oil to help improve retention.

Leadership

General Uses: Administration, authority, direction, guidance, and control.

Timing: Months of July and October. Moon in Sagittarius, Leo, or Aries. Tuesday or Sunday. Daylight hours.

Props/Focals: Medals, crowns, a rod of leadership, or an elevated chair. Lions and grasshoppers. Amethyst. Bay, black tea, saffron, and allspice. Honey wine. Broccoli or spinach. The numbers one and eight. The colors gold and reddish purple.

Secondary Listings: Adaptation, Communication, Doubt, Negotiation, Organization, Teachers teaching, Wisdom.

Sample Spells:

In much of Western culture, the cartoon "Popeye" is among many easily recognized images of strength amid adversity. His component for aid is spinach. This spell borrows the power of that symbol to improve leadership skills.

Place a bowl of warm spinach on your altar or in a sacred space. Take a moment to call on an appropriate divine visage to bless the food for authority and control. Stir the spinach clockwise eight times, then eat it.

Find a deep-purple rope or cord (try shopping at a curtain shop). Soak it in black tea, then dry it in the sunlight. Next, tie the rope with eight knots, each of which secures a bay leaf or allspice berry. As you tie each knot, add a verbal component if you desire. If not, simply visualize yourself in a positive leadership position. Then, each time you need extra administrative skill, untie one of the knots and place the spice in your mouth for a moment. This endows authoritative speech and wisdom.

Several figures in history, including Julius Caesar, have been noted as drinking spiced honey wines to improve their personal command abilities. If you would like to make a similar wine for yourself, pour a bottle of dry apple wine into a saucepan and add about 2 tablespoons of honey. Add a bay leaf and dash of allspice and warm this over a low flame. Test for a comfortable level of spice and sweetness, adding more honey or herbs if necessary.

Meanwhile, empower a small amethyst crystal by saying: *"Strong words, strong deeds, help me in my wish to lead."* Place the amethyst in the bottom of the empty wine bottle, then refill it with the spiced beverage. Store the wine in a cool place and drink a small amount whenever you need improved leadership skills.

LIBERATION

General Uses: Freedom from constraints. Liberated thought.

Timing: The waning moon. Noon or daylight hours (to banish the shadows). July and October. Thursday. Moon in Sagittarius, Gemini, Aries, or Capricorn. Independence Day.

Props/Focals: Birds or wings. Broken chains and cords or untied knots. Cleansing spices like garlic and pepper. Tulip petals, amethyst, or ashes. The numbers four and forty.

Secondary Listings: Banishing, Choices, Courage, Fear, Justice, Overcoming, Victory.

Sample Spells:

Knots are very useful emblems of release. For this spell, take a symbol of whatever (or whomever) you feel enslaves you, and tie it securely with four knots to a string. Attach the end of the string to your waist or belt loop. Then, hold the image tightly with your hands and visualize yourself lifting away from it like a bird.

When you experience the sensation of becoming lighter, take a pair of scissors and swiftly cut the end of the string attached to you. At the same time, drop the image from your hands so that the problem no longer weighs you down. Turn and walk away, taking care not to look back. Continue making positive efforts toward change in that situation.

Take forty tulip petals and forty feathers (ones from a feather duster work well). Mix them together with a fistful of pepper. Release the entire batch to either a southerly wind (for purification) or a westerly wind (for healing), saying: *"Liberate me as these petals fly free. Like a bird on the wing, let my freedom sing."* Turn away from the direction of the wind, allowing the petals and feathers to disappear totally from sight. Leave that place with confidence in your victory.

LOVE

General Uses: Romance, adoration, devotion, esteem, attachment, and infatuation.

Timing: Valentine's Day and May Day. Full moon. The month of June. Moon in Aquarius or Pisces. Friday.

Props/Focals: The numbers two, three, and twelve. Hearts, doves, lovebirds, flowers, and Cupid images. Anise, apricot, cardamom, clove, lemon, peppermint, strawberries, and roses. Mead.

Secondary Listings: Communication, Forgiveness, Friendship, Harmony, Kinship, Lust, Passion, Relationships, Unions.

Sample Spells:

Warning! Love spells should not be manipulative. It is best to use these enchantments for two people who are already involved and who wish to increase their feelings toward each other. Alternatively, release your magic outward to the universe, asking for guidance in bringing a positive relationship your way.

Since love magic is one of the most popular types of folk magic in history, I have devoted a little more space to examples here.

A medieval love charm is made by carefully poking twelve small holes in a lemon (using a toothpick) and then placing a whole clove into each hole. Then, give the lemon to the person desired. If they want to return your love, they will take a clove to freshen their breath and kiss you. If not, the lemon will not be accepted.

Speak three times the name of one you love. Then, carry a personal item of theirs for the three nights of the full moon. According to Romani tradition, this increases the intended's tenderness toward you.

Vervain and rose petals steeped together in water was a potent love elixir used in medieval France. If vervain is not available, appropriate substitutes include cloves, nutmeg, ginger, lavender, powdered almonds or cashews, cardamom, and lemon.

Take some rose petals to a moving water source. Rivers that move away carry energy outward, searching for a response. Those moving toward you draw love inward. If no river is available, turn on a lawn hose and point it away from you to make your miniature river.

When you find an appropriate spot on the river or a flow large enough from your hose, toss the petals into the water, saying: *"As this rose moves out to sea, so true love will come to me."* Visualize your ideal mate while repeating the incantation. The water transports the magic to its target.

According to Z. Budapest in *The Grandmother of Time*, this spell is more powerful when enacted on Summer Solstice. Then, the rose petals carry your wishes directly to the Goddess.

A couple wishing to improve either their relationship or their fertility can plant acorns together. The people involved need to gather one acorn for each letter in their full names. After digging a small hole in the ground, add to the acorns a snippet of each person's hair, a sprig of vervain, and some Saint John's wort. Cover and water the site. English and rural American customs say that when the acorns are tended carefully, by the time they sprout, love will grow as well.

In Victorian days, it was believed that you could tell your love was true by heating hazelnuts. A handful of nuts was placed on a fire, but only one of them bore the name of your love. If this nut jumped from the flames when it became hot, the person's feelings for you were genuine.

To make a candle that you can burn to attract love to your life, warm dried apple peels (or apple-scented oil) and 2 teaspoons of dried basil together with a cup of pink or red wax. Once the wax has fully melted, remove the apple peels and pour the liquid into an oiled flower planter, old milk carton, or other heat-resistant container. For easy removal after the wax has hardened, the size of the top of this container should be equal to or larger than the bottom. Make sure to include a wick suspended from the top of the container.

Once the wax has set, remove the candle from the mold and carve into it symbols of love (hearts, a bow and arrow for direction, etc.). Burn the candle for two hours—at a time during the full moon (for companionship), visualizing your desire and meditating during that time. If you wish, add a chanted incantation, like: *"Light the night with my dreams, bring love with the full moon's beams."*

This is a tasty magical snack to make for two lovers. Hull a quart of strawberries and soak them in a cup of schnapps for three hours by the light of a full moon. Good choices for schnapps flavors include raspberry for joy or peppermint for zest.

Before removing the berries from this bath, add a verbal component. For example: *"As the abundant berries fill the Earth, so too shalt love fill our hearts."* Next, chill the fruit. The following night, serve them to each other beneath the stars with a little sweet cream and talk of your dreams.

Luck

General Uses: Serendipity, fortuity, good fortune, fate, destiny, and chance.

Timing: Daylight hours. Sunday. Moon in Virgo and Pisces. The month of April and the season of spring.

Props/Focals: The numbers one, four, and seven, or your lucky number. The dragonfly or a rabbit's foot. Allspice, fish, and cabbage. Rainbows, wind, ships, champagne, and found items, especially pennies.

Secondary Listings: Openings, Wishes.

Sample Spells:

Our ancestors were wont to overlook nothing that might improve their lives a little bit. This led to a myriad of luck charms, potions, and spells to encourage good fortune.

Old European lore includes a recipe that mixes cold cream with seven drops of rose water to bring you good fortune. Stir the mixture with the found feather of a white bird, then anoint yourself. This preparation will also settle disputes between people.

A version of this says to gather four chrysanthemums just before the sun rises and place them in a bottle with scented rose oil. The next day, rub a little on your face, and good fortune and amiability will be yours.

A third alternative is to steep petals from seven marigolds for one hour in a liter of warmed red wine. Strain this thoroughly, rebottle it, and drink a little every day for a month.

If you write your wish for luck on a sage leaf and then sleep on it, your dreams will tell you if your desire will come to pass. If you do not dream, the sage is to be planted so the wish may grow.

Japanese folklore says that placing pieces of bamboo around the threshold of your door attracts good luck to your home. In the US, planting cabbage in your garden is said to achieve the same thing. If you cannot find bamboo, place some canned bamboo shoots (available at the supermarket) and some fresh cabbage leaves in the ground instead. This will not hurt the soil and will encourage the same type of energy.

To create a meditative bath that will bring serendipity into your life, add small quantities of pineapple and orange rind with a sprinkling of poppy seeds to bathwater. Let the aromas carry good fortune to you!

To make a wind chime that will draw providence whenever it sounds, string together seven strands of hazelnuts, nutmeg beads, star anise, and tonka beans. From strings adjacent to these, hang seven oak twigs to act as ringers. Hang this in a northerly window and add a personal blessing.

In the Old West, if people thought something needed to change, they would quite literally demonstrate this by sitting backward on a chair or by wearing an apron backward. You can follow this magical twist by turning yourself counterclockwise (to relieve bad luck) four times, turning your socks the opposite side out, walking backward, and so on.

Add to this action an empowering phrase, like: *"What once was lingering I command out the door, turned away from me now, bad luck is no more."* Keep your reversed token the way it is until there is an obvious change in the fates.

A lucky amulet can be made from a found penny, a picture of a dock or a sailing ship at port (so your ship will come in), allspice berries, nutmeg, orange rind pieces, and a candlewick that has been burnt.

Gather a personally lucky number of these ingredients together and bless them by saying: *"Luck be agile, luck be quick, luck burn bright like this candle wick. Each component here I bind, that good fortune will be mine."* Wrap these securely in rainbow-colored cloth or paper so you can carry the amulet with you in your wallet or purse.

Finding a broom in a new home is considered good luck. The broom should not be thrown away lest you likewise toss out your fortune. This belief was predominant in rural Europe from about 1600 onward and during the Victorian period in the US.

Lust

General Uses: Passion, desire, sensuality, sexual ability, and eroticism.

Timing: Moonlight. Wednesday or Thursday. Moon in Virgo, Pisces, or Scorpio.

Props/Focals: Asparagus, carrot, celery, onions, parsley, caraway, dill, mint, garlic, passion fruit, strawberries, chocolate, cherries, and bananas. The color red. Mullein tea and oats.

Secondary Listings: Love, Passion, Relationships, Unions, Zeal.

Sample Spells:

For a potion to enhance desire, prepare a juice with carrots, celery, a hint of dill, and a little water. Use a blender or food processor. Strain the juice for a smoother texture. Before drinking, take the elixir into the moonlight and visualize a reddish fire burning in its center. Quaff the glass to bring that fire into yourself.

To heighten sensuality, consider creating a flaming banana split for two, filled with ingredients that accentuate the passionate nature. Prepare with vanilla ice cream, chocolate nuggets or strawberry pieces, cherries, passion fruit, bananas, and a topping of brandy. Light the brandy carefully while incanting together: *"Passion and desire, fill us with Fire!"* Blow out the flames in unison. Feed small spoonfuls of the dessert to each other, and be creative while you're eating. Play tempestuous music and share your personal fantasies. Let nature take her course.

Find a romantic, secluded area where you and your lover can build a fire legally and safely. Walk clockwise around the fire pit, visualizing a reddish-purple light surrounding it and spreading outward. Then, on top of that ground, sprinkle kindling in a pattern symbolic of passion. On top of this pattern, lay more kindling and your logs, then light the fire. If possible, use only natural fire-starting techniques since the chemicals in lighter fluid can impede magical results.

Once the fire is burning well, add a mixture of cinnamon, mint, seven strands of each person's hair, and some musk-scented wood powder. Sprinkle this on the coals, saying: *"Burn in us, flames of desire, as these embers rise up, so passion burns higher."* An incantation like this can be transformed into a chant that reaches a crescendo at the same time as your feelings. If the area is secluded enough, slowly undress and enjoy lovemaking right where you are.

Magic

General Uses: Energizing mystical, supernatural, or metaphysical functions and rites. Psychic shielding from negative magic.

Timing: For banishing negative magics, use a waning moon or bright sunlight. For increasing positive magic, use waxing to full moons. Months of September, November, and December. Moon in Capricorn. Wednesday.

Props/Focals: Moonstone, amber, silver, and quartz. The numbers seven and thirteen. Elder, nutmeg, bay, eggs, mace, and garlic (to break hexes). Athame, wand, and other magical tools. The circle and pentagram. The color purple. Woven items, candles, and "Witch animals" (such as cats, rabbits, and birds).

Secondary Listings: Banishing, Cleansing, Discernment, Elements, Energy, Ghosts, Protection, Quarters, Unconscious Mind.

Sample Spells:

Spells can be used to break enchantments or to enhance positive magic or the learning thereof.

To Break Enchantments:

An old folk spell from Brittany says to mix ashes and vervain together. When dusted on your forehead and the soles of your feet, this will negate any malicious magic that has been directed toward you.

To protect your home from enchantment, make a Witch bottle containing sharp items like broken glass, nails, and pins. To this, add some of your hair, a mirrored surface, and vinegar. If you recently broke a mirror, this is a perfect way to put those pieces to good use and turn the misfortune into something positive!

Bury this in a safe place near your threshold so that any negative energy is either trapped there or returned to its source. You may also want to ask your personal god or goddess to bless this tool for protection before burying it.

In Medieval and Renaissance Europe, a brown or black agate with a white center was considered a potent charm against the evil eye. Other stones for this purpose included carnelian, brightly colored corals, jasper, malachite, topaz, and stones with holes (in the Romani tradition). Together, these seven stones make a potent combination for a medicine bag. Once gathered and empowered, the stones provide continuous warding.

When you sense negative energy coming your way, grasp the pouch with your weak hand while pointing away from you with your strong hand. Say: *"Away from me all negativity. Protection is mine, all evil I bind."* Repeat your chosen incantation seven or thirteen times. As you do, turn counterclockwise. This action makes you the focal point of a protected circle while you guide the energy away.

Wintergreen, thistles, hot pepper, pine needles, basil, dried beans, leeks, onions, and garlic are all potent herbs for warding off hexes. Greek, Roman, and European herbalists felt that the stronger an item smelled or the more severe its exterior appeared, the more powerful it was against magic. To put this idea to use, make a poppet of yourself in white cloth (the color of protection) and stuff it with your choice of seven of these herbs.

As you work, strongly visualize a sparkling, blue-white light being absorbed into each herb and the cloth fiber until the poppet virtually glows with energy. Mark the poppet as a representation of yourself by anointing it with your own cologne or perfume and/ or a personal piece of jewelry. Sleep with the poppet under your pillow to keep nightmares at bay.

A poppet such as this may also make a nice gift. In this case, however, the jewelry and perfume should be one of the recipient's choosing.

To Enhance Positive Magic or the Learning Thereof:

Make an empowered altar mat. Start with seven purple strips of cloth and thirteen white strips, all of which should be about 1–1½ inches wide and 7 inches long. Weave the strips together in an over-under pattern, the thirteen going left to right and the seven moving top to bottom. While you work, sing a magical song or add a chant to store power within the mat. One example is: *"Weave the cloth, weave it well, all the while I weave my spell. Wrought with magic that I impart, weave the power with my art."* The finished mat can become part of your altar or make an effective covering for one of your magical tools.

As a side note, you can make these mats more durable by starting with a base material of colored construction paper and by laminating the finished product. In this form, this spell is an excellent project for children ages six through nine. Laminating materials are available at most photocopying stores.

Before working magic, enjoy fluffy scrambled eggs (productivity) with a hint of bay (power and success) and cheese (manifestation). Beat your ingredients together until frothy, then pour into a warm, oiled frying pan. As the egg mixture rises, visualize it being filled with light. Hold your hands above the pan and extend positive energy toward your meal while it cooks. Then bless and eat it to internalize growing power.

British lore claims that a Witch's power is multiplied by letting their hair down during a spell. If you try this, release your hair at the same time you release and direct your magic for proper sympathy. If you have short hair, try gathering and releasing the hem of a robe, unfurling a scroll of fabric, or untying a belt as a substitute. Or snip a little strand of hair and release it to the wind.

Mental Ability

General Uses: Alert discernment. Intellectual and cognitive functions of the mind. Rationality and reason.

Timing: Tuesday. During times of strong natural light. Moon in Aries, Leo, or Scorpio. May and October.

Props/Focals: Vanilla, walnut, apple, pansy, mustard seed, rosemary, lilac, coriander, coffee, and cauliflower. Amethyst. Books, eyeglasses, computers, keys, or diplomas. The numbers six and ten. The colors yellow and gold.

Secondary Listings: Conscious Mind, Doubt, Grounding, Judgment, Knowledge, New Endeavors, Quick-Mindedness, Understanding.

Sample Spells:

To enhance learning, during May (or around spring recess), plant cauliflower seeds in a yellow pot filled with rich soil. To the soil add six strands of rosemary and 6 teaspoons of coffee grounds. Name your seeds after the topic you wish to learn more about. Tend to them with care. When the seeds start to sprout, your knowledge should likewise show signs of growing. Keep the plant nearby while you study, but otherwise, move it to a sunny area because the sunshine reinforces cognitive energy.

For an edible treat to improve mental functions, make an apple walnut pie. Use a normal recipe, adding ½ teaspoon of vanilla and 1 teaspoon of fresh-brewed coffee to the apple mixture. When you weave the crust, add an emblem that you feel is appropriate. As the pie bakes, visualize it being filled with the golden rays of the sun. Add a verbal component, like: *"Even as this food is warmed by fire, so it will spark my mind. In you, knowledge I seek and find."* Spend a lot of time in the kitchen while this bakes to strengthen your hunger for learning, then eat the pie so the magic starts growing in your heart.

To make a magical diploma, find a piece of professional quality art paper. With a gold-colored pen or marker, write yourself a diploma in the area of study. Dab the edges with vanilla extract while you say: *"Success is mine, success I claim, within me burns a growing flame."* Keep this bound by a gold-colored ribbon to which six sprigs of rosemary are attached. Have the bundle nearby whenever you study this particular topic. Once your goal is achieved, the diploma makes a nice keepsake commemorating your ability to create positive change.

Money

General Uses: Financial improvement or stability. Improved cash flow and resources. Prosperity.

Timing: The month of April. Full and blue moons. Moon in Taurus, Virgo, Aquarius, or Pisces. Sunday.

Props/Focals: The colors green, silver, or gold (all associated with currency). Anything that grows or expands. Wallet, debit card, pay stub, piggy banks, and wishing wells. Alfalfa, allspice, almond, basil, cinnamon, clove, dill, ginger, maple syrup, mint, nutmeg, orange, parsley, pomegranate, oats, rice, beef, and fish. Moss agate and moonstone.

Secondary Listings: Abundance, Blessing, Employment, Goals, Jobs, Overcoming, Prosperity, Thrift, Wisdom.

Sample Spells:

To release money magic energy, make yourself a green paper airplane with the word "prosperity" written on the wings. Take this outside with a stick of cinnamon incense. Light the incense and set it so the wind catches the smoke. Launch your airplane into a northerly wind, saying: *"On the winds and through the smoke, prosperity I now invoke."* Allow the breeze to take the airplane freely, carrying your magic toward its goal. If the wind is not cooperative, anything traveling in a northerly direction, including the roof of your car, can substitute as a place from which to launch the plane.

Pierce a large navel orange with a needle, making the pattern of a dollar sign. Insert a clove in each of the piercings. Wrap the orange using green, silver, and gold ribbons in between the rows of cloves. At the top, make a loop of the three ribbons. Decorate the base with a favored crystal. Bless this little token for improved finances, then hang it in a window to release its scented energy with every breeze. When the aroma of the orange fades (the fruit will shrink as it dries), simply anoint it with essential oils for a refreshed fragrance.

In the center of a large fishbowl, place a green candle marked with symbols and words that are personally meaningful for financial abundance. Anoint the candle with mint extract before affixing it to the bottom of the bowl. Every day for a month, beginning on a waxing moon, toss a coin into this magic well (the bowl) and light the candle for a few minutes. Add a brief incantation, such as: *"Saving for a rainy day will help more money come my way."*

Have this bowl nearby and the candle lit when you go over your finances at the end of the month. When the bowl is filled or the candle burns too low, put the funds to charitable use so the universe can return your kindness.

MOVEMENT

General Uses: Change, manifestation, and action. Improved personal drive. Overcoming red tape.

Timing: Spring months, specifically April. The waxing moon increases movement, and waning slows it. Thursday. Moon in Aries, Taurus, Sagittarius, and Pisces.

Props/Focals: The colors red and yellow or other vibrant hues. Sources of energy such as batteries or electrical generators. Sneakers and activity-related clothing. Automobiles, bikes, trains, airplanes, clouds, water, roads, blenders, or matches (Fire). Animals and insects known for swiftness, such as bees and birds. Vanilla, baking soda or powder, and ginger. The element of Air (wind). The number forty (only to be used for solitary movement as was experienced by Noah and Jonah).

Secondary Listings: Adaptation, Energy, Inspiration, Justice, Liberation, Openings, Transformation.

Sample Spells:

To help keep yourself on schedule and motivated, bless your shoes with vanilla-scented baking soda. To prepare this, place 1 cup of baking soda in a bowl and stir in 2 teaspoons of vanilla oil or extract, mixing clockwise. As you stir, add a verbal component, like: *"Movement swift, movement fleet, motivation on my feet."* Leave this mixture to dry completely before using it. To keep the scent strong, put a vanilla bean in your storage jar. Then, sprinkle about a tablespoon in each shoe once per week.

This mixture lasts for eight weeks if used daily. It has the additional benefit of keeping your shoes smelling fresh. For other tough odors, add a bit of powdered lemon rind and orris root. Leave a container of this open in any area prone to pungent smells, like the inside of your refrigerator or near the kitchen trash.

To light a fire underneath a situation that seems stagnant, draw a symbol of this circumstance on paper and bind the paper with red string. Then, neatly burn it on any fire source while saying: *"Wait no longer, the magic urges, even as the fire surges. When the flames consume the string, movement will my magic bring."* Keep the ashes as a charm to maintain activity until you achieve some type of conclusion. Then, release the ashes to the winds with gratitude.

To move something away from or toward you, begin by waiting for a day when the clouds are moving in an appropriate direction. Visualize a braided yellow and red beam of light streaming in a straight line from yourself to a cloud. On that line, imagine the name of your need written clearly in your own hand. Allow this to travel along the line into the cloud until it is completely engulfed. Your verbal component to this spell should reflect the direction of movement needed. For example, with sickness, one might say: *"As the clouds move far away, keep this illness long at bay. When the clouds all abate, so my cold evaporates!"* Finally, disengage the light beam in your visualization to release the magic.

NATURE (CONNECTION TO)

General Uses: Reconnecting with the "wild" within. Better understanding of natural cycles. Empathy with animals and the Earth.

Timing: Spring, Earth Day, full moon.

Props/Focals: Animal or plant costumes, masks, and pictures. Seasonal representations. Gardens, woods, and other places that typify and accent natural beauty. The colors green and brown. The numbers nine and twelve. Catnip, valerian, or other herbs known to attract certain creatures.

Secondary Listings: Ecology, Elements, Quarters, Weather.

Sample Spells:

Some day in early spring, take yourself for a nature walk. If you live in a city, go to a street with lots of curbside trees, a garden, or a park. As you go, pick up items that strike your fancy, such as acorns, daisies, and rocks. Each time you take something, thank the Earth in your own way, then return home.

Next, place the collected treasures inside a brown or green pouch. Add nine pinches each of catnip and valerian and draw the pouch closed. Bless the finished amulet by saying: *"From Earth you were born, now to be worn, as a reminder to me, live in reciprocity!"* Each time you take notice of the pouch, do something nice for Gaia. Leave breadcrumbs out for birds, begin a recycling effort, or perhaps plant a tree.

Commit yourself to studying one plant type carefully for a full year, taking time out for your studies at least once a month. During your study time, imitate the plant's movements by watching how it sways in the wind or turns in the sun. Wear similar colors and make notes about your feelings regarding that natural being. What can it teach you?

After the year is over, sit down before the plant with a small crystal. Place it at the stem's base as a gift, then ask to learn from the plant deva who abides there. Put yourself into a meditative state of mind and wait patiently for insight. At this point, any earthy magical song, done in a whispered chant, can augment the encounter. Make notes of your experience. Repeat as desired with other natural objects.

NEGOTIATION

General Uses: Diplomatic exchanges, mediation, arbitration, intercession, and reconciliation.

Timing: Tuesday. During a waning moon (to decrease negative feelings). In bright sunlight. The months of February, April, August, and December. Moon in Libra, Gemini, or Aries.

Props/Focals: Items known to aid vision like binoculars. Things that have the ability to smooth or cool, such as ice and blenders. Herbs with a calming influence, including chamomile and lavender. The colors white, pink, yellow, and gold. Apple (wisdom), basil (accord), blackberry (success), tomato (love), and almond (moderation). Amethyst and carnelian. An open hand. Flexible items and the number two.

Secondary Listings: Anger, Balance, Communication, Conscious Mind, Discernment, Forgiveness, Harmony, Leadership, Relationships, Understanding, Wisdom.

Sample Spells:

Place one tomato for each person involved in a negotiation in a blender and name the tomato for that individual. As the mixer stirs up positive energy, add your verbal ingredient: *"Move together, become as one, let the magic spell be spun. Peace among you, truce to find, let us become of one mind."* Repeat the incantation twice, then either drink this as tomato juice or warm it (to bring warm feelings) and eat it as soup. For the latter, add a little basil while the soup heats for flavor and enhanced symbolism.

Before going into arbitration, prepare a white sachet bearing two crystals and two peaceful herbs (like lavender and basil) for each person who will be present. Charge these bundles for two hours in sunlight to encourage truth, then for two hours by a waning moon to disperse anger.

If the attendees are open to New Age ideas, present one cache to each of them for supportive energy after explaining the significance. Otherwise, keep the sachets and ritually destroy them after the meeting to dissolve any grudges.

When trying to negotiate for yourself or someone else, wait until the moon reaches its waning phase, write the name of the perceived antagonist on a piece of paper, and then put the paper on a plate. On top of the name, put two pieces of ice. Leave this in sunlight until the ice melts. That evening, take the water outside and pour it onto the Earth, saying: *"As water flows out to the sea, so I release all enmity. As freely as this water is poured, so I extend peace and accord."* Keep a strong image of the other person in mind while you work. Take the paper to your negotiations as a charm for success.

NEW ENDEAVORS

General Uses: Blessing any new effort. Bountiful beginnings. Commencement and generation of specific ideas/energy.

Timing: New and early waxing moon. Sunrise or the beginning of a personally significant season. March and April. Moon in Virgo, Sagittarius, or Pisces. Thursday.

Props/Focals: Pinkish orange, like the sun at dawn. New brooms, keys, chimes, open doors, and seedlings. Kelp or parsley, rice, ginger, honey, birch, chicken, cheese, cabbage or lettuce, coffee, allspice, apple, and berries. Agate. The numbers three, four, and six.

Secondary Listings: Adaptation, Blessing, Courage, Goals, Luck, Openings, Tenacity, Visions, Zeal.

Sample Spells:

Like some European folk beliefs, in Japan, they say that using kelp to wash the floors of a new business ensures success. This can be adapted for other commencements by keeping kelp under your pillow to aid conception or by anointing the tools of your trade with a kelp solution. An alternative to kelp is parsley.

Rice is traditionally thrown at weddings to assure the couple of happiness and providence. Using this idea, keep a special jar of rice mixed with any of the above-mentioned herbs and an emblem of a new effort. Seal the jar with orange wax. Place this charm near the area where you will be working on your goal most often. Wheat may be substituted for rice in this spell.

Ginger is an herb of achievement, and honey encourages the pleasant things in life to come our way. This spell combines these two into an easily stored edible. Take fresh gingerroot and peel off the bark carefully. Slice into six very thin (¼ inch) pieces. Place them in a little peanut oil (for solid foundations) and sauté until the ginger turns very translucent. Drain the slices on a paper towel and rinse out your pan.

Return the ginger to the cooking dish and add 1 cup of honey. Cook this over a very low flame until the honey crystallizes on the ginger. Dry the slices on waxed paper and charge them by saying: *"Ginger, once a food of kings, to me now victory brings. Sweet success I savor each time I fancy your favor!"* Store the ginger in a jar and nibble a piece just before working on a novel idea. This also makes an effective breath freshener and digestive aid.

A less complicated version of the previous spell is to drink a hot cup of coffee flavored with allspice or ginger just as dawn meets the horizon. With this, eat an apple or fresh berries and add the same type of incantation.

NIGHTMARES

General Uses: Shelter against bad dreams.

Timing: January. The waning moon. Moon in Gemini or Capricorn.

Props/Focals: Agate, amber, malachite, and pyrite. Garlic and cleansing herbs. Protective herbs including anise, caraway, mullein, rosemary, cedar, cypress, hyacinth, bluebell, and cranberry. Herbs that aid sleep, such as valerian and chamomile. The colors white, blue, and gold. The number six.

Secondary Listings: Banishing, Fear, Peace, Protection, Sleep, Unconscious Mind, Victory.

Sample Spells:

Nightmares are often reflections of our own fears and tensions. Because of this, a calming drink such as chamomile tea or cranberry juice just before bed can have both physical and magical effects. Your verbal component should be fun to ease your stress and encourage a lighthearted attitude: *"Past the gums and through the lips, peaceful sleep is in each sip."*

For a child, a terrific charm against nightmares is a favored blanket or stuffed toy. If the child is old enough, let them pick the item out. Empower the item together in whatever way seems apt. Explain how the love you both place there will help keep bad dreams away.

Divine blessings and protection will shelter the child's sleep each time the token is taken to bed.

To take this further, also anoint the four points of the child's bed with cedar oil or a cedar-scented polish as you say: *"Fears of things that bump and fright, you're not welcome here tonight. As my child dreams in sleep, only good thoughts will they keep."* Lemon juice or oil is a suitable substitute for cedar to cleanse negativity.

A favorite gift among magical folk is a dream pillow. This is made from two pieces of square cloth sewn together (use white and blue fabric with golden thread, if possible). Stuff the pillow with six herbs believed to ensure pleasant dreams. Choose the spices from the list above or according to your own insight.

The final seam of the pillow should be stitched by hand. As you sew, empower the filling using a chant, like: *"Stitched with a thread of gold, peace and joy this pillow holds. Herbs within will bring good dreams, pouring from the pillow seams."* I like to add decorative lace edging and/or a specially appliqued symbol to personalize each pillow.

OATHS

General Uses: Sealing vows, promises, contracts, and agreements.

Timing: Moon in Aries to break down barriers, Virgo for fruitful alliances, Libra for fairness and equity, Sagittarius for self-control, and Aquarius for sharing. Tuesday for legal matters, Thursday for commitment.

Props/Focals: Lemon and lettuce for accord. Beans bring good judgment. Vinegar to inspire truthfulness. Carnelian for communication, agate for blessing, and amethyst for making sound decisions. Cardamom, nutmeg, apple, basil, and rose. Knots and communal cups. Neutral places like the middle of a bridge. The number two and the rune of partnership.

Secondary Listings: Choices, Dedication, Friendship, Harmony, Kinship, Love, Relationships, Unions.

Sample Spells:

A single shared cup participated in a myriad of ancient ceremonies to seal a promise to one's lips. Notably, Pagans, Romani, and the ancient Celts used this symbolism repeatedly. In Germany, they also employed a special cup for vows of love called the *minne* cup. With these examples in mind, nearly any promise may be sealed using a magically prepared beverage and a specially chosen cup.

To these ends, I recommend apple wine or apple juice stirred clockwise with nutmeg and cardamom to ensure that only good things will come. Empower the beverage with both sunlight and moonbeams. The sun will encourage forthright commitments, while the moon will engender the sensitive insight necessary for productive partnerships and relationships. Once prepared, place the beverage in a cup and drink together after vows are spoken or paperwork is signed.

If you find you sometimes have trouble keeping your promises, consider making an amulet for yourself. In a brown or green pouch (for foundations and development, respectively), place two agates, two nutmeg beads, and two dried rose petals. Use a prayer, like: *"God and Goddess, let me now be heard. Keep me ever true to my word. Two agates, two nutmegs, incentive in both, then a rose for sweetness, fulfilling my oath."* Decorate the outside of this pouch with the rune of partnership.

When promises are jointly made in a group setting, a celebratory feast often follows (weddings and initiations, for example). One excellent choice of food for such gatherings is a simple lettuce salad with lemon-vinaigrette dressing. This food mirrors the reason for your gathering and amplifies the magical energy on an internal level.

To make the vinaigrette, combine ½ cup of olive oil with ½ teaspoon of lemon juice, 2–3 tablespoons of wine vinegar (to taste), salt, and pepper (also to taste). Shake the mixture vigorously while saying: *"Vinegar for truth, lemon for unity, oil binds the magic, spices for energy! As over this lettuce, the dressing is poured, bind here our promises and grant us accord."*

OBTAINING (ITEMS AND GOALS)

General Uses: Capturing, securing, safeguarding, and achieving.

Timing: Spring months, especially March and April. Moon in Taurus, Leo, and Sagittarius. Waxing, full, and blue moons. Tuesday or Thursday.

Props/Focals: Brussels sprouts, berries, cheese, cinnamon, ginger, anise, and tulip. Agate, beryl, jade, or hematite. Spiders, targets, brass rings, and pointers. Anything that helps solidify other items, like flour and cornstarch. The number four. The colors red and orange.

Secondary Listings: Goals, Inspiration, Movement, Openings, Tenacity, Victory.

Sample Spells:

Cheddar cheese Brussels sprout soup is a good one for obtaining something. To begin, name each Brussels sprout after your need. Use about 3 cups, which equates to about 1 pound. Slice the sprouts to release their energy and put them into a pot of boiling water for increasing power. Once they are tender, put them into a blender with the water, 1 pound of cheddar cheese, 4 cups of milk, and any spices you like. As the blender spins, whipping up your magic, add an incantation suitable to your situation. For example, if you are seeking a new job, something like: *"Food with power, start to perk, help me find some decent work!"* would be appropriate.

Return the soup to the stove to warm. Stir regularly to keep the cheese from burning and sticking to the bottom of the pan. If you have trouble with the consistency, 2 tablespoons of cornstarch mixed into a paste with cold water will help. Add this slowly while warming the soup. Serve when all the cheese is melted and the texture is creamy. Remember to visualize while you eat!

Find a piece of brass or brass-colored paper or ribbon and place it on a nearby wall so that you can just reach it. Try to attach it so it can be clutched. Every morning and night, from the new moon to the full moon, stretch upward to grasp the brass, positively stating your goal in the present tense as if it is already a reality.

Using our previous example, someone looking for a new job would say: *"I am working at a great job!"* Follow this routine every month until your ambition is fulfilled.

This spell functions because of two important factors. First is the power of positive speech to bring change into our lives. Second is the building of energy from a daily routine of repeating affirmative words to achieve success. To realize victory, any such spell must be followed by honest effort on the mundane level.

For a little bit of symbolic magic, make a paste using equal amounts of cornstarch and flour and just enough water to create a dough. Tint this with two drops each of yellow and red food coloring to make it orange. Form this into an object symbolizing your dream. As you work, recite an affirming chant or incantation.

One example would be: *"Born in my heart, my ambitions will see a brand-new beginning in reality!"* Glaze and keep the image you create, blessing it periodically with this incantation, or one personally devised, until you obtain your desire.

OMENS

General Uses: Foretelling the future. Interpretation of signs and omens. Uncovering harbingers.

Timing: Full moon. The months of September, November, and December. Halloween or May Day (for love). Moon in Cancer or Libra. Monday and Wednesday.

Props/Focals: All divination tools. Emblem of the eye. A gray streak of hair (the mark of a seer). The color yellow and the number five. Yarrow, dirt, beans, birds (especially feathers), nutmeg, bay, beer, candles, carrots, copper, elder, willow, dandelion, grapes, mace, reflective surfaces, and bowls. Round crystals and moonstones.

Secondary Listings: Discernment, Divination, Identifying, Intuition, Understanding, Visions, Wisdom.

Sample Spells:

Before doing meditations aimed at increasing your psychic perception, cut out a picture of an open eye. Wrap this around a moonstone and place it over your third eye. You can do this by either lying down or using a handkerchief to hold the moonstone in place.

As you breathe deeply, visualize a clean, yellow light pouring into the region of your third eye until an open eye appears in your inner vision. As this image grows stronger, focus the energy by adding a verbal component, such as: *"Pouring inward, my soul to fill. Grant discernment through power and will."* Continue repeating the incantation until you feel like you're about to burst with energy. Take that momentum into whatever divinatory attempts you have planned. Just be careful not to move too quickly or to make sudden, loud noises. Either action may disrupt your meditative attitude and leave you with a headache.

To make a divinatory wand, find a five-inch-long copper tube (check hardware and plumbing stores). Using a leather thong or ribbon, affix a bit of willow bark, a found feather, and a bay leaf so they dangle decoratively from one end. At the other end, using good epoxy, attach a crystal. Bless the wand by the light of a full moon for five hours. Once each hour, walk around the wand clockwise, saying: *"Light of intuition, by magic, now bond divining energy to this metal wand."* This instrument can now be used to scribe magic circles for divinatory or oracular attempts. Improve or restore its energy in the future by returning it to charge under a full moon.

Many oracles of the ancient world, including the inner sanctum at Delphi, used Fire as a central focus. To do this, make the Fire from four different components, one for each element. Willow, ash, and pine wood with a bit of fem is one option. As you place each item on burning kindling, recite an appropriate verse, like: *"Willow for Water, so insight may flow. Fern for the Earth so vision can grow. Pine is for Air, that the omens I'll sight, Ash for the Fire, divination ignite!"* Next, listen closely. Look to the sky, the animals in your home, and the fire itself for interpretable signs.

Please note that if you cannot make a full-blown fire, using an incense burner or small brazier and the four elemental ingredients is a good alternative.

OPENINGS

General Uses: Opportunity. Positive chances. New beginnings and spiritual doorways.

Timing: Waxing to full moon. Moon in Taurus and Pisces. The month of April. Tuesday and Thursday.

Props/Focals: Open windows, doors, books, etc. The starting line of a race. Keys and handles. Hammer or shovel (items that create openings). Archways and can openers. Cameras or other items that can capture energy. The number one (beginning). Allspice, apple, vanilla, nutmeg, and daisy. The colors yellow-green or brown.

Secondary Listings: Adaptation, Choices, Discernment, Goals, Jobs, New Endeavors, Versatility.

Sample Spells:

If opportunities seem evasive, lightly anoint your door frame with watered-down apple juice or vanilla extract. Then, each day upon returning home, knock on your door once before entering. As you knock, use one word to describe the domain you want to open.

Good examples include love, employment, knowledge, etc. Then, step through the door carrying that sympathetic energy. Continue this routine until you see change.

Gather some daisy petals, apple peels, allspice berries, or nutmeg. Take your chosen component in the same hand you receive handshakes with. Holding it securely, say: *"New beginnings in my hand, my magic with the winds released. Circulated to the land, opportunities be increased!"* Let go of the herbs when you say *"released."* Visualize your magic as a green light spreading outward while the components fly away.

Watch neighborhood garage sales or secondhand shops for an interesting old skeleton key. In older homes, these keys often fit every door of the house, giving them marvelous symbolism for opening and opportunity. Once you find a key you like, cleanse it and charge it during the full moon of April. Afterward, wear it on a chain to help open doors in your life, wherever you may be.

ORGANIZATION

General Uses: Improving or bringing to bear a design. Plans, structure, and patterns.

Timing: Daylight hours. Fall and spring cleaning times. Moon in Leo, Taurus, and Sagittarius. The month of July. Tuesday and Sunday.

Props/Focals: Computer, calculator, pen and notepad, clocks, and brooms. Anything that is sorted or helps to sort items (like filing cabinets or drawers). The numbers two, three, and ten. The colors gold or yellow to highlight the logical, conscious mind. Rosemary, almond, apple, walnut, and fish (brain foods). Amethyst and coral.

Secondary Listings: Conscious Mind, Leadership, Understanding, Viewpoints, Wisdom.

Sample Spells:

Prepare some incense using rosemary, apple peel (dried and powdered), pine needles (for clarity), and wood powder. The last ingredient can often be gathered from any woodpile. I've also had some success grinding small pieces of aromatic wood (cedar, for example) using pencil sharpeners. Mix the ingredients together thoroughly. Empower the incense for organization using an incantation, like: *"Apple grants wisdom, pine outlines the way, rosemary remembers, bringing structure today."* Burn on any fire source whenever you feel disorderly. To preserve the extra incense, store it in a dry, airtight container.

To make an orderly household decoration, snip a few strands from your kitchen broom. Each strand needs to be several inches long. Bind them at one end with a piece of gold or yellow thread wrapped snugly around ten times. Similarly, wrap a piece of coral and a walnut with string, leaving extra to tie them onto the top of the broom handle. At the top of the charm, add a ribbon long enough to suspend it from another object. Use this to affix the charm to a key ring, the rearview mirror of a car, or other place where it can help you complete specific tasks in an orderly fashion.

OVERCOMING

General Uses: To conquer, master, surmount, or subdue.

Timing: Waning, dark, and blue moons. The month of March. Moon in Aries, Gemini, Sagittarius, or Capricorn. Thursday.

Props/Focals: Items that can be climbed, stepped on, or turned backward. Iron (for strength), balloons (for lifting burdens), cleansing herbs (like pepper and garlic), and broccoli. The element of Fire. Salt, fir wood, and items that are loosened (untied shoes, for example). The numbers four, eight, and ten. The color red.

Secondary Listings: Anger, Banishing, Doubt, Fear, Habits, Heartbreak, Liberation, Nightmares, Prejudice, Tenacity, Victory.

Sample Spells:

Find a tangled lace or cord. Place it on a table in front of a red candle into which you have carved the word *"self-mastery."* Light the candle and slowly untangle the cord. Chant as you work, *"Life's a web, a silver braid, here within my future's laid. Confusion transcend, all knots be undone, soon my battle will be won."* Once you straighten the mess out, carry a snippet of the string with you. This becomes a portable charm encouraging improved control over your circumstances.

To protect your home from negativity and encourage energy-enabling in any situation, try this: sprinkle a combination of salt, iron filings, and cleansing herbs around the perimeter of your living space. Walk the full circuit counterclockwise either four, eight, or ten times while reciting, *"Overcome all doubts, there's nothing to fear, no negativity is allowed in here. Overcome all trials, banish all dread, assurance abide here forever instead."* Repeat this procedure any time you feel the energy at home shifting to a less positive mode.

This particular procedure was adapted from the Roman festival known as *Terminalia* (February 23). At this time, people walked the boundaries of their land and left offerings to Terminus, the god of borders. The Romans believed this gesture protected their land and crops from sickness, natural disasters, and other difficulties.

Passion

General Uses: Increasing desire, adoration, or yearning for a person, job, art, etc.

Timing: Waxing to full moon. During hours of potent sunlight (the Fire element). Seasons of spring and summer, especially May Day. Wednesday and Friday. Moon in Virgo, Aquarius, or Pisces.

Props/Focals: Plum, grape, asparagus, banana, carrot, cherry, chocolate, orange, cucumber, eggs, and lettuce. Cloves, cardamom, sweet relish, and "energy" foods. Vibrant red and orange. Onyx. Candlelight and other Fire-related items. The number two.

Secondary Listings: Energy, Joy, Love, Lust, Relationships, Unions.

Sample Spells:

Prepare a salad from lettuce, cucumber, carrot slices, and chopped eggs. Make sure to tear the lettuce by hand instead of cutting it so emotions aren't also cut off. Also consider carving the carrot slices into heart shapes by chilling the fresh carrot, using ¼-inch pieces, and carefully cutting out a small indentation on one edge.

Toss this salad with cardamom dressing to hold the energy together. Add a verbal component, like: "With greens to grow, and carrots to light an inner glow, cucumber adds some zest, eggs and dressing do the rest. Passion from this bowl now turned, within me, let those Fires burn." Serve by the light of two red candles.

After your passionate salad, try this special froth. Put 2 cups of passion fruit juice, two small bananas, and two slices of orange into your blender. Add some crushed ice, then whip up the romantic energy. Serve from one large glass adorned with two straws and two cherries.

During your preludes to passionate moments, have two candles lit in the room, one for each person. Have a third, vibrant red candle that remains unlit until an appropriate moment. As you notice your mood shifting, have each person take one candle and place its flame simultaneously with the other on the central red taper to signal igniting desire. Together, whisper: *"With the lighting of this flame, so too my desire. One candle burns in two hearts."* Blow out the individual candles and let nature have her way.

To accentuate this magic further, carve a word or emblem into the upper third of the candle and dab it with a favorite cologne or perfume. Alternatively, use an oil associated with romance, like rose, clove, or vanilla.

PASSAGES

General Uses: Coping with drastic life changes, including births, deaths, coming of age, eldership, etc.

Timing: Moon in Gemini, Capricorn, or Aries. November, December, and August. Times of transition such as New Year, dawn, dusk, and changing tides. Monday and Thursday.

Props/Focals: Butterfly, peony, chameleon, hoops, fire pits, keys, doors, and archways. Woven or flowing things. Almond, butter, salves, and clover. Agate. The element of Air (change and movement). The colors purple or blue.

Secondary Listings: Adaptation, Balance, Courage, Grief, Kindness, Overcoming, Remembrance, Victory.

Sample Spells:

In Celtic regions, the act of jumping a fire pit marked the end of any phase, whether it was physical, emotional, or spiritual. At an outdoor gathering, this is still possible to do with a small, burnt-down fire that is safely made and tended. A more contemporary alternative is to use a covered candle.

In either case, the movement from one side to the other indicates the change in status. Accentuate this by an alteration in clothing or adornment or by taking a ritual bath and anointing. For a group, this activity is enhanced when all members chant phrases like: *"The wheel turns, it never ceases, turn and change, turn and change. Over the Fires of rebirth, you move, turn and change, turn and change."* Release symbols of the past to the ritual fires (or a fireproof pot or cauldron) and don new emblems.

Put on a blue item of clothing, then take yourself to an area where a noticeable breeze will be present. Stand facing into the wind and anoint your pulse points with almond oil, saying: *"My life's blood never ceases to move, so too I must move. Maiden and*

Crone, Boy and Grandfather, I accept your example and accept my new position as_____. Help me grow in wisdom. So be it." Next, drop an emblem of your old life where you stand. Turn away from it, moving into your new position with the wind at your back and fortune as your guide.

Unlike other spells of this nature, it is not improper to look back if you feel guided to. The past has made us what we are; rejoice in it.

Go to a beach before high tide, and with a piece of driftwood, draw in the sand an image of any outmoded ways. Say: *"As water must have its way, this part of me cannot stay. Into the sands, I now convey, be freed with water, washed away!"* Watch and meditate as the tides slowly smooth away that image, drawing it into the sea. Afterward, either return the wood to the sea with thanks or keep it as a magical wand for future spells.

If you cannot get to a beach, use a hose and dirt on a nearby driveway, sidewalk, or street. In this case, your scribing tool should be something more urban, like a hose nozzle or crowbar. Another alternative is to sprinkle a little salt in your sink, draw your chosen image, and then turn on the faucet!

PEACE

General Uses: Serenity, harmony, reconciliation, accord, tranquility, composure, and ceasing hostilities.

Timing: August or November. Waning moon to decrease hostility. Moon in Gemini, Aries, or Libra. Dawn. Monday.

Props/Focals: Ash wood or leaves; hawthorn flowers; linden (community); willow or yew (flexibility). Bridges and open hands. Lettuce, violet, olive, almond, basil, blueberry, and celery. Amethyst. The number two and the colors white or pale blue.

Secondary Listings: Balance, Blessing, Forgiveness, Harmony, Negotiation, Quiet, Understanding.

Sample Spells:

To make a peace wreath, gather tiny ash wood shards (or alternatives) that naturally fall to the ground and glue them together into a circle. To the top of this, add dried violet petals around a focal point of whole almonds, a few basil leaves, and amethyst for decoration. Braid white and pale blue ribbon together as a final touch. These wreaths can be made small enough to hang from a keychain or large enough to become a protective amulet for your home.

Create a biodegradable image of your anger out of dirt, cloth, or anything that seems appropriate. Bury this under ashes and leaves, saying: *"Dust falls to dust, and leaves fly away, let peace find a foothold, keeping anger at bay."* On top of the mound, place an amethyst crystal. Depending on the location, this should remain undisturbed for as long as possible to transmit your magical energy.

On a piece of paper, trace your dominant hand (the one normally extended in a handshake). In the center of the tracing, write the name of the person to whom you wish to extend peace. Wrap this carefully around a green olive (or olive leaf) and tie it with two circuits of white thread. Bless this amulet by saying: *"I open my hand and heart so all anger can depart. Let peace now grow between me and thee."* Carry this to your next meeting with that individual to encourage resolution. Once the problem is reconciled, bury the amulet so the past remains buried.

If your words with this individual were unusually harsh, you may wish to substitute a honey-flavored candy or honeycomb for the olive. In India, honey represents wise words. In this form, the amulet stimulates discourse tempered with gentle speech.

Make or find an image of the person who is showing intolerance. To this image, apply skin cream over the area of their heart and say: *"Let healing have its way; let understanding flow. Peace be between us."* Keep this image close to your heart whenever possible. At other times, wrap it in the white cloth of peace. When the problems have been resolved, burn the bundle so that harmony can be carried on the winds.

POWER

General Uses: Increasing energy, vigor, and stamina. Potency, force, and command/control of oneself or a situation.

Timing: Month of March. Waxing to Full Moon. Spring and summer. Thursday. Moon in Taurus, Virgo, Aries, Scorpio, or Pisces. During times of increasing temperature or bright sunlight.

Props/Focals: Electrical outlets, batteries, blender. Quartz, topaz, or gold. The colors red or orange. The number eight. Ginger, pepper, vanilla, baking powder, bay, yeast, fig, lilac, your own hair, and elder wood or bark. Powerful animals like the lion.

Secondary Listings: Energy, Grounding, Health, Leadership, Overcoming, Victory, Zeal.

Sample Spells:

Open a box of animal crackers and remove all the images of vigorous beasts. Set aside eight of the best ones, dipping them lightly in a mixture of vanilla extract (eight drops), ¼ cup weak coffee, and powdered ginger. As you eat the crackers, visualize the energy of that creature in its natural setting. Feel this power like a growing warmth in your stomach that spreads up your back and then throughout your body. When you feel about to burst from the energy, stop eating and direct the energy toward your goal(s). Save leftover crackers for another time of need.

During a full moon, gently pull eight strands of hair from your head. Say: "*From my will, eight strands I pull, to give this magic the strength of a bull. With these stones and herbs inlaid, let the power now be stayed,*" as you place the strands with eight quartz crystals and eight bay leaves into a small pouch. Wear this during spells or rituals, hang it from a staff or wand, or keep it in your home to release its energy as needed.

From small bits of elder bark, dried lilac petals, and ginger powder, make an empowering incense. Mix them in the proportion: ¼ cup of powdered bark to eight lilac petals and 1 teaspoon of ginger powder. Burn on self-lighting charcoal in a heat-proof container. As the mixture sparks and burns, add an incantation, like: "*Smoke, rise higher with my power! Will, with magic, might rise through the night! Through the air, embark directly to my mark!*" Leave this burning while you meditate on a goal or work a ritual to increase its accuracy.

Prejudice

General Uses: Banishing prejudice, predisposition, bigotry, racism, favoritism, intolerance, or partiality. Encouraging diversity and tolerance.

Timing: Waning moons to decrease hostility. Waxing moons to increase tolerance. Daytime hours to bring truth into "light." August, October, November, and December. Moon in Aries or Gemini. Monday or Wednesday.

Props/Focals: Easterly winds. Radish, grass, clove, basil, pine, vanilla, caraway, chives, violet, oak, or salt. Purgative herbs and foods. Anything that softens or smooths, like an iron or skin cream. Carnelian and amethyst. Breaking bread, an open hand, eyes, and ears. The numbers two and three. The colors blue, white, and black.

Secondary Listings: Balance, Banishing, Communication, Forgiveness, Friendship, Gossip, Intuition, Judgment, Kindness, Liberation, Overcoming, Understanding, Wisdom.

Sample Spells:

To make a tasty sauce for tolerance, combine 2 cups of cider vinegar and 4 cups of salad oil in a saucepan. Warm over a low flame with personally pleasing amounts of basil, caraway, chives, and garlic. Stir counterclockwise and chant: *"Warm their hearts, intolerance depart!"*

Once the mixture smells heavily of the herbs, cool it. Then, place it in an airtight container to use on salads or as a marinade for meats. Name your meal after the area where prejudice is being experienced. Let your dressing act as a healing, softening salve, and internalize it by eating.

Break a slice of fresh bread into two equal pieces. Eat one as an emblem of your willingness to forgive. Bury the other with pine needles, cloves, and a flowering seed named after the person showing prejudice. Speak words of healing, such as *"peace," "understanding,"* and *"respect,"* to the seed as you tend it daily. By the time the plant blossoms, some positive change should take place.

PROSPERITY

General Uses: Abundance, affluence, success, accomplishment.

Timing: Month of April. Waxing to full moon. Friday and Saturday. Moon in Pisces, Aquarius, Virgo, or Taurus. The season of spring.

Props/Focals: The numbers four and twelve. Northerly winds. The colors gold, silver, and green. Oak, almond, alfalfa, tulip, tomato, ash, banana, saffron, pumpkin, pineapple, parsley, oats, rice and other grains, lettuce, fish, blackberry, beef, allspice, and basil. The dragonfly. Anything that thrives abundantly in your region (see the third spell in the sample spells provided).

Secondary Listings: Abundance, Blessing, Goals, Jobs, Luck, Money.

Sample Spells:

Note: Prosperity spells can be used to bring abundance to any endeavor, including gardening and creative crafts.

Every day during the month of April, eat a cereal that contains oats, rice, corn, barley, or other grains. During this time, also regularly wear items of clothing whose color is sympathetic to prosperity (green, gold, or silver). Each morning, light a green candle with the word "prosperity" carved into it. Let this burn for four to twelve minutes as you eat or dress. Then, go out into your day, making positive efforts to fulfill your needs. By the end of the month, some measure of success should come.

On a day when the wind is blowing from the north, go outside with a handful of oats, wheat, and rice, holding them in your receiving hand. Visualize your need in detail, then release the handful to the wind with your wish: *"As oats and wheat and rice go free, bring to me prosperity. As o'er the ground they twist and blow, let my _____ start to grow."* Fill in the blank with the area needful of prospering.

Hollow out a small pumpkin or a squash and line it with tinfoil. Fill this with twelve pineapple bits, twelve chopped almonds, twelve banana slices (optional), twelve blackberries, and a dash of allspice. As you add each ingredient, stir clockwise, saying: *"Pineapple for golden luck, almonds to bring wealth, banana is for energy, blackberry for joy and health. Last to mix is allspice, bronzed powder in each bite, and with it, stir my magic so the power can ignite!"* Keep covered tightly in your refrigerator, eating a little each morning over the next twelve days. If time is of the essence, eat one or two good-sized bites every hour for twelve hours.

To give this magical snack greater longevity, mix your fruits with a berry gelatin dessert (follow the directions on the box).

Berries represent the abundance of the Earth, and gelatin adds happiness to the equation.

To avoid waste, use the pumpkin to make a prosperity pie after the magic has been worked.

PROTECTION

General Uses: Safety, shielding, warding, preservation, care, and security.

Timing: Tuesday and Thursday. Moon in Virgo or Leo. The month of January. In bright sunlight.

Props/Focals: Chili, cranberries, dill, horseradish, hot sauce, clove, garlic, frankincense, myrrh, pineapple, rhubarb, mints, thistle, or onion. Coral, malachite, and topaz. Birch and ash. Image of a shield, sprinkled water, a fence, white light, a dog, a circle, and the number six.

Secondary Listings: Banishing, Cleansing, Ghosts, Quarters, Victory

Sample Spells:

To make a protective charm, take a picture of the person or item you wish to protect and wrap it carefully in white cloth so that it is not bent or soiled. Bless this bundle regularly by sprinkling a circle of water around it in a clockwise fashion, envisioning white light encompassing it. Ask your personal god or goddess for favor on your efforts. Keep the item safe with other magical charms.

A practical, refreshing, and useful anointing oil for your living space can be prepared as follows: place 6 teaspoons of dried mint, six cloves, and six each of frankincense and myrrh tears in 1 cup of warm almond oil. Allow these to soak for six days in bright sunlight to empower them, then dab on all your windows, doors, and other openings around the home. As you anoint the area, add a brief chant, such as: *"Where there is light, darkness may not dwell."*

Envision each anointed area being bound together by a network of white-light webs. This strengthens this spell.

If you want the oil to have a stronger smell, warm it over a low flame for fifteen minutes or so at the end of the six-day period. This enhances the fiery, protective nature and incorporates the herbal aromas into the oil base. Additionally, keep the herbs sealed in the oil bottle to continue refreshing the scent.

A piece of coral worn as jewelry has long been regarded as a potent protective amulet, especially in ancient Greece. If you can find a piece by yourself, be sure to thank the sea for its gift. Take it to a private place to bless the talisman, saying: *"In my life, light shall flow, smooth as the sea. Let this token keep safety ever with me."* If the coral ever breaks, that will destroy the energy within.

At that time, return the pieces to the water with gratitude before making a new amulet.

Quarters of the Magic Circle (Spells to Invoke)

General Uses: Empowering, charging, and invoking the four quarters of a magical circle (Earth, Air, Fire, and Water). Becoming more attuned to each element.

Timing: Wednesday. September and November. As desired for spells and rituals. Possibly during appropriate elemental moon signs (like Pisces for Water) to create permanent sacred space.

Props/Focals:

- Earth/North: The number three. The colors brown, black, and green. Apple, barley (most grains), beets, peas, and potatoes. Plants, a globe, soil, or crystals.
- Air/East: The number five. The colors yellow, white, and pale orange. Fans, feathers, incense, windows, doors, flags, and wind chimes. Anise, dandelion, lavender, and mint.

- Fire/South: The number one. The colors orange and red. Candles, fireplaces, stoves, heaters, and light sources. Cinnamon, fennel, radish, orange, ash, bay, carrots, cloves, and pepper.
- Water/West: The number seven. The colors blue, deep green, and purple. Sink, tub, seashells, sand, grapes, peach (or any juicy fruit), coconut, willow wood or leaves, and cauliflower.

Secondary Listings: Blessing, Elements, Energy, Magic, Protection, Wisdom.

Sample Spells:

Each quarter's invocation will be different according to your working space, personal preference, and the quarter's function. One example of each is given below:

Earth: Find three seeds of any flower-bearing plant that thrives well in an indoor environment. Place them in a pot and say: *"Guardians of the Earth, sacred soil of my birth, with these seeds, your power shall glow, throughout this sacred space to grow."* Place the pot somewhere in the Northern quarter of your magical space or home. If the lighting is not good there, use a grow light or keep the plant elsewhere between magical gatherings.

Air: Intersperse five feathers and five bells on a string. Add mint leaves if available. Affix the string to a window that is either in or near the East, and say: *"Guardians of the Air, changing winds on each now bear, ringing safety through our home, as magic moves within this poem."* Leave it in the window to ring out warm, protective energy throughout your living area.

Fire: Get yourself one large red, orange, or golden candle and affix it to a safe container. Place it somewhere in the Southern area of your magical space. Anoint the candle with cinnamon oil and say: *"Guardians of the Fire, embers that brighten the darkest night, let your sparks within me burn, and protect this space with eternal light."* Light the candle any time you feel negative energy infringing on your home.

Water: Gather seven seashells in a small, decorative glass canning container. Fill this with boiling water or sand and seal it shut immediately. When cooled, decorate the edge of the seal using blue or green wax. Set this in the Western quarter of your sacred space, saying: *"Guardians of the Waters, the flowing, endless grail, move your waves upon this shore, let magic take to sail!"* If this token ever looks dirty within, the contents should be completely changed, and the invocation repeated.

Quests

General Uses: Pursuits, crusades, inner journeys, searches, endeavors, or undertakings. Also, oaths and promises.

Timing: July and from September to December. New moon and dawn. Thursday. Moon in Sagittarius and Capricorn.

Props/Focals: Primary colors (for delineated purposes). The numbers four, thirteen, and forty. Mustard (faith), mint, lemon, grass, squash, thyme, oak, birch, elder, Brussels sprouts, and pansy. Birds and horses (for movement or messages), grail or chalice, shoes, and thread. Moonstone or rock crystal. Footpaths. Easterly winds.

Secondary Listings: Adaptation, Balance, Courage, Dedication, Goals, Inspiration, Leadership, Obtaining, Recovering Items, Tenacity, Virtue, Zeal.

Sample Spells:

In medieval days, a quest was a journey of personal honor. European folklore also portrayed it as an adventure toward self-discovery and refinement. In both instances, the quest was often preceded by an oath to fulfill a sacred mission.

To keep faith strong during a quest, make an inspiring talisman by wrapping a mustard seed with an oak leaf. Tie this round thirteen times with strands of red, green, and blue thread. Say a brief prayer reflecting your goals over the item. Carry it with you until your quest has been successful, then keep it in a safe place. Any time you feel a need to strengthen your convictions, begin carrying it again.

In a chalice, place a full cup of lemonade and four mint leaves. Drink half the cup, then pour the rest to the Earth as a libation, saying: *"The cup of truth and perseverance has touched my lips. By this liquid, accept my promise to _____ ."*

Such an action brings universal energy to bear witness to your pledge. Therefore, it is best not to enter into such an oath lightly or without forethought.

If a friend or a loved one is embarking on some type of quest, it is traditional to give them some token of your love. In the Middle Ages, this was called a "favor." These gifts bring luck and honor to the recipient's efforts. Most often, an embroidered piece of cloth was created.

For magical quests, the token should be made during the full moon using personally significant symbols. Cross-stitch patterns are particularly effective in this type of magic, as each stitch forms an "X" that can emblematize the four elements in balance (like a Celtic cross). Sigils and runes are a nice touch, along with some type of central emblem. The finished piece can then encompass a quartz or moon tone.

Before presenting the favor, take a moment to meditate with it close to your heart and pour as much love into it as possible. Then, deliver it to your loved one and explain the symbolism. In the pattern above, a griffin was used to impart the strength of a lion and the vision of an eagle.

Quick-Mindedness

General Uses: Mental alertness and attentiveness. Fast decision-making. Increased cognitive and rational ability.

Timing: During sunlight hours. Tuesday. May and October. Moon in Aries, Leo, or Scorpio.

Props/Focals: The colors yellow and gold. The number ten. Amethyst. Rabbit, apple, vanilla, carrot, coffee, coriander, lilac, mace, mustard, and rosemary. The snap of a finger, coin flips, alarms, light bulbs, or sharp items. Easterly winds.

Secondary Listings: Choices, Communication, Conscious Mind, Judgment, Knowledge, Leadership, Mental Ability, Organization, Understanding, Viewpoints.

Sample Spells:

Flip a favorite coin (perhaps one with the year of your birth on it). After it returns to your hand, put it with some coffee, coriander, and ten rosemary sprigs in a golden pouch. Bind the top with yellow yarn, turn it around ten times, and overstitch it. Then, incant: *"With a flip of the coin and a finger snap, let my judgment quickly adapt."* Make sure to snap your fingers at the appropriate moment.

Any time you need to make a fast decision, hold the pouch in hand and repeat the phrase while focusing on your question. The pouch can be used for this purpose ten times, then should be filled with new ingredients and empowered again.

To make an empowering perfume or cologne, put a couple of apple peels, some carrot tops, vanilla extract, and an amethyst into warm oil. Set this in the sun for ten days. On the final day, bless the oil for alertness. Each time you need agile wits, anoint either yourself or a light bulb in your home. As you turn on the light, say: *"Touched by the*

light of the sun, my mind will see clearly. Scented with the aroma of reason, my decisions will be sound." Then, make your choice with conviction.

Note that the aroma in this recipe may be improved by adding a few drops of apple and vanilla essential oil to the finished product.

QUIET

General Uses: Silence, serenity, or tranquility. Knowing when to be still, both verbally and spiritually.

Timing: Monday. Dark moon. Moon in Gemini or Aquarius. The month of August and the season of winter.

Props/Focals: The colors white, pink, black, and dark blue. Stars, snow, an ear, a finger to one's lips, and a bed. Rose petals (especially pink and white), tea, oak, ash, violet, pansy, basil, or blueberries. Northerly winds.

Secondary Listings: Banishing, Beauty, Cleansing, Forgiveness, Harmony, Peace, Sleep.

Sample Spells:

Gather a bowl of snow or shaved ice and add some red food coloring, mixing until the whole pile appears pink. Place this in an area where it will melt slowly. Add your incantation: *"As the snow melts away, so too all disruption. Let peace fall on this house like winter's blanket."* This spell is enhanced by laying a white blanket over the bowl for symbolic emphasis.

Once the snow has melted, pour the liquid outdoors, saying: *"Harmony and peace here shall stay. Negativity is banished and flows away."*

Gather a handful of black tea. Next, go outside on a moonless night. Keep the finger of your free hand against your lips in the signal for silence. Walk out to the night, saying nothing but focusing your mind on the need for quiet. Toss the tea to the stars along with your wish.

Recovering Items

General Uses: Finding lost people or things. Rejuvenating and regaining composure. Reclaiming health.

Timing: March and August. Waxing moons. Moon in Taurus and Libra. Wednesday.

Props/Focals: Westerly winds. The numbers two and four. The colors yellow or blue (health). Agate, allspice, amethyst, apple, nutmeg, barley, brussels sprouts, chicken, date, lilac, and hazelwood. A string or circle, boomerang, magnet, magnifying glass, or dowsing rod.

Secondary Listings: Adaptation, Balance, Energy, Health, Identifying, Mental Ability, Tenacity, Visions.

Sample Spells:

To find a lost item, tie a piece of string four times around a description of the article. Leave enough string dangling so that you can place the paper across the table from you and still keep the end of the string in hand. Focus intently on the object and the places where it might have been lost. Slowly pull the string (and thereby the object) toward you until it is in your hand. Carry the string and paper while conducting your search.

Cut open a rubber band so that it can be laid out straight. At one end, glue two small agates. Hold the other end of the rubber band in your strong hand while visualizing the item that was lost. Try a simple repeated incantation, such as: *"Return to me, return to me...."* Then, gently snap the rubber band outward, allowing its natural force to bring the energy back to you. Carry this as a charm until you feel your goal has been met.

For returning good health, pour apple juice into a glass or goblet. Add four drops of blue food coloring. To increase positive energy, look at the goblet through a magnifying glass before drinking it and say: *"Where sickness dwells, health shall grow, carried with this liquid, well-being I sow."* Now enjoy the juice!

RELATIONSHIPS

General Uses: Friendship, family ties, love, romance, and general associations.

Timing: Friday. June and August. Waxing to full moon. Moon in Pisces, Gemini, or Aries.

Props/Focals: Bridges, cake, cups, jade (dedication), knots, a dog, and woven or connected items. The numbers two, three, nine, twelve, and thirteen. The colors pink and orange (friendship). Cocoa (warm feelings), buttercup, anise, lemon, caraway, cardamom, orange, peas, plum, berries, rose, tomato, apple, rosemary, basil, bread, and nutmeg. Paper clips or things that join and unite other items.

Secondary Listings: Communication, Forgiveness, Friendship, Harmony, Kinship, Love, Lust, Passion, Versatility, Unions.

Sample Spells:

Line a basket with a pinkish-orange linen or cotton cloth. Find a recipe for gingerbread ornaments or salt dough and prepare according to the sample directions provided. To this base, add a bit of basil or rose for love and harmony.

Before baking or drying, devise an image of each person in your group or home, and decorate each appropriately. Cook until the images harden, adorn them with other reflections of the season, and then place them in the basket. Bless the finished basket by saying: *"Woven together in love. Bound in harmony. Freely shared, freely accepted."* This is a lovely decoration and gift item.

In medieval Germany, a loving cup, sometimes called a *minne* cup, was used to improve unity in a relationship. People filled this special chalice with fruity wine (for joy) and a dash of cardamom (or another "love" herb). It was believed that when two parties partook of the goblet, their lives and destinies were linked. To drink was to accept that bond.

We can use this tradition as it stands, adding a chant performed by all parties to empower the spell. The phrase used should be repeated once for each person participating.

One way to improve the strength of friendships or other close associations is through weaving. Simple over-under patterns are fine. Each member of the group brings along a fabric swatch, preferably from an old piece of clothing. These pieces are then woven together with white swatches (for peace) brought by the leader of the group. Each time someone new comes into the group, add a new piece of fabric to the weave. Anoint the edges of the weave with a mixture of orange and lemon oil (watered-down juice may substitute), saying: *"Weave and braid and twine, my life is joined to thine. Once the spell is woven, so be joined in trust and love."* The oldest member of the group retains the fabric and passes it on when the time is right.

Remembering

General Uses: Recollection/retention of knowledge. Forgetfulness.

Timing: October and March. Moon in Leo, Scorpio, Sagittarius, or any Air sign. Tuesday and Sunday. Waxing moon to improve knowledge; waning moon to alleviate absent-mindedness.

Props/Focals: Apple (health), rosemary, fish, coffee (alertness), coriander, pansy, mace, mustard, walnut, and vanilla. Southerly winds. The numbers five, eight, and ten. Books and notebooks, photographs, computers. Carnelian. Dragons, elephants, tortoises, and other long-lived creatures. The colors yellow and gold.

Secondary Listings: Conscious Mind, Knowledge, Mental Ability, Overcoming, Teachers/teaching, Understanding.

Sample Spells:

A pleasant memory-enhancing beverage to enjoy on a hot summer day consists of one large scoop of vanilla ice cream, 5 tablespoons of brewed coffee, five sprigs of rosemary, and 1 cup of apple juice. (One teaspoon of instant coffee dissolved in water may be used if fresh brewed is unavailable.) Place these in a blender. Focus strongly on the area where you need better retention. As the blender works, visualize a bright golden light filling every drop. Then enjoy!

Find a children's coloring book with an image of a kindly dragon from which you can make a book cover. Carefully remove this page and color the dragon using a gold or a yellow crayon. As you work, repeat this incantation ten times: *"As your life is long, so too is my memory. With golden light now drawn, retention come to me."* Use this sheet as a protective book cover or fold it to carry to school or work. Anoint it with eight drops of apple juice and surround the image with appropriate symbols to enhance the energies further.

Roles

General Uses: Coping with new and unique situations. Functioning well in diverse positions and capacities.

Timing: Waxing moon for personal development; new moon for the art of disguise. July and October. Moon in Aries, Cancer (for creative adaptation), Leo, or Sagittarius. Monday or Wednesday for resourceful solutions.

Props/Focals: Masks and costumes. Chameleons. Flexible, fluid, or variegated items. The numbers four, six, eight, and ten. Eastern winds (transformation). Coconut (variety), gravy (smooth changes), apples, and vanilla (perceptions). Curtains, makeup, and mirrors.

Secondary Listings: Choices, Dedication, Goals, Harmony, Intuition, Jobs, Movement, Overcoming, Quick-Mindedness, Versatility, Visions.

Sample Spells:

Before working magic, it is important to remove the more mundane cares of the world so you can participate fully. To prepare for your role in personal or group workings, it helps to change your clothes (perhaps donning a ritual robe) behind a curtain or door. This divider marks the line between the mundane world and the space "between the worlds."

As you change, breathe deeply and meditate to bring your metaphysical senses and gifts to the forefront. When you are ready, reach for the divider, saying: *"The temporal is behind, the mundane I here bind. Open the curtain and be free, the magic in me!"* Open the curtain at the appropriate moment and step into your spiritual role. This process may be reversed to return to a normal level of awareness.

Another incantation suggested for this spell by my friend, MayRose, is: *"This is a time that is not a time; in a place that is not a place; on a day that is not a day. I stand before the eternal gateway, before the veil of mystery."*

In all of our lives, there are circumstances that make us ill at ease. To help yourself adapt to your role in difficult surroundings, try this visualization. Imagine that situation or environment with as many details as possible. See yourself in the center. In your mind's eye, let the edges of your physical body get fuzzy until you become one with your surroundings. The effect should be like watching a chameleon adapt to the color of a leaf onto which it has jumped. While in this state, extend your senses so that you can feel and hear subtle undercurrents and attune yourself to them. Finally, return to a solid image, seeing yourself effectively dealing with the situation. Repeat this visualization as often as necessary until your confidence improves.

When preparing for work or a difficult task, let your clothing represent an aspect of the job or a particular professional attitude. For example, a shirt can be buttoned while you speak an incantation, like: *"From my neck down to my hip, remind me when to button my lip!"* As you don each item, name it according to the characteristic you are integrating. When you come home at night, reverse the process to leave your stress behind you.

SAFE TRAVEL

General Uses: Adventure. Voyages. Any time you are going out of the home (by foot, by car, or whatever).

Timing: January. Waxing moons. Moon in Gemini, Virgo, or Sagittarius. Weekends.

Props/Focals: Your vehicle, small portable tokens, an airplane, inspection stickers, road maps or guidebooks, the rune of protection, and cameras. For sea voyages, champagne, and coins. For land travel, moonstone, turquoise, or shoes. Mint, catnip, and chives. The color white. The number fifty-five.

Secondary Listings: Luck, Movement, Protection, Weather

Sample Spells:

Mark a toy car or paper airplane with the rune of protection. Additionally, dab a little mint extract on the vehicle, then release it in the direction you will be traveling. Add a memorable verbal component like *"Powers of light, protect my car, when I travel near or far."* Preserve both the incantation and the object to use as needed within that mode of transportation.

Find a small bell whose sound is pleasant to you. These can be found at flea markets, thrift stores, craft shops, and other novelty-type businesses. Place it in the light of the moon and then the light of the sun for fifty-five minutes each. Afterward, bless it by saying: *"Each time the bell rings, with it, safety brings."* You can affix the chime to any number of items, including your shoelaces, a bicycle wheel, or the rearview mirror of a car to act as a portable amulet. When you hear the bell, repeat your power phrase silently or out loud to reinforce the magic.

A Victorian folk spell for safe travel is to place mint in a wallet, purse, or briefcase. This was believed to encourage prosperity, as well. To accent this effort, use a fresh mint leaf wrapped neatly around a small moonstone or other favorite good luck charm.

Stuff a white cloth with any combination of comfrey, catnip, turquoise, pieces of champagne cork, and Irish moss. To this, add a slip of paper with your destination written on it. Stitch this bundle together with white thread while repeating the phrase *"Wherever I roam, return me safely to home"* until the sewing is complete. Leave this token somewhere in your house as a magical beacon to draw you back, safe and sound. Snip it open and change the paper before your next trip, then repeat the procedure. Should the cloth or ingredients get dirty, replace them.

SEPARATION

General Uses: Divorce. Estrangement of relationships. End of business partnerships. Long absence from loved ones.

Timing: February, April, August, and November. Waning to dark moon. Sunset. Moon in Gemini, Capricorn, or Pisces. Friday and Thursday.

Props/Focals: A division sign, fire, cut cords or apron strings, scissors and knives, partitions. Things that can be stored or put out of sight. Ashes, dates, blueberries, basil, wheat with chaff, oil, and salves. The colors blue and black.

Secondary Listings: Adaptation, Banishing, Cleansing, Courage, Forgiveness, Doubt, Grief, Relationships, Remembering, Wisdom.

Sample Spells:

For two individuals to end a business relationship in a positive manner, they should come together with one copy of their contract and two pairs of scissors. With their contract stretched between them, each cuts from their end until they meet in the center and say: *"I release you as our partnership wanes. You liberate me, but friendship remains."* Burn the paper and release the ashes to an easterly wind for a new beginning.

Have two handfasted people who wish to part go together to the spot where they initially exchanged vows, bringing with them any tokens they kept from the occasion. Set up a sacred space at the site and invoke the gods or goddesses of peace and understanding for assistance. Next, ritually burn, bury, or break the tokens of the commitment, saying: *"What was done, we now freely release, while our union is ended, perfect love does not cease."* Your last words at this point should be personal, nonjudgmental, and freeing with the best intentions. When finished, the people should turn their backs to each other and walk away in opposite directions, not looking back.

When you or a family member is moving away for a long period of time, set up a mutual time to work magic aimed toward easing separation anxieties. Begin with a meditation where you visualize each other and a pinkish-red beam of light that connects you. Once you feel each other's presence, begin repeating simple, one-word phrases that empower your relationship. Examples include *"love," "peace," "harmony,"* and *"unity."*

This exercise acts as a reciprocal spell. Accentuate by burning a pink or red candle with similar words carved into it or by releasing rose petals to the winds to carry your feelings.

At sunset before the first night of a dark moon, take an emblem of your separation to a private spot. Dig a small hole in the Earth while the sun moves to the horizon. When only a small trace of light is still visible, place the item within the Earth and say: *"Everything returns to dust; _____ ends here, as it must. I place this token in the clay to sow new beginnings, come light of day."* Put a little water on the icon before covering it with soil to help the magic to grow. As you leave the spot, resolve in your heart to make a fresh start tomorrow.

SLEEP

General Uses: Banishing or easing insomnia. Peaceful rest.

Timing: Winter. Moon just rising in the sky. Night in general. August. Moon in Gemini or Aquarius.

Props/Focals: Pillows, valerian, black tea, quiet music, your bed, blankets, and yawning. Topaz. Anise, barley, rosemary, rose, blueberry, catnip, and bluebells. Sheep and bears. Caves.

Secondary Listings: Banishing, Blessing, Harmony, Liberation, Nightmares, Peace, Protection, Quiet, Visions.

Sample Spells:

Sometimes the old tried-and-true methods for anything are best. A favorite folk remedy for sleeplessness is to drink weak chamomile tea and warm milk before bed. To this, you can add an incantation like, *"As this drink is taken deep, soon I will be fast asleep!"*

To emphasize your goal further, repeat this phrase while stirring the tea, either clockwise to bring sleep or counterclockwise to keep wakefulness at bay. Also, quietly whisper it to yourself like a mantra when you lie down.

Take your pillow to a dry area beneath the moonbeams. Sprinkle a rosemary infusion around it. Work in a counterclockwise manner as you repeat, *"Away from me the thoughts of day, away from me my*

worried ways." Then change your direction to clockwise, altering the incantation to: *"When Luna smiles through night's sky, so sleep will come to tired eyes. No more to wake, no more to roam, rest is welcome in my home."*

As with the last spell, repeat this last phrase as you put your head on the pillow every night.

Another favorite country spell, while a little unconventional, was also one that apparently ensured undisturbed rest for at least ten hours. European Cunning Folk recommended taking a little dirt gathered from a graveyard and sprinkling it around the perimeter of one's home. They did this because death was likened to a long sleep for the soul.

Get a white candle and light it without a word. Walk counterclockwise around your bedroom three times. As you do, project simple protective phrases into the walls, floors, and windows. Next, go clockwise thrice in silence, meditating on positive, restful phrases. Finally, blow out the candle, whisper the word "sleep," and turn in for the night.

This spell does not have to be repeated to continue working. Instead, simply light the candle for a few minutes each night, then whisper "sleep" again before getting into bed. When the candle is completely spent, repeat the original spell with a new taper.

SPEECH

General Uses: Communication, conversation, articulating ideas. Potent lectures and positive dialogue.

Timing: October and December. Waxing to full moon. Moon in Aries or Leo. Tuesday and Wednesday.

Props/Focals: Wax lips, a silver tongue, and cue cards. Soup (especially alphabet soup), coffee, figs (power), and ham. Quartz and carnelian. The colors gold, red, or yellow. The number eight.

Secondary Listings: Communication, Conscious Mind, Courage, Energy, Inspiration, Leadership, Mental Ability, Negotiation, Quick-Mindedness, Wisdom.

Sample Spells:

Make yourself a small coffee cake that includes some chopped figs (¼ cup is a good amount). Cut off one end and shape it into the image of a tongue. Place this on top of the cake with toothpicks. Decorate the image using cake decorators' silver balls. As you do, visualize yourself making your presentation (or whatever your task is) with great success. Eat this to internalize strong oratorical powers.

Take a small jar with a secure lid to a private area and shout into it words or short phrases appropriate to your situation like, *"leadership"* or *"positive conversation."* When finished, cap it quickly and tightly. Place the jar beneath a waxing to full moon on Tuesday night for eight hours. At 8 a.m. on the next day, open the jar and inhale to accept the breath of magic you have placed within!

To create a portable amulet for stimulating better articulation, combine four quartz crystals with four carnelians in a small jar of instant coffee. Wrap this jar with a red or yellow cloth saying: *"Grow stronger today, each word I say. When drunk hot and pure, all stammers will cure!"* Prepare yourself a cup whenever you feel inarticulate.

Teachers/Teaching

General Uses: Instruction, education, and guidance of others. Finding spiritual teachers.

Timing: May, June, July, September, or any time before a school semester begins. Waxing to full moon. Moon in Scorpio, Virgo, or Pisces. Thursday and Sunday.

Props/Focals: Pointers, chalk, and white robes. Amethyst and agate. Rosemary, caraway, pansy, hazelnut, magnets, mustard, apple, rosemary, saffron, or elder. Books, keys, and magnets. The sun. The colors gold, green, and brown. The numbers four, eight, ten, and twenty-one; possibly the number twelve (i.e., years of elementary and secondary school).

Secondary Listings: Communication, Conscious Mind, Dedication, Goals, Knowledge, Leadership, Mental Ability, Understanding.

Sample Spells:

To Find a Teacher:

Make a white robe from a new sheet. Come the next new moon, rub the neckline with eight sprigs of rosemary, saying: *"I make this for my teacher to come, it will stay safely here until this magic manifests with the fullness of the moon."* Keep the robe in a safe place.

A teacher will appear to you sometime during the three days of a full moon, at which time you should offer the robe in acknowledgment. If the teacher does not accept the gift, dye it an appropriate color for your novice training.

Using greenish-yellow chalk on the sidewalk, write all the attributes you desire in a teacher. Let these sit undisturbed beneath a full moon in September or another positive month. As the moonbeams first touch your words, say: *"Silver light, my wishes see, let a teacher come to me. Come the morning, when washed with sun, manifest my magic, the spell's begun."* Leave the words on the sidewalk until they naturally wear away.

To Improve Teaching Skills:

Find a refrigerator magnet that depicts the "sun in splendor" (fully shining). Place this in a bed of associated herbs (see "Props/Focals") beneath the sunlight for four hours. Before removing the token, call upon an appropriate god or goddess to bless your efforts. Add a verbal component like *"As the light shines, so shine my words. Let students attend, let only truth be heard."* Keep this with you in your classroom.

In keeping with the age-old tradition of giving an apple to the teacher, eat one every morning. Name the fruit after a particular teaching ability that you need to enhance that day.

To strengthen this effort, store your apples in a loose-weave gold or green bag with an amethyst or agate crystal in the bottom.

TECHNOMAGIC

General Uses: Improving the performance of technology. For example, getting a temperamental car started, making a computer run smoothly, or getting enough phone service.

Timing: Will depend upon your goals. Waxing moons encourage improvements while waning moons can help banish difficulties. The month of March (success). Moon in Taurus (resolution), Sagittarius (obtaining a goal), Pisces (miracles), or Aquarius. Tuesday and Thursday, which are more attuned to the conscious, logical mind.

Props/Focals: The item in need of repair or improvement, any tools you may need, and instruction manuals. Almond or apple incense to improve personanal composure and attentiveness. An amethyst crystal.

Secondary Listings: Adaptation, Conscious Mind, Judgment, Knowledge, Luck, Mental Ability, Overcoming, Quick-Mindedness, Tenacity, Victory

Sample Spells:

Technomagical spells can be viewed in two ways: first, that you are trying to heal a sick object, and, second, that you are trying to improve your own abilities to correct a problem.

Healing the Object:

When a car, computer, tablet, cellphone, or other object is giving you trouble, try adapting any symbolic remedy you like to make it appropriate to the situation. For example, set a whole egg on top of a laptop, visualizing the virus or other issue being transferred to the egg like a dark sludge. Add an incantation like *"Bytes and bits, within you sit. Where disarrayed, order now inlaid."* Afterward, crack open the egg into a trash container to effectively "can" the problem. Reapproach your system with a more positive attitude.

Another spell I use for mechanical or electronic objects entails drawing a banishing pentagram before them seven times (for completion). To this motion, I may add a silently repeated component such as *"Problems be gone, problems away, I have work to do today. Troubles be free. When I return I will see that this is working effortlessly!"*

Improving Personal Abilities:

Before beginning repairs, prepare an incense of almond or apple, and move your tools through the vapors. This will purge them of any negative energy and allow them to absorb the traits necessary for success.

For growing understanding, charge an amethyst crystal by a waxing moon. Hold this crystal in your receiving hand before beginning your project and say: *"Problems decrease, power release, and like the moon, my skill increase!"* Visualize the silvery rays of the moon pouring out of the crystal into your hands and eyes to illuminate your talents.

TENACITY

General Uses: Determination, perseverance, or persistence. Steadfastness and unwavering conviction.

Timing: October, July, June, and May. Moon in Taurus or Leo. Tuesday and Thursday. When the sun is shining.

Props/Focals: Sticky items (bubble gum, peanut butter), red coals, and immovable objects (such as anything set in concrete). Ants and "*The Little Engine That Could.*" Southerly winds. The colors red or orange. Lilac, lemon, molasses, nutmeg, pine, and beets. The number three.

Secondary Listings: Courage, Dedication, Energy, Goals, Obtaining, Zeal

Sample Spells:

Put a slightly chewed piece of gum on a symbol of the area in your life needing determination. Affix the other side to a spot where it will be visible to you often and say: "*Perseverance stuck like glue, keep my mind trained on you.*" Repeat this phrase each time you see that item. Leave it there until you have completed your task.

An alternative is to pour some strong household adhesive into a paper cup that holds an image of the area where you need improved conviction (for faith, use a religious symbol). While the glue dries, finish the spell by adding a verbal component similar to the one above or with strong visualization.

Ignite some self-lighting charcoal in a fireproof container. When it has turned red, toss some dried lemon rind, pine, and nutmeg on the coals, saying: "*As you burn higher, so sparks my desire. Scent rising in the room, persistence shall bloom. From the coals to my heart, never to depart.*" Use the same procedure any time you feel your determination waning.

Find a kinetic toy or knickknack (one that will not stop unless external force comes upon it, like "drinking birds") and name it after your aspiration. On the day you begin pursuing that goal, start the item moving, saying: "*Never stop moving, devotion ne'er end, my will grows ever stronger, it shall not bend.*" Put this object where it can keep your magic in motion until the goal has been achieved. If you cannot find such a toy, an alternative is an hourglass, turned over daily with a rephrased incantation like "*Time unending, with a turn of my wrist, to all that needs tending, my conviction persists.*"

THRIFT (PRACTICALITY)

General Uses: Frugality, budgeting, sensibility, pragmatics, prudence, conservation, and realistic outlooks.

Timing: Winter. May and July. Waning moon (resources shrinking). Any "dry" or "barren" moon sign. Tuesday and Wednesday.

Props/Focals: A mouse image, shopping coupons, pennies, leftovers, a bank, change purse, jars and bottles, food wrap or measuring cups. Macaroni and cheese, bread, alfalfa, almond, apple, and cords or twist ties. The colors yellow and green. The number ten. Anything that stretches.

Secondary Listings: Adaptation, Choices, Discernment, Judgment, Organization, Quick-Mindedness, Versatility, Virtue

Sample Spells:

Pinch as many pennies between the thumb and forefinger of your strong hand as possible. As you squeeze them together, visualize a dollar stretching like a rubber band in your mind's eye and say: "*Times are hard, and money is scant, frugality I now incant. Let funds and food both stretch and span until prosperity reigns again.*" Keep the pennies with you as an amulet.

An alternative to using pennies is drawing a dollar on a large rubber band or balloon, then stretching either for visual effect.

Place all your shopping coupons on the table before going to the supermarket. Behind them, burn a short green candle (symbolic of short funds) while reviewing your list. Chant "*Sales be plentiful, bargains be mine, upon the shelf your names will shine.*" When you get to the store, take a deep breath and relax. Let your spell guide the choices you make. When uncertain, repeat the incantation to yourself, then look again for a bargain.

Find a mouse magnet for the refrigerator. Beneath it affix a yellow paper with a little poem like:

Heart and soul are nourished
from leftovers and love
so it is we're thankful
for our blessings from above.

This is not so much a spell as a gentle reminder that a grateful heart is powerful magic in itself.

Collect some of your leftover meats, vegetables, and sauces. Dice the meat and vegetables into stew-size pieces, adding enough water to cover them and a few noodles or potatoes to fill out the dish. Once heated, stir in sauces to create a mock gravy. Stir clockwise while cooking, adding a verse like "*A bit of this and a dash of that, all good things from a Witch's hat. Around my cauldron stirred and blessed, let sensibility herein rest!*" Enjoy!

TRANSFORMATION

General Uses: Evolution, metamorphosis, and change.

Timing: September, October, and May. The season of spring. During Fire signs. Moon in Pisces or Scorpio. Monday. Dawn. Cusps or transitory periods like midnight on New Year's Eve.

Props/Focals: Fires and ashes, caterpillars and butterflies, eggs, flower buds, seeds, food processor, moon phases, the Phoenix, and masks. Pepper, fir wood, easterly winds. The number eight. Anything that can show a state of change.

Secondary Listings: Adaptation, Banishing, Cleansing, Energy, Habits, Overcoming, Passages, Viewpoints

Sample Spells:

Place two apples before you. Consider for a moment what you have. Most people will say "two apples." Then, before your eyes, smack the two apples together (or mash them in a bowl) and say: "*What about applesauce?*" The idea here is to awaken yourself to things beyond surface impressions so that the potential for change is visible. As a bonus, you can bless and eat the results of your experiment!

In a cup-shaped piece of eggshell place a little dirt and a seed. Set this in a larger container filled with more good planting soil. Name the seed after the situation or attribute you wish to transform. Each time you water the seedling, speak words of affirmation to the soil that specifically aid your goal. For example, if you are trying to quit smoking, you might encourage your seedling with words like "*self-control,*" "*restraint,*" or "*freedom.*" Continue to pursue your goal on other levels while the plant grows. Once it is ready for transplanting, you should see signs of positive transformation in your life.

This is an exercise especially designed for people who want to lose weight. Go to a toy store and buy yourself a hula hoop. Swirl it around yourself so it is moving counterclockwise (to reduce excess weight) and say: "*Turn, turn, turn, calories burn, burn, burn.*" Do this for eight minutes at 8 a.m. and 8 p.m. every day until your goal is reached.

The time can vary if 8 o'clock is not feasible with your schedule. The important thing is to establish a routine that creates a positive energy flow. It's also good exercise!

Visualize yourself inside a cocoon. Each strand of the sphere is made up of words that name your restraints. Within this shell, you have a pair of scissors marked with the word "transformation" on both blades. When you can see this image clearly, use the power of change to cut your way to liberation!

In the future when you feel tempted to return to those old ways, find a pair of scissors. Hold them tightly while repeating the word "transformation." See that you are still free of those binding threads. Don't take them back!

Unconscious Mind

General Uses: Latent spiritual gifts. The lunar nature. Intuitive self, instinct, and subconscious influences.

Timing: December and November. Night. Full moon. Moon in Cancer, Libra, or Capricorn. Monday and Wednesday.

Props/Focals: Ink or wax blots. Bay leaves. The colors silver and white. Westerly winds, the moon, and water. Elder, black tea, and your eyes. The number seven.

Secondary Listings: Art, Discernment, Doubt, Fear, Imagination, Inspiration, Intuition, Nightmares, Visions

Sample Spells:

An incense that inspires unconscious awareness is made by mixing 7 teaspoons of ground elder wood or leaves, 7 crushed bay leaves, and 7 teaspoons of black tea. Burn this at the seventh hour (a.m. or p.m.) while meditating. Please note, however, that evening hours tend to emphasize the unconscious mind more than daytime does.

This exercise helps to uncover your own unconscious impressions by using an ancient Greek technique. Drop a bit of ink or melted wax into a bowl of cold water. Un-focus your eyes and say: "*Let the hidden be revealed, all that was and will be. From my mind and my heart, let me see the unseen.*"

Repeat this phrase softly to yourself until you naturally fall into a light trance. Eventually an impression of the floating image will come to you. Note all the feelings you have at this moment. Look the image up later in a book of symbols for possible interpretations. If you don't have wax or ink handy, a fun alternative is to use the shapes made by an old fully heated lava lamp.

To stimulate the exposure of repressed spiritual talents, find an old key around your house. During the next waxing moon, bathe the key in moonlight (waxing-to-full moon phase) for seven hours. The next time you meditate, place the key atop your third eye as a talisman to unlock those gifts. Otherwise, carry the key to inspire a consistent flow of energy.

If you want to use the key immediately, let it stay in the moonlight for seven minutes instead, but return it when you are done meditating, so it can finish charging.

Some evening during a waxing to full moon (full is best), when the weather permits, get yourself all dressed for a beach outing. Grab a towel and other accoutrements and take a moon bath for any amount of time that is a multiple of seven (thirty-five minutes, for example). As the beams reach you, focus on those that illuminate your chakras. Visualize little doors opening at each point. Now the light of intuition will permeate them. Continue until you are overflowing with energy.

UNDERSTANDING

General Uses: Comprehension, discernment, perception, compassion, and sympathy.

Timing: February, August, and November. Water signs. Moon in Capricorn. Monday and Friday.

Props/Focals: An ear or open hand. Binoculars, glasses, or other items that improve vision. Amethyst, keys, light bulbs, or candles in a dark room. Air element, vanilla, apple, rosemary, black tea, walnut, and sunlight. The numbers forty and five. The color orange.

Secondary Listings: Anger, Forgiveness, Identifying, Kindness, Relationships, Viewpoints, Virtue, Wisdom

Sample Spells:

Cut the picture of an ear out of a magazine. Next, find an orange cord, piece of yarn, or string, and knot it five times while it is in sunlight. Name each knot after the specific attribute you want either to release in yourself or encourage in someone else. Lay it on top of the image of the ear and place both outside to soak in the sun for forty minutes.

On the next Monday or Friday, begin untying each knot, one every five minutes. As you do, visualize the sunlight pouring out of the knot toward either yourself or that other individual. Add an appropriate incantation, repeating it with each knot you untie. Afterward, keep the cord wrapped around the picture in order to draw understanding into your life.

To share sympathy with someone you can't go to see, make a small stuffed image of the person, and fill it with dried apple peels and rosemary. Take this poppet to your personal sacred space while you meditate. Strongly visualize that individual while you hold the

poppet close to your heart and speak words of consolation. If you can't make a poppet, try using a pillow instead. Continue pouring out supportive energy as long as you like.

Put a magnifying glass on a symbol of the area of your life where you lack comprehension (this approach is also excellent for learning). Slowly lift the glass to your eye and observe the emblem as it becomes larger and clearer. Just before it becomes perfectly distinct, add a verbal component such as "*Confusion shall wane, discernment to gain. Though turmoil still blows, assurance grows. Puzzlement tamed, comprehension I claim.*" Keep either the emblem or the eyeglass as a charm for emphasizing comprehension.

Unions

General Use: Consolidation, affiliation, alliance, mergers, weddings or handfastings, initiation, and conception rites.

Timing: June, March, and August. Waxing to full moon. Moon in Gemini, Virgo, or Aquarius. Thursday, Friday, and Saturday.

Props/Focals: Rings, flower garlands, contracts, cups, triangles, and wax seals. Tied knots, celebratory decorations, or cake. Agate. Almond, anise, apple, basil, rosemary, rose, and cardamom. Easterly winds. Ash wood, birch, and pine. The numbers one (unity) and two (partnership).

Secondary Listings: Balance, Blessing, Friendship, Harmony, Kinship, Love, Negotiation, Relationships, Web Weaving

Sample Spells:

For a marriage or handfasting, make a long garland of roses, apple blossoms, and decorative leaves by binding them together with florist's wire. As you secure each, empower the decoration by saying something like "*Joined in love, in unity, bring happiness to _____ and*

_____." The garland is then wrapped around the couple's joined hands after the vows are recited. An alternative is to use scented silk flowers so the garland can be preserved as a memento of that special day.

All individuals involved in an affiliation should partake of a single glass filled with apple wine and almonds (one almond per person). Once everyone has sipped from the communal cup, together they voice a promise before witnesses and the gods and goddesses. Next, the glass should be placed in a cloth pouch or covering of some sort and put on the ground while the group forms a circle around it. After everyone has joined hands around the glass, together they shatter it with their feet (perhaps taking turns to avoid broken toes). By doing so, the group symbolically shows that the oath cannot be broken without everyone's agreement. The shards in the pouch can then be distributed—carefully—for people to use as part of Witch bottles near places of business or homes.

A lovely union keepsake is a homemade lace doily hat. The lace itself is in keeping with the idea of tying knots. At a craft store obtain one six-inch diameter doily and a hat form. Glue the doily to the form, then add decorations meaningful to the couple, along with two rings bound in blue for happiness. Anoint the finished hat with oil of rose, then enchant the piece with an incantation like *"Bound in blue, joy rings true. Circles unite, magic take flight. Sweetness and peace, may love never cease."*

Note that this ornament is serviceable for other magical ends too. Affix other emblems to the hat, like crystals to capture positive energy, or feathers to give flight to your dreams. Adjust your verbal component accordingly, then mount the decoration in an appropriate area, such as over your work desk or your bed.

To bring a friendship into closer harmony, bind together apple, birch, and pine twigs using blue and pink ribbons. From the end of the ribbons, hang herbs or other focals along with something personal. Make this token either small enough to be carried by your friend or large enough to be a home decoration. Empower it with an incantation such as *"You and me and we, bound together, but always free. Within this thread of pink and blue, I place my friendship, that it will always be true."* Explain the significance of the gift to the recipient.

VERSATILITY

General Uses: Multifaceted ability. All-purpose learning, awareness, or experience. Flexibility.

Timing: April and October. Wednesday and Saturday. Any times when the weather or wind is shifting. Change to or from daylight saving time. Moon in Pisces, Gemini, Aquarius, Libra, or Sagittarius.

Props/Focals: Modeling clay or dough, a rubber band, water, chameleons, and cats. Vanilla, coconut, willow, soup, and winds. The numbers five and twelve. Anything that shows a visible change of state; wax, for example, which melts, solidifies, and even evaporates.

Secondary Listings: Adaptation, Choices, Knowledge, Movement, New Endeavors, Virtue

Sample Spells:

Create an image of yourself out of modeling clay. To make a stronger connection, add a bit of saliva or a favorite perfume or cologne to the clay while working it into your likeness. Hold this image in your hands as you think about where you need more flexibility. Then reshape the clay into an emblem of that domain, working in five drops of vanilla and repeating a chosen incantation five times.

Keep this image in a safe place until your goal is achieved. After that, reuse it for similar ends in other areas of your life.

Gather a pitcher of water and twelve containers of different shapes and sizes. Name the water after yourself, then pour it sequentially into each of the twelve containers and say: "*Flexibility's a must; adjust and conform. As this water transforms, versatility is born.*" Drink the water afterward to internalize your magical energy.

Gather several small, flexible items such as a reed, a willow branch, or a rubber or elastic band to make an amulet. Take pieces of each and place them in a container with twelve ice cubes. Watch as the ice melts and, until its change of state is completed, chant, "*Learning to change, learning to bend, versatility this magic will send. As the ice melts away, the magic will stay, within me, versatility's freed.*" Keep the container somewhere in your home where its power can continue to help you in this goal.

VICTORY

General Uses: Achievement, mastery, success, or triumph.

Timing: March. Moon in Taurus or Virgo. Blue moon. Tuesday and Sunday. Daybreak.

Props/Focals: Finish lines or flags. The thumbs-up sign. Agate and hematite. Oats, blackberry, banana, tulip, ants or a rubber tree plant, and grass. The number four. The colors blue, red, and gold.

Secondary Listings: Anger, Courage, Energy, Fear, Health, Joy, Justice, New Endeavors, Overcoming, Liberation

Sample Spells:

Take into your hands an image of the thing you wish to conquer and crush it. This effectively breaks apart its energy on a symbolic level. Take the remnants somewhere private, place those pieces under your foot, and say: "*Your power and control over me is gone. I am the master of my destiny.*" Leave that area and do not look back. If you are concerned about the remnants being unsafe, return later to clean them up and dispose of them appropriately.

Gather the implements of the trade or craft in which you hope to achieve mastery. Sprinkle each with four pinches of oats, moving clockwise as you incant, "*Success I claim, my art to master, let achievement come faster!*" Repeat this spell each time you begin working on a project. Continue making efforts on all levels to reach your goal.

Make a figurine of yourself stuffed with grass and tulip petals. Using markers, trace on the poppet a symbol for deliverance, overcoming, or liberation. On the back of the image, glue feathers and a swatch of cloth from some of your old clothing. Take this to any outdoor area, like a cliffside or a beach, where you can easily throw the token far away. Hold it in both hands and focus on the thing that binds you. Let negative energy pour into the item, then toss it, saying: "*Fly and be free, seek out my victory.*" Leave this place and don't look back.

In the interest of our environment, use only ingredients that will biodegrade rapidly. For example, use a lightweight cotton cloth or a paper exterior, seeds or breadcrumbs as alternative fillings, and water-based nontoxic markers.

Repeated affirmations work nicely as mini-spells. In this case, your only component is repetition of chosen phrases for a prespecified period of time. Sample affirmations for victory in an uncomfortable social situation might include "*I am a good listener,*" "*I am confident,*" and "*I accept success.*" Keep your affirmations short and simple so you remember them. Repeat them any time you feel the need, whenever they come to mind, or at a preselected time. Let this build harmonic, positive energy in and around you until you reach your goal.

Viewpoints

General Uses: Beliefs, convictions, ideas, opinions, concepts, and perspectives.

Timing: February, August, November, and December. Moon in Scorpio, Libra, or Cancer. Monday.

Props/Focals: Anything that provides or improves long-distance vision like ladders, telescopes, etc. Birds, apples, carrots, lamps, and the "chicken and the egg." Easterly winds. The number five.

Secondary Listings: Balance, Communication, Discernment, Judgment, Negotiation, Prejudice, Wisdom

Sample Spells:

Take yourself to a high place like a tree branch or safe rooftop to meditate. Focus your eyes on the horizon. As you do, bring the image of the farthest spot you can see into closer scrutiny without losing sight of the surroundings. Quietly repeat an incantation like *"Grant perspective, my mind is free, bring clear concepts, help me see."* The more you practice this exercise, the more it broadens both your horizons and your vision.

Get some charcoal or a makeup stick and carefully draw eyeglass rims around your eyes. Then, on the area of your third eye, moving clockwise, inscribe the infinity sign five times as you chant, *"Judgment and discernment in the eye of the soul, help my vision be pure and whole."* Try meditating afterward, visualizing the image of the infinity sign glowing with silver light. Repeat your verbal component, breathe deeply and rhythmically, and extend your senses. See what impressions you pick up.

If you have an allergy to makeup or prefer not to have marks on your face, just trace the patterns with your index finger. Try to visualize the pattern so that the meditation afterward is more effective.

Go to the room where your TV is located and begin to meditate. In your mind's eye, visualize yourself sitting on a cloud looking comfortably downward. Once you have that perspective firmly in mind, direct your attention to the blank TV screen.

Let images of your situation form upon it. Observe from your cloud as if you are a spectator. Watch closely to discover the different facets this perspective offers. To heighten the experience, add a verbal component similar to those already presented under this topic.

To help improve perspective and to maintain balance and harmony, make this decorative bird and animal feeder. Begin with a wooden rectangle that has five holes along the bottom of one long edge. On the wood, paint the image of an item such as an eye that symbolizes perspective. Then tie five sturdy strings into the holes. At various junctures in the strings, knot dried apple and carrot pieces. Hang this token in a tree where it can be reached by the birds or squirrels so your magic can move!

VIRTUE

General Uses: Morality, purity, and goodness. Developing positive attributes or characteristics. Honor.

Timing: October, September, and July. Moon in Pisces, Aries, Sagittarius, or Capricorn. Monday, Thursday, and Saturday.

Props/Focals: A glove, a sword, and a coat of arms. Jade, agate, amethyst, or rock crystal. Pine, rose, banana, mustard, and thyme. The numbers nine and thirteen.

Secondary Listings: Adaptation, Dedication, Habits, Obtaining, Quests, Tenacity, Zeal

Sample Spells:

In medieval times, the gift of a glove was a sign of acceptance and honor. With this in mind, you can make one for yourself to encourage a specific trait in your life. This can be done in one of two ways. Cloth can be stitched together in glove form, or an old winter glove can be reused. In both instances, stuff the glove with herbs that reflect your goals. For example, to improve your sense of honor in relationships, combine roses (for love) with amethyst (to tame your wilder nature). Once completed, carry this token into situations that require a strong moral character.

Another remarkable medieval item that indicated honor, respected professions, and represented family ties was a coat of arms. This was an artistic rendering that told anyone looking at it who you were and what you could do.

To update this, we can use the idea to create pins, t-shirts, or other wearable items that are enchanted to empower specific personal characteristics. During a waxing moon take the blank form of your chosen medium and then sketch or paint an image of your goal onto it. Complete it over the next nine days, concentrating diligently as you work. Then place the finished piece beneath the full moon, adding an incantation that reflects your intentions. Wear this as often as possible, repeating your own verbal component each time it is donned, until the target is reached. Afterward, consider sharing it with a friend who needs help in the same area.

Two-edged items teach us balance and how to cut away old, outmoded ideas. For this exercise, slide one edge of a blade along your aura to cut away habits no longer desired. As you do so, name the habits out loud. For safety, keep the edge three inches above your skin or use a dull blade. Move counterclockwise. Visualize dark, muddy guck being sliced away.

Then, to apply new attributes, turn the blade completely over and move clockwise as if you were spreading butter on yourself. Envision a clean, sparkling light that saturates your pores as you move the blade. Name the quality you are applying out loud. Continue until you feel fully revitalized.

VISIONS (DREAMS)

General Uses: Prescience, foresight, revelation, discernment, prophecy, fantasy, imagination, and participatory dreams.

Timing: Night. November and December. Samhain or New Year. Moon in Capricorn or Libra. Monday and Wednesday.

Props/Focals: Angelica, mugwort, rose, onion, or marigold. Pizza and unusual combinations of food. Vanilla, beans, beer, carrots, and grapes. The color yellow. Eye pads. Topaz.

Secondary Listings: Discernment, Divination, Imagination, Inspiration, Omens, Nightmares, Unconscious Mind

Sample Spells:

To make a visionary pillow, gather two large scraps of cloth approximately eight inches by eight inches. Stitch these together and fill the center with peaceful herbs such as pine, lavender, chamomile, or any of the herbs listed above. As you sew the final seam, verbalize your magical goals in the form of a repetitive, lulling chant like *"Rest your head, don't stay awake; eyes grow tired, good dreams to make; let this pillow your worries keep while you quickly fall to sleep."* Keep this in your bed to grant peaceful slumber or give it to a friend who suffers from insomnia.

Make a cup of angelica tea and place it in moonlight. Use 1 teaspoon of herb to 1 cup of water. On top, float either a fresh rose petal or a bud. Drink the tea, retaining the rose to put on your pillow until

you retire for the night. As you set the bud down on your pillow, whisper, *"Like this flower, soon I will rest, no more be busy, no more to fret. Let sleep come quickly to my eyes when upon this pillow my head lies."* Leave the flower where it lies until you go to bed; then slip it under your pillow.

To dream of the person you love, place something of theirs under your pillow or near your heart. Arrange some fresh marigolds or mugwort near your bed, too. As you start to drift off, visualize your loved one, and extend a welcome. Make notes of your visions as soon as you wake up the next morning.

A great sleep aid for children is a patchwork dream blanket. For this, you will need to save bits of favored old clothing and stuffed animals as the child grows. When you have enough for a small lap blanket, hand stitch the strips together using white thread or thin yarn. In the middle, add the image of a heart (you can often get premade ones at fabric stores). Paint on the applique a rune of protection using nontoxic fabric paint. Once completed, bless it in any way with which you feel comfortable; then give it to the child. Explain that it came from all the things they love best and that the magical power of that love can keep them safe.

WEATHER

General Uses: Moderating or changing certain weather patterns.

Timing: November and December. Waxing moon to bring a specific type of weather, waning moon to stop it. Water signs and Wednesday to encourage precipitation, Fire signs and Sunday for dryness. Earth Day.

Props/Focals: Rice, water, drums, and fires. Corn, leaves, bird calls, or smoke blown in a specific direction. Jasper, knots, elemental colors, or weather symbols. Creatures of very specific climates. Objects associated through folklore with specific weather patterns like a red sun portending rain.

Secondary Listings: Banishing, Ecology, Judgment, Nature, Safe Travel

Sample Spells:

Please take care with weather spells and use them wisely. This magic interferes with natural patterns and should only be resorted to when real need exists.

An old bit of sympathetic magic still used in California and many parts of the U.S. is washing your windows or washing your car any day you wish to bring rain. Let this water spill and drip on the ground for a real downpour.

Many of our childhood rhymes have a great deal of magical potency. Consider using *"Rain, rain, go away"* the next time you need a clear sky. Perform the rhyme while moving counterclockwise and holding a towel in the air to dry the moisture.

Sprinkle rice clockwise while another person or a musical tape plays slowly increasing drumbeats. This sympathetic magic can work to bring rain or snow; for rain, I suggest dyeing the rice blue. This type of rain magic was common in ancient Asia.

Alternative tools here include shaking a rattle or rain stick (an African tradition), turning on a sprinkler, or even using a spritzer bottle. In European folklore, it is said that hitting wet rags against stone or shaking a wet broom on the ground can similarly encourage precipitation.

In Norse tradition, if you offer the first toast at a wedding or other special gathering to Thor, you are ensured good weather. To accentuate this further, move clockwise and pour the wine over small decorative bundles of garlic that have been carefully hung around the perimeter of the area.

Seafaring superstitions tell us that the herb broom, tossed into the air, encourages the winds. If you do this while whistling, it increases the power of the wind from a breeze to gusts. To stop the wind, simply bury the herb when your work is done.

Bury some sage near water (a hose faucet is one good place) at sunrise to bring rain by sunset. Once enough rain has fallen, dig another hole and fill it with water. Stir the water in even strokes moving counterclockwise, strongly visualizing the skies clearing. Do not cease until magic has begun to take effect in the sky.

Web Weaving (Networks)

General Uses: Creating a mesh of individuals whose lines of communication are strong and helpful to your spiritual well-being.

Timing: November, August, June, and April. Moon in Aries or Gemini. Friday and Saturday.

Props/Focals: Spider webs and other items that connect things such as tape and string. Paperclip chains, baskets, phones. Trees and basil. Easterly or northerly winds.

Secondary Listings: Choices, Communication, Friendship, Goals, Identifying, Openings, Relationships, Wisdom, Versatility

Sample Spells:

Gather twelve long pieces of pink ribbon or heavy string. Connect one end of each to yourself and hold on to the others. With your back to a northerly wind, release the strings from your hands saying: "*These ribbons are my desire to find others of a like mind.*" Then start drawing them back in, saying: "*Come to me.*" Keep repeating the final phrase until the ribbons are securely back in hand. When you are finished, keep these for other rites that deal with connections or as a portable amulet to help manifest your magic.

To divine how long it will be before you find the networking contacts you are hoping for, find an area of fairly still water. Pick up a small flat stone to focus your desire on. Skip the stone on the water, counting the number of times it jumps. This answer is indicative of the number of days, weeks, months, or years it might sometimes take to establish a network.

The following is an expanded version of this spell. Before skipping the stone, engrave or paint your name on it. Next, drop it carefully in shallow water out of which you can retrieve it easily. Watch as the waves roll outward from the central point (symbolic of Self) and say: "*With the waves of time, my wishes are free; bring companions near to me!*" Retrieve the stone and proceed with the aforementioned divinatory process.

To strengthen the emotional bonds between you and someone who is far away, arrange to meditate together at the same time (take into account your time zones). As you center yourself, visualize a red-pink light connecting the two of you. Once this connection is secured, repeat simple, one-word phrases that echo across this line of energy. Good choices include "*unity,*" "*accord,*" and "*love.*" When you are done with your meditation, write a letter or make something special for your companion and send it as a token of those feelings.

Wisdom

General Uses: Sagacity, judgment, prudence, erudition, insight, and Shrewdness.

Timing: July and September to December Moon in Leo, Sagittarius, or Capricorn. Wednesday, Thursday, and Saturday.

Props/Focals: Sage, elder, pansy, hazelwood, and peach. The number five. Westerly winds and the owl. Agate and amethyst. The color purple.

Secondary Listings: Balance, Discernment, Judgment, Leadership, Virtue, Negotiation, Quests, Teachers/Teaching, Understanding.

Sample Spells:

Take one strand of silvery white thread or one of your own gray hairs and bind it to a sprig of sage. Wrap the sage with the strand five times. Then hold it in your strong hand and visualize a purple light filling it as you say: "*Wisdom and prudence be my guide. Insight and judgment stand by my side.*" Keep this as an amulet in your side pocket to bring the spirit of wisdom into your life.

Gather a bowl of fresh peaches. Let the fruit soak in sunlight for five minutes for alertness, refrigerate them, and then bathe them for five minutes in moonlight for intuition. Eat them to manifest the energy. Set aside the pits for drying.

String together the dried pits, alternating them with pieces of a hazel branch (See List C). This makes an effective wind chime that will ring wisdom into your home.

For wisdom leading to improved profits in business, bind into a green cloth: basil, yellow dock, cinnamon, elder bark, and dried peas. Keep these where decisions are made in your workplace.

Wishes

General Uses: Fancy, whims, dreams, ambitions, objectives, and longings.

Timing: Waxing to full moon, blue moon. Nighttime in general. Wednesday. Moon in Virgo or Pisces. The month of April.

Props/Focals: Wells, coins, candles, bottles, rainbows, and four-leaf clovers. The number seven. Dandelion, hazelwood, pomegranate, sage, sandalwood, violet, walnut, ginseng, lavender, driftwood, dogwood, sunflower, or feathers. The first star that appears at night.

Secondary Listings: Blessing, Goals, Joy, Luck, Youthful Outlook

Sample Spells:

Go outside at sunrise. Pick a morning glory or other flower strongly associated with the movement of the sun. Make a simple wish upon it as the sun peeks over the horizon. In Brittany, it is said that, if the wish is uncomplicated, it should come true by sunset.

Pick a dogwood flower at midnight on Midsummer Eve. As you do, whisper your wish to the spirit of that plant. European superstition claims that your wish will be fulfilled by the following year. If dogwood is not blossoming in your region in June, choose another flower from "Props/Focals" above.

Get a small piece of driftwood. On it, either write your wish or carve it into the wood. Turn your back to the waves, throwing the stick over your left shoulder for luck. Let the sea carry your desire to its goal.

To make an amulet that will bring wishes into reality, carefully crack open a walnut and save the two halves of the shell. Inside them, place a bit of sage, ginseng, seven shelled sunflower seeds, and the tuft of a dandelion. Secure the two halves with sturdy glue and carry the token with you as often as possible.

YOUTHFUL OUTLOOK

General Uses: Spirited, optimistic, energetic, and fresh perspectives. Reclaiming innocence and trust.

Timing: Spring and early summer. Crescent moons. Moon in Aquarius. Wednesday and weekends.

Props/Focals: Falling stars, chalk, crayons, toys and games, and balloons. Gelatin desserts, cookies, candies, and other traditional "children's" foods. The colors white or pale yellow. Hawthorn, daisy, sprouts, buttercup, mint, or rosemary. Open windows, swing sets, and slides.

Secondary Listings: Adaptation, Humor, Intuition, Joy, Luck, Visions, Viewpoints, Zeal

Sample Spells:

Create a hopscotch board for yourself on some pavement. Write the word "joy" on the winner's line at the end of the board. Then, as you skip toward happiness, add a liberating rhyme such as *"Jump on one foot, then both to the ground, jump again and the sun comes around. First to the left, then to the right, then both together, let my magic take flight!"* Make sure your footing matches the words and have fun!

Buy or pick the brightest-colored bundle of daisies you can find. Note that daisies take very well to being tinted by food coloring, so you can dye them to match your magical goals.

Arrange the flowers rather wildly in a container, naming each after a youthful aspect you wish to reclaim. Before getting involved in activities that encourage those traits, pluck the petals off the appropriate daisy, and give them to the winds with your desire. Let the magic and your heart fly free!

While this spell is also appropriate for wish magic, it is so strongly associated with children that it functions just as well in this scenario. At dusk, go outside and wait to see a falling star or the first star that appears. Use the "Starlight, Star Bright" rhyme as your incantation, then visualize your youthful aspirations as your wish.

ZEAL

General Uses: Enthusiasm, fervor, or vigor. Zest for any activity or project.

Timing: Spring. October. Waxing to full moon. Moon in Pisces or Leo. Thursday. In bright sunlight to bring fiery energy.

Props/Focals: An exclamation mark. Cheering and pom-poms. Young, playful animals. The color red. The number six. Anise, pine, juice, element of Fire, ginger, sausage, peony, mint, and red pepper.

Secondary Listings: Energy, Obtaining, Tenacity, Youthful Outlook.

Sample Spells:

Cut an exclamation point out of fiery red paper. Affix it to a symbol of the project where you need more enthusiasm. Dab the paper with pine or mint oil and bless it, saying: *"Exclamation point, I now anoint, when here my gaze rests, magic kindles new zest!"* Leave this in a highly visible area.

Make a handful of confetti and sit on the floor. Cup the confetti in both hands and as you do, visualize a brightly colored light filling your whole being from your toes upward. You may feel warm or tingly. When this happens, slowly start to stand up extending your hands toward the ceiling to release the light. As you sense this experience reaching a pinnacle, release the confetti to pour vigorous energy onto yourself. Keep the remnants as a portable charm or recycle the paper to symbolically keep your zeal refreshed.

At one time or another we have all heard the expression, "*Put a fire under it!*" Why not put this to the best possible use in a magical construct? Make an incense from anise, ginger, pine, mint, a little pepper, and a piece of paper with your goal written on it. Place this to burn in a brazier or fireplace, allowing the smoke to surround you. Inhale a bit of the energy from the herbs along with your intentions in the form of smoke. As you exhale, repeat this phrase six times: "*With the power of smoke, zeal is invoked!*" Let the fire burn itself out naturally—as long as it is safe—and go immediately to your tasks.

COMPONENTS, SYMBOLS, AND COMMON MAGICAL ASSOCIATIONS

THE FOLLOWING IS AN ALPHABETIZED INVENTORY of components to use for folk magic. Their applications to your craft are as varied and unique as your imagination can invent. Use them as emblems, as parts of visualizations, in incenses or oils, as parts of medicine pouches, as accents to cooking magic, for props or tools, or in any other manner that will accent your magical goal.

In the interest of space and convenience, this list reflects items and symbols readily found in or near your own home. Many more associations and components can be added from outside that realm by referring to dream books, encyclopedias of folklore and superstition, and astrology books. Also keep in mind unique, personal meanings for items. These connotations are usually the best to use when considering potential magical applications.

In reviewing this list, keep in mind that some items gain their attributes through puns or plays on words. Butter, for example, has associations with calming anger. This comes from the old phrase "buttering someone up." These kinds of correlations are immensely useful in folk magic because of their familiarity. Try to think up your own.

A good illustration of this came to me in my own home. l was very distressed and had a lot of chores to do, including washing the dishes. I needed a component to lift burdens when I spied a bottle of Joy dish detergent on my counter. The connection made me laugh. I grabbed the bottle and added that Joy to the dishwater. I visualized smiling bubbles rising to the surface as I worked. Sure enough, I felt better afterward.

The magic here was not in the ingredient, but in the transformation in my personal attitude. When you do something constructive to change circumstances or emotions, it provides a stronger feeling of control in your life.

ITEM ASSOCIATIONS

Agate: Divine blessings or favor

Alcohol, rubbing: Cleansing, pain relief

Alfalfa Sprout: Never wanting, prudence, sustenance

Almond: Composure, happiness, moderation, well-being

Allspice: Fortune, health

Aloe: Healing, safety, well-being

Amethyst: Constructive decision-making, control of the disorderly self

Animals:

Bird: Enlightenment, perspective, swiftness, vision

Cat: Goddess energy, mystical power

Dog: Companionship, health, service

Fish: Miracles, providence, sea magic

Frog: Healing and cleansing, messages

Mouse: Frugality, rebirth

Rabbit: Fertility, moon magic, speed

Anise: Love, protection from nightmares, zeal

Apple: Earth magic, fitness, harmony, romance

Apricot: Courtship

Apron: Domestic affairs, neatness, turning luck

Archway: Passage into safe havens, victory

Artichoke: Protection

Aroma: Please note that aromas have slightly different magical/therapeutic applications than the use of whole herbs or a plant does. Inhale lightly to internalize the energy or release the scent into a room to fill your working space.

Apple: Perceptive decisions, shrewdness
Basil: Accord, peace
Cloves: Love, safety
Nutmeg: Supernatural awareness
Pine: Cleansing, revitalization
Rose: Dedication, love, serenity
Rosemary: Memory, relationships, well-being
Vanilla: Increasing power, perception, romance

Art: Varies with spell purpose
Ashes: Atonement, cleansing, new beginnings
Asparagus: Sexuality, especially male aspects
Aster: Celestial vision (this plant's name means "star"), variety
Avocado: Physical Beauty
Bacon: Magic for employment, prosperity
Baking Soda/Powder: Increasing energy or hopeful expectations
Balloon: Air element, inflated notions, lifting burdens
Bamboo Shoots: Health, long life
Banana: Male sexuality, valiant acts
Bandage: Healing, maternal nature
Bank: Finances, prosperity, saving
Barbecue: Fire element, kinship, pleasant gatherings
Barley: Celebration, love, regulating discomfort, sleep
Basil: Associations, especially romantic ones; prosperity
Basin: Alternative emblem for a cup, cleansing
Basket: Networking, weaving of fate
Bathmat: Safety and warmth
Bay: Spiritual powers, vigor, and fitness
Bean: Judgment calls, oracles, prosperity
Bed: Dreaming, peacefulness, rest
Beef: Abundance, foundations
Beer: Dreams, purifying, offerings, visions
Beet: Desire, devotion, grace
Blackberry: Fortune, success
Blanket: Comfort, rest, warmth
Blender: Socialization, stimulating energy
Blueberry: Composure, peace, serenity
Bone: Strength, structure
Book: Enjoyment, knowledge, learning

Boot: Protection from the elements, weather magic

Bottle: Reserving, wishes

Bowl: Alternative emblem for a cup, especially for pet magic

Box: Hidden things, storage, surprises

Bread: Friends and family, sustenance

Breadcrumbs: Animal magic, bird kinship, sufficiency

Bridge: Building communication, crossing gaps

Broccoli: Authority, bodily refinement, fortitude

Broom: Domesticity, Goddess energy, organization

Brussels Sprouts: Perseverance, resolution, stability

Butter: Determination, healing anger

Cabbage: Fortune, moon magic, security

Cake: Festivals, happy gatherings, welcome

Calculator: Careful planning, determination

Calendar: Appointments, cycles, time awareness

Camera: Adventure, special moments, travel

Candle: Color symbolism, divination, the Fire element, focus, illumination

Candy: Indulgence, sweetness, tender gifts

Canned Goods: Economy, preservation, safeguarding

Can Opener: Hidden promise, opportunity

Capers: Passion, stamina

Carnelian: Hope, improved communication, safety, strength of speech, truth

Car: Mobility, movement

Caraway: Confidence, safeguards from theft and dissenting energy

Cardamom: Increases the strength of unions/partnerships

Carrot: Foresight, masculine energies

Catnip: Cat magic, contentment, happiness, leisure

Catsup: Blood substitute, smooths relationships (also tomato sauce)

Cauliflower: Lunar and Water-related magics

Celery: Desire, grounding, harmony

Cereal: Check the type or name of the grain for clues to use; generally, providence

Chain: Bondage, control

Chair: Recess, turning bad fortune, welcome

Cheese: Happiness, manifestation, well-being

Cherry: Female sexuality, love

Chessboard: Forethought, intellect, mastery

Chicken: Health, new beginnings, sunrise magic

Chili Pepper: Protection, purification

Chive: Safety, security, turning negativity

Chocolate: Lifting emotions, love

Cinnamon: Abundance, energy, love, prosperity

Clock: Alertness, punctuality, time management

Clove: Piercing, misconceptions, protection, young romance

Coconut: Flexibility, spirituality, variety

Coffee: Increased attentiveness, mental astuteness

Coffee, Gourmet: Hospitality, luxury, prosperity

Colander: Sorting out or saving only the best things

Colors: Use paper, cloth, candles, crystals, or even personal clothing of a specific hue to encourage the appropriate vibrations in your magic

 Black: Banishing, rest, the void

 Blue: Contemplation, healing, joy, peace, water

 Brown: Earth, foundations, nature, new endeavors

 Green: Faith, growth, health, prosperity

 Orange: Compassion, energy, harvest, warmth

 Pink: Kinship, leisure, positive attitude, relaxation

 Purple: Devotion, sensitivity, spirituality

 Red: Courage, fire, strength, vitality

 White: Innocence, protection, purification

 Yellow: Air, creativity, divination, mind, movement

Computer: Accuracy, knowledge, retention of information

Cookbook: Perfection, positive personal qualities, spell book

Cookie: Maternal instincts, nurturing love

Copper: Mirror divination, Venus energy

Coral: Fertility, health, protection

Cord: Promises, restraint, security, ties

Coriander: Intelligence, love, well-being

Corn: Cycles, Earth magic, timelessness

Corn Syrup: Solidifying plans or ideas

Costume/Mask: Imitative and sympathetic magic

Coupons: Budgets, planning, thrift

Cranberry: Energy for security and protection

Crisper: Enlivening or revitalizing energy

Crockpot: Slow, consistent increase in energy; things taking shape in reality

Cross: Four elements in balance

Cucumber: Beauty, fertility (male), healing, rest

Cupboard: Frugality, reservoir of energy, savings

Cup: The Goddess, offerings, Water element

Curtains: Commencement, hidden matters, privacy

Date: Eternity, resurrection, spirit

Dew/Rain: Cleansing, fertility, Water element

Dill: Protecting children

Dish Towel: Cleaning, resolution

Dishwasher: Amenities, freedom, the Water element

Door: Openings, safety, welcome

Doorbell: Guests, messages, news, welcome

Doughnut: The circle, one's attention being in the wrong place

Drain: Failure, hardship, misgivings, negativity

Drawer: Necessary tangibles, secret things

Dryer: Air element, refreshment, warmth

Egg: Ancient questions, fertility, mysticism

Elements:

Air: Change, creativity, the East, movement, sprites, whimsy, windy places

Earth: Dwarves, gnomes, grounding, growth, the North

Fire: Conscious mind, drastic change, energy, the God aspect, illumination, noon time, purification, salamanders, the South, summer

Water: Evening, Goddess energy, healing, the moon, nurturing, peace, unconscious mind, undines, the West

Envelope: Communication, news, secret missives

Fan: Air element, change, movement

Feather: Dreams taking wing, hopes and wishes (see the "Bird" entry under "Animals")

Fence: Protection and sanctuary

Fig: Physical strength, power

Finger: Alternative wand or athame, getting to the point, the direction of energy

Fish: Fertility, improving the mind, miracles, transformation

Flour: Consistency, revealing hidden matters

Flowers:
- *Bluebell:* Permanence
- *Buttercup:* Love, pleasure, youthful energy
- *Clover:* Luck, triune nature of the God and Goddess and humankind
- *Daisy:* Commencement, dawn, simplicity
- *Dandelion:* Divination, fertility, oracles, wishes
- *Lilac:* Energy, lucidity, symmetry
- *Pansy:* Contemplation, thoughts
- *Peony:* Inspiration, life, light
- *Rose:* Goddess energy, love, health, relationships
- *Sunflower:* Creativity, illumination, sun magic
- *Tulip:* Awareness, foundations, victory
- *Violet:* Accord, gentleness, quiet

Food Processor: Diverse energy blending, transformation
Food Wraps: Conservation, control, prudence, secrets
Fork: Penetrating, perception, piercing
Funnel: Flow, following a course, precision
Garlic: Banishing, health, hex breakings, protection
Gelatin: Adventure, childlike pleasure, fun, solidifying uncertain circumstances
Ginger: Cleansing, health, vibrant energy, zeal
Gold: Leadership, logical mind, strength, sun energy
Grape: Dreams, fecundity, visions
Grapefruit: Cleansing, health
Gravy: Congruity, smooth transitions, uniformity
Gum: Holding fast, sticky situations
Hair: Energy, power, strength
Ham: Dramatic energy, theatrical flair
Hazelnut: Fertility, luck, wisdom, wishes
Hematite: Legal matters, victory
Honey: Happiness, health, sweet things in life
Horseradish: Fiery energy, protection
Hot Cocoa: Kinship, peacefulness, satisfaction, warmth
Hot Sauce: Energy, Fire magic, protection
Insects:
- *Ant:* Community, industry, remarkable strength
- *Bee:* Divine messages, love
- *Butterfly:* Reincarnation, the soul, transformation

Dragonfly: Good fortune, magic, vision
Grasshopper: Nobility, prosperity
Spider: Destiny, fate
Worm: Earth magic, getting to the bottom, grounding of matters that seem hidden
"Instant" Dinners: Promptness, quick action, rapid movement
Jade: Love, luck, morality, well-being
Jasper: Protection, weather magic, especially rain
Jelly: (see "Fruit," by type)
Juice: Energy, rejuvenation, vitality
Keys: Opportunity, understanding
Knife: Alternative emblem for an athame, cutting away, separation (two-edged knives for balance), sharpness of mind
Knots: By opening, to release energy toward its goal; by tying, to bind energy
Lamp: Awareness, illumination
Lemon: Commitment, faithfulness, long life, refinement
Lettuce: Accord, peace, prosperity
Mace: Conscious mind, increasing psychic gifts
Magnet: Attraction, affixing energy
Malachite: Protection, especially for children; warning of problems to come
Margarine: Health, weight loss
Measuring Cup: Partitioning, prudence, weighing options
Meat Tenderizer: Empathy, increasing receptiveness, sensitivity
Microwave: Acceleration, legal expedition
Milk: Goddess energy, maternal instinct, nurturing
Mineral Water: Awareness of health and fitness
Mint: Energy, refreshment, safe travel
Mirror: External images, personal reflection
Molasses: Adherence to an idea or way of life, slowing movement
Months:
January: Safety and protection
February: Forgiveness, healing, motivations
March: Success
April: Good luck, openings, opportunity
May: Development, growth, and maturity
June: Commitment, love

July: Authority, self-regulation

August: Accord, peace, and symmetry

September: Spiritual development and growth

October: Personal modifications

November: Empathy

December: Discernment, understanding of universal truths

Moon: Creativity, Goddess energy, intuitive nature, nurturing, Water element

Blue Moon: The second full moon of a month (time for miracles)

Full Moon: Completion, fulfillment, maturity

Dark Moon: Banishing, quiet, rest

Waxing Moon: Fertility, growth, positive energy

Waning Moon: Banishing negative energy, reduction, reversals, slowing

Moon in Aries: Breaking down barriers; cleansing and personal development of talents or crafts

Moon in Taurus: Productivity and abundance, stubborn tenacity, well-earned respite

Moon in Gemini: Balancing diverse energies, banishing negative personality traits, change

Moon in Cancer: Creativity, fruitfulness, moon magic

Moon in Leo: Development of new skills or qualities, especially for strength

Moon in Virgo: Fertility, financial improvements, fruitfulness, victory

Moon in Libra: Balance, development of discernment, revealing secrets

Moon in Scorpio: Fiery energy, passion, sexuality, uprooting negativity, scrutiny, and study

Moon in Sagittarius: Foundations, frugality, and mastery of the self, reaching goals with accuracy

Moon in Capricorn: Focus on the hidden self, gathering fruits, inner development, support

Moon in Aquarius: Enjoyment, gathering the fruit of one's labors, inspiration, sharing, simple pleasures, trying something new and adventurous

Moon in Pisces: Improved movement, intuition, miracles, profuseness, Water energy

Moonstone: Good fortune, oracular activities, safe travel, spiritual perception

Mop: Cleaning up messy situations
Mushroom: Awareness, luck, intuition, spiritual vision
Mustard: Faith, mental alertness
Newspaper: Opinions, world affairs
Notebook: Memory, organization
Numbers:

1: Cooperation, self, the sun, wholeness
2: Agreement, symmetry, sanctification
3: Balance, body-mind-spirit, determination
4: Elements, goals, time, victory/success
5: Awareness, psychic endeavors, versatility
6: Dedication, finishing projects, safety
7: The moon, variety, vision
8: Authority, personal transformation, power
9: Service to others, universal law
10: Follow-through, logic, rationality
12: A full year, durability, fruitfulness
13: Convictions, fidelity, forbearance
21: Excellence, honor, remembrance
40: Drastic cleansing, hermitage, rejuvenation, sanctuary

Nutmeg: Commitment, fidelity, love
Oat: Prosperity, sustenance
Olive: Peace, spiritual pursuits
Onion: Protection from negative energy
Onyx: Cooling passion
Orange: Fidelity, health, love
Oven: Fervor, fertility
Paper clip: Fire element, passion, warming a cold shoulder
Parsley: Consolidation, joining, order, unity
Peach: Luck, prosperity, protection from accidents
Peanut: Joy, long life, wisdom
Peanut butter: Earth magic, male energy
Pear: Finishing projects, follow-through, grounding
Pea: Longevity, luck
Pen: Goddess magic, love
Pencil: Authorization, communication, endorsement, permanence
Pepper, Black: Ability to correct errors, experiments, tests
Pepper, Green: Banishing, cleansing, purification, protection

Pepper, Red: Growth, prosperity, energy, strength, vitality, empowered creativity

Pepper, Yellow: Good memories, family gatherings, joyful times

Photo Album: Healing, prosperity, protection

Pineapple: Rest, revitalization, stimulation

Pitcher: Cycles, modern life, quick nourishment, social activities

Pizza: Development, Earth element, grounding

Plants:

    Foxglove: Fairy kinship

    Grass: Conquering problems or foes, success, victory

    Ivy: Captivation, druidic energy, enchantment

    Juniper: Sacred to elves and fairies

    Thistle: Fertility, marriage, protection

    Vine: Adherence, connections, life

Plastic Food Keepers: Adequate supplies, preserving, protection

Plate: Service, utility

Plum: Aphrodisiac, attraction

Pointer: Direction, guidelines, instruction

Pomegranate: Fruitfulness, hospitality, wishes

Popcorn: Easing financial constraints, lifting burdens, recreation

Pork: Fertility, profuseness

Potato: Earth magic, folk medicine, grounding, health

Potholder: Protection specifically from a situation that has grown too heated

Pumpkin: Abundance, full moon magic

Punch Bowl: Alternative to cauldron, celebration, parties

Quartz: Holding or increasing energy (like a battery)

Radio: Information, leisure

Radish: Overcoming difficulties, protection

Raspberry: Love, stamina, vigor

Razor: Cutting away, keen judgment, sharp wits

Refrigerator: Cooling temper, preservation, protection

Relish: Enhanced passion (sweet), protection (dill)

Rice: Abundant blessings, fertility, weather magic

Ring: Commitment, longevity, relationships

Robe: Comfort, rest, warmth

Rock Crystal: Purity of faith

Rolling Pin: Chastisement, regulation, restraint

Rose: Faithfulness, friendship, love
Rosemary: Remembrance, youthful energy
Rubber Band: Holding together, return of energy
Rug: Cleanliness, exploitation
Runes:

ᛗ *Mannaz:* A beginning, direction, growth, modesty, self, willingness to change

ᚷ *Gebo:* Gifts freely given, partnership

ᚨ *Ansuz:* Communication, listening to wise counsel, messages, signals and signs

ᛟ *Othila:* Hermitage, leaving behind outmoded views, separation

ᚢ *Uruz:* Gestation, maturity, self-change, strength

ᛈ *Perth:* Initiation, surprises, the unknowable

ᚾ *Nauthiz:* Limitations, moderation, personal shadows

ᛜ *Inguz:* Deliverance (especially from uncertainty), fertility, intuition, the moon

ᛇ *Eihwaz:* Foresight, knowing when to act, overcoming barriers, tenacity

ᛉ *Algiz:* Emotional stability, positive personal conduct, protection

ᚠ *Fehu:* Conservation and protection of that which has been achieved, satisfied goals

ᚹ *Wunjo:* Blessings, fruitfulness, joy, well-being

ᛃ *Jera:* A full season, following the natural flow of cycles, harvest

ᚲ *Kano:* Clarity, the Fire element, opportunity

ᛏ *Teiwaz:* Cutting away the old, the rewards of patience, warrior energy

ᛒ *Berkana:* Development, increased awareness, progress

ᛖ *Ehwaz:* Development of virtue, movement, transition

ᛚ *Laguz:* Emotional needs, fluidity, Water element

ᚺ *Hagalaz:* Inventive psychic energy, liberation, new sense of reality

ᚱ *Raido:* Communication, balance among multiple factors into unity, reunions, travel

ᚦ *Thurisaz:* The moment of contemplation before moving into new responsibilities, passion

ᛞ *Dagaz:* Accomplishment, extreme transitions, prosperity, seizing the moment

| *Isa:* A lone road toward releasing the past, gestation, impasse

〉 *Sowelu:* Completeness, power of life force, the sun

Odin: Creative power, destiny, fate, potential (blank rune)

Saffron: Bounty, leadership, prosperity

Sage: Longevity, wisdom, wishes

Salt: Cleansing, grounding, purification

Sausage: God magic, variety, zest

Scale: Overindulgence, monitoring health, weighing different options

Scissors: Craft work, separation

Sesame: Opportunity, sexuality, waning moon magic

Shoe: Fertility, luck, movement, productivity

Shortening/Oil: Emotional detachment, objectivity, smoothing a difficult path

Sifter: Filtering out clutter, organization

Silver: Intuitive senses, the moon, unconscious mind

Sleeping Bag: Adventure, exploration of nature, outings

Snow: Cooling heated arguments, rest, thoughtfulness

Soap: Cleansing, purification, watching words

Sofa: Brief repose, casual conversation, relaxation

Soup: Steady change and improved communication

Soybean: Good luck, nourishment

Spatula: Altering course of action, conservation

Spinach: Growth, observance, strength

Sprouts (all types): Energetic awareness, spirituality

Squash: Sacred honors and duties

Stapler: Focus, security, stability

Starfruit: The pentagram or pentacle, protection

Stationery: Communication, personal flair

Strawberry: Intensity, romance, zest

Steamer: Consistent disposition, revealing the hidden

Stool: Overcoming, reaching goals

Sun: Cleansing, drastic change, fire, God energy, leadership, strength

Sweet Potato: Gentle love, well-founded

Symbols:

▲ *Triangle:* Body-mind-spirit in balance, threefold nature

∞ *Infinity:* Immutable human spirit, reincarnation, timelessness

✝ *Cross:* The four elements/directions

★ *Star:* Celestial influences, five-pointed stars are similar to the magical pentacle, universal energy, wishes

♀ *Ankh:* Health, life, sexual compatibility

X: Adventure, discovery, hitting the goal

→ *Arrow:* Aspiration, direction, keeping on track

$$: Financial security, prosperity

!!: Announcements, excitement, improved energy

=: Balance, equity, justice

O: Cycles, protection, the sun

^^: Inclusion or addition of ideas/customs

<: Increasing power, waxing moon

>: Decreasing power, waning moon

◉: Insight, the true self, vision

Syrup: Amiable meetings, tree magic

Tea: Divination, insight, meditation, restfulness

Telephone: Communication, messages, networking

Thermometer: Monitoring, scrutiny, supervision

Thread: Destiny, fate, ties

Thyme: Bravery, health, rest, romance

Tie: Propriety, refinement, societal constraints

Tomato: Attracting love

Tools: Consider each according to its function: a screwdriver might be used to tighten up loose ends, while a hammer might help bring a point to bear; a saw might provide a cutting edge, while a nail pierces and connects.

Toothbrush: Attention to personal needs

Topaz: Protection from nightmares and negative magic (most potent bound to left arm)

Toy: The child within, the spirit of play

Trees: Flowers, fruits, leaves, pictures, use wood

    Ash: Health, motherhood, world unity

    Birch: Beginnings, creation

    Elder: Ancient wisdom, magical energy

    Elm: Female/Goddess energy

    Fir: Immortality, rebirth

    Hawthorn: Love, spring, youthful energy

    Oak: Haven, power, sacred magical energy

Pine: Longevity, nature spirits
Willow: Divination, flexibility, Water element
Tuna: Frugality, sea magic
Turkey: Family gatherings, holiday feasts
Turquoise: Healing, luck, protection from falling, timeliness
TV: Distraction, power of media, timely announcements
Vanilla: Conscious love, mental awareness
Vase: Alternative to cup, feminine aspect of divinity
Vinegar: Piercing truth, purification, refreshment
Vitamins: Energy, health, personal maintenance
Waffles: Gathering or preserving amiable feelings, indulgence
Walnut: Mental faculties
Washer: Cleansing, Water element
Water: Creativity, healing, insight, moon magic
Watermelon: Peace for the dead, protection from spirits
Wedding Ring: Commitment, relationships, unending love
Weekdays:
    Monday: Creativity, fertility and Goddess-related efforts, insight, maternal nature
    Tuesday: Athletics, combat, law, strategy, strength
    Wednesday: Imagination, mystical energy, poetry, resourcefulness
    Thursday: Commitment, devotion, stamina, strength
    Friday: Relationships and fertility
    Saturday: Harvests and planting positive attributes
    Sunday: Leadership, logic, solar magic, study
Whisk: Abundance, enthusiasm, improving energy
Winds:
    East: Changing ideas, new beginnings, refreshment
    South: Cleansing, determination, Fire energy
    West: Healing, instincts, productivity
    North: Finances, growth, providence, rest
Window: Air element, cleansing, fresh ideas
Wine: Celebration, honoring positive actions, joy
Worcestershire Sauce: Action, energy, livening things up
Yeast: Active energy
Yogurt: Goddess magic, health, spirituality attributes

Appendix B

GODS, GODDESSES, SPIRITS, AND HEROES FOR SPELLCRAFT

CALLING ON SPIRIT ENTITIES can help magic but must be done with care. Gods, goddesses, and other spirits are not simply handy energy sources sitting around to manifest our will. They are powerful beings who are due a healthy portion of respect. If you're planning on invoking the blessing or requesting aid from a particular higher power, learn to pronounce the name of the deity or spirit correctly, prepare the proper offerings and altar regalia, and familiarize yourself with the cultural context in which they reside.

This takes a little time, it but is very important in helping you properly honor that power in your sacred space. It is also ethically important not just to randomly call upon a power when you don't really know anything about them. The learning process helps you connect with that specific energy, venerate it in a suitable manner, and thereby improve dialogue with it.

To choose a god, goddess, spirit, or heroic figure for folk magic, you might consider one who has magic as part of their domain of influence. Or you could petition your own personal god or goddess. Another alternative is to call upon an entity whose jurisdiction is associated with your goal. Any one of these three approaches is perfectly fitting. Choose whichever one feels right for your magical path and techniques. Following is a list of names arranged by topic for you to consider. Note that next to each name is an indication of that being's gender, culture, and, sometimes, specific sub-dominions for which they are known. To illustrate, the goddess Ida-Ten, who may be helpful in general spells for obtaining truth, appears under that heading, but I have also noted her special power for the realm of legal matters. An asterisk* accompanying an entry indicates a plural deity or spirit.

Additionally, this is an incomplete listing. For more information on gods and goddesses of the world, refer to *The Witch's God* and *The Witch's Goddess*, by Janet and Stewart Farrar, or *Ancient Shining Ones*, by D. J. Conway (see the Bibliography).

Communication

Amergin (M, Irish)
Baduh (M, Semitic—Messages)
Bharati (F, Hindu)
Fides (F, Roman—In good faith)
Gadel (M, Irish)
Hashye-Altye (M, Navajo)
Hermes (M, Greek)
Hu (M, Egyptian—Authority in)
Ikto (M, Sioux)
Imbaluris (F, Hittite)
Iris (F, Greek)
Mercury (M, Roman)
Nabu (M, Babylonian—Written)
Oghma (M, Irish—Written)
Pairikas (F, Persian)
Tashmit (F, Chaldean—Hearing)
Yach (F, Hindu—Mystical discourse)

Creativity

Apollo (M, Greek/Roman)
Athene (F, Greek)
Bragi (M, Norse)
Brighid (F, Irish)
Luonnotar (F, Finnish)

Maya (F, Hindu)
Muses* (F, Greek)
Namagiri (F, Hindu)
Odin (M, Norse)
Ptah (M, Egyptian)
Tvashtri (M, Hindu)
Veveteotl (M, Aztec)

Destiny, Fate

Agathadaimon (M, Egyptian)
Ananke (F, Greek)
Arachne (F, Greek)
Fa (M, Beninese)
Fortuna (F, Roman)
Meri (F, Chaldean)
Moerae, The* (F, Greek)
Nabu (M, Babylonian)
Shai (NB Egyptian)

Dedication, Devotion

Aramati (F, Hindu)
Ebisu (M, Japan—To occupation)
Fides (F, Roman—Promises)
Gaia (F, Greek—Oaths)
Ida (F, Hindu)

Divination, Oracles, Prophesy

Adraste (F, British)
Apollo (M, Roman)
Bannik (M, Slavic)
Carmenta (F, Roman)
Dione (F, Phoenician)
Egeria (F, Roman)
Evander (M, Roman)
Filia Vocis (F, Latin name for
   a Hebrew figure)
Gaia (F, Greek)
Gwendydd (F, Welsh)
Hecate (F, Greek)
Ida (F, Hindu)
Inanna (F, Sumerian)
Ishtar (F, Babylonian)
Kwan Yin (F, Chinese)
Mari (F, Basque)
Namagiri (F, Hindu)
Odin (M, Norse)
Phoebus Apollo (M, Greek)
Shamash (M, Babylonian)
Shaushka (F, Hittite)

Fertility, Fruitfulness, Productivity

Acat (M, Mayan)
Ahurani (F, Persian)
Aima (F, Hebrew)
Althea (F, Greek)
Amahita (F, Persian)
Anat (F, Canaanite)
Apollo (M, Greek/Roman)
Astarte (F, Canaanite)
Atargatis (F, Syrian)
Baal (M, Phoenician)
Bacchus (M, Greek)

Berchta (F, Teutonic)
Bona Dea (F, Roman)
Brimo (F, Greek)
Cupra (F, Etruscan)
Damara (F, British)
Dionysus (M, Greek)
Freya (F, Teutonic)
Isis (F, Egypt)
Lono (M, Polynesian)
Ma (F, Lydian)
Neith (F, Egyptian)
Phoebus Apollo (M, Greek)
Sati (F, Egyptian)
Wadj-wer (M, Egyptian)

Friendship

Maitri (F, Hindu)
Mithras (M, Persian)

Happiness, Joy

Amaterasu (F, Japanese)
Ataksak (M, Inuit)
Baldur (M, Norse)
Fu-Hsing (M, Chinese)
Hathor (F, Egyptian)
Hotei (M, Japanese)
Omacatl (M, Aztec)
Samkhat (F, Babylonian)
Tien Kuan (M, Chinese)

Health, Well-Being

Asclepius (M, Greek)
Apollo (M, Greek/Roman)
Brighid (F, Irish)
Diancecht (M, Irish)
Eir (F, Teutonic)

Eshmun (M, Phoenician)
Gula (F, Babylonian)
Hygeia (F, Greek)
Karusepas (F, Hittite)
Kedesh (F, Syrian)
Kwan Yin (F, Chinese)
Liban (F, Irish)
Salus (F, Roman)
Tien Kuan (M, Chinese)

Home Matters

Bannik (M, Slavic)
Cardea (F, Roman—Protection)
Da-Bog (M, Slavic)
Ougnai (F, Slavic)
Gucumatz (M, Mayan)
Hastehogan (M, Navajo)
Hestia (F, Greek)
Kikimora (F, Slavic)
Kitchen God (M, Chinese)
Neith (F, Egyptian)
Penates* (M, Roman)
Vesta (F, Roman)

Knowledge, Insight

Binah (F, Hebrew)
Buddhi (F, Tibetan)
Cerridwen (F, Welsh)
Deshtri (F, Hindu—Learning)
Gwion (M, Welsh)
Namagiri (F, Hindu—Teaching)
Hanuman (M, Hindu—
    Learning)
Hermes (M, Greek)
K'uei Hsing (M, Chinese—Tests)
Ormazd (M, Persia)
Shing Mu (F, Chinese)

Sia (M, Egyptian)
Tenjin (M, Japanese)
Toma (F, Tibetan)

Love, Romance

Amun Ra (M, Egyptian)
Anat (F, Canaanite)
Angus (M, Irish)
Aphrodite (F, Greek)
Belili (F, Sumerian)
Belit-ilanit (F, Chaldean)
Benten (F, Japanese)
Cupid (M, Roman)
Erzulie (F, Haitian)
Ishtar (F, Mesopotamian)
Kama (M, Hindu)
Venus (F, Roman)

Luck, Fortune

Agathadaimon (M, Egyptian)
Benten (F, Japanese)
Bonus Eventus (M, Roman)
Chala (F, Hindu)
Diakoku (M, Japanese)
Gansea (M, Hindu)
Kichijo-Ten (F, Japanese)
Lakshmi (F, Hindu)
Muses, The* (F, Greek)
Tamon (M, Japanese)

Magic (General, Including Psychic Ability)

Amathaon (M, Welsh)
Aunt Piety (F, Chinese)
Aradia (F, Italian)
Ayizan (F, Haitian)

Cemunnos (M, Celtic)
Cerridwen (F, Welsh)
Dakinis* (F, Tibetan—Psychic)
Diana (F, Roman)
Ea (M, Babylonian)
Etema (F, Chinese)
Gulleig (F, Teutonic)
Habondia (F, Medieval)
Hecate (F, Greek)
Herodias (F, Gaulish)
Holle (F, Teutonic)
Kwan Yin (F, Chinese)
Mari (F, Basque)
Odin (M, Norse)
Rangda (F, Hindu)
Untunktahe (M, Dakota)

Moon Magic

Al-Lat (F, Persian)
Anumati (F, Hindu)
Artemis (F, Greek)
Ashima (F, Samaritan)
Belili (F, Sumerian)
Callisto (F, Greek)
Diana (F, Roman)
Fati (M, Polynesian)
Gou (M, Beninese)
Hecate (F, Greek)
Iah (M, Egyptian)
Almaqah (M, Semitic)
Jerah (F, Canaanite)
Levanah (F, Chaldean)
Luna (F, Roman)
Mah (M, Persian)
Máni (M, Norse)
Re (F, Phoenician)
Selene (F, Greek)

Peace, Harmony, Restitution

Athene (F, Greek)
Concordia (F, Roman)
Forseti (M, Norse)
Harmonia (F, Greek)
Kuan-Ti (M, Chinese)
Pax (F, Roman)

Prosperity

Anna Koun (F, Hindu)
Anna Perenna (F, Roman)
Anu (F, Irish)
Benten (F, Japanese)
Buddhi (F, Hindu)
Daikoku (M, Japanese)
Inari (NB, Japanese)
Jambhala (M, Buddhist)
Lakshmi (F, Hindu)
Lu-Hsing (M, Chinese)
Ops (F, Roman)
Plutos (M, Greek)
Vasudhara (F, Buddhist)

Protection

Aditi (F, Hindu)
Atar (M, Persian)
Oichomage (F, Chilean)
Mars (M, Roman)
Nahmauit (F, Egypt)
Padmapani (M, Buddhist)
Prometheus (M, Greek)
Sheila-na-gig (F, Irish)
Shui-Kuan (M, Chinese)
Syen (M, Slavic—Home)
Thor (M, Norse)

Sexual Prowess/Enjoyment

Aphrodite (F, Greek)
Arami (F, Hindu)
Bes (M, Egyptian)
Hathor (F, Egyptian)
Heket (F, Egyptian)
Indrani (F, Hindu)
Lalita (F, Hindu)
Min (M, Egyptian)
Rati (F, Hindu)
Venus (F, Roman)
Yarilo (M, Slavic)

Strength/Courage

Achilles (M, Greek)
Athena (F, Greek)
Atlas (M, Greek)
Bellona (F, Roman)
Hercules (M, Roman)
Mars (M, Roman)
Morgan (F, Breton)
Muilidheartach (F, Scottish)
Neith (F, Egyptian)
Perseus (M, Greek)
Sita (F, Hindu)
Suwa (F, Arab)
Zorya (F, Slavic)

Solar Magic

Amaterasu (F, Japanese)
Amun Ra (M, Egyptian)
Apollo (M, Greek/Roman)
Asva (F, Hindu)
Aya (F, Babylonian)
Baldur (M, Norse)

Bast (F, Egyptian)
Bochica (M, Muisca)
Da-Bog (M, Slavic)
Dyaus (M, Hindu)
Eos (F, Greek)
Helios (M, Greek)
Hsi-Ho (F, Chinese)
Hyperion (M, Greek)
Igaehindvo (F, Native American)
Li (F, Chinese)
Maui (M, Polynesian)
Sul (F, British)
Surya (M, Hindu)

Travel

Akaru-Hime (F, Japanese—Water)
Bielbog (M, Slavic, Forest)
Ekchuah (M, Mayan)
Glaucus (M, Greek—Water)
Hasammelis (M, Hittite)
Kunado (M, Japanese—Roads)
Mercury (M, Roman)

Truth, Validity, Justice

Aleitheia (F, Gnostic)
Anase (M, African—Intermediary)
Apollo (M, Greek/Roman)
Astraea (F, Greek)
Erinyes* (F, Greek)
Filia Vocis (F, Latin)
Forseti (M, Norse)
Gibil (M, Babylonian—Arbitration)

Ida-Ten (M, Japanese—
 Legal matters)
Kukuri-Hime
 (F, Japanese—Mediation)
Ma'at (F, Egyptian)
Misharu (M, Babylonian—Rules)
Mithras (M, Persian)
Nusku (M, Babylonian)
Sin (F, Teutonic)
Tyr (M, Teutonic—Rules)
Varuna (M, Hindu—Justice)

Victory/Success

Hercules (M, Roman)
Korrovai (F, Hindu)
Nike (F, Greek)
Victoria (F, Roman)
Vijaya (F, Hindu)

Weather

Aeolus (M, Greek, Wind)
Agni (M, Hindu—Rain and
 Lightning)
Awhiowhio
 (M, Māori—Whirlwinds)
Gwalu (M, Nigerian—Rain)
Hadad (M, Babylonian—Storms)
Holle (F, Teutonic—Snow)
Jupiter (M, Roman)
Mama Quilla (F, Incan—Rain)
Mari (F, Basque)
Peroun (M, Slavic—Thunder)
Rainbow Serpent (M/F,
 Aboriginal Australian)
Rodasi (F, Hindu—Storm)
Sadwes (F, Persian—Rain)

Sarama (F, Japanese—Wind)
Saranyu (F, Hindu—Clouds)
Thor (M, Scandinavian—
 Thunder)
Tien Mu (F, Chinese—
 Lightning)
Tallai (F, Canaanite—Rain)

Wisdom

Atri (M, Hindu)
Baldur (M, Norse)
Bragi (M, Norse)
Buddha (M, Buddhist)
Dainichi (M, Japanese)
Ea (M, Babylonian)
Gasmu (F, Chaldean)
Heh (F, Egyptian)
Ekadzati (F, Tibetan—Mystical)
Metis (F, Greek)
Minerva (F, Roman)
Oannes (M, Babylonian)
Prajna (F, Hindu)
Shekinah (F, Hebrew)
Sophia (F, Gnostic)

* Indicates a plural deity

Appendix C

Handcrafting Magical Compounds

THROUGHOUT THIS MATERIAL SHARED HERE, crafts have been used to combine symbolic components into completed spells. The bonus in this process is that you can fashion durable items that radiate your magic, please the eye, and are inexpensive.

This section is a hands-on aid for readers who do not ordinarily make crafts. While it is easier to purchase an item to suit your magical goals, I strongly encourage making your own components. This saturates the tokens with personal energy and improves the outcome of your spellcraft.

CANDLES

A favorite childhood pastime to reclaim is making milk carton candles. For this, you will need to buy or save wax in a hue that matches your magical intention. Cut this into small pieces, then melt this slowly in a double boiler, over a low flame on the stove. Once it is melted, you can add extracts, oils, or finely powdered herbs that are coordinated to your spell's design. To accentuate this effort, work during an appropriate moon phase or sign.

Let the wax cool until a thin layer of solidified wax forms on top, then pour it into an empty, washed milk carton. Dangle your wick from the top of the carton, secured in place by a paper clip or clothespin. Once the wax has totally cooled, cut the paper away, carve any emblems you desire with a warm toothpick, needle, or knife, and store the candle for use. Light it any time you need that specific energy in your life.

Please be sure not to use the same pot for melting wax as you do for preparing food. Some waxes have dyes that are toxic. Keep old pots and pans for this job set aside from your other cookware.

Herb Pendulum

Herbal pendulums, usually employed for divinatory spells, are easily made with a bit of yarn or string and the herb you have chosen. Normally, the string or yarn is tied tightly around one end of an herb bundle with enough thread left over so the bundle can dangle freely when one end of the string is held in one hand. For spices like garlic buds that do not tie so easily make a small hole in the top of the herb using a needle or fine knife, then thread your string through as you would with a bead. The bay leaf pendulum shown here would be used for questions pertaining to personal fitness or psychic powers; the garlic pendulum is better suited to questions about safety, health, and protection.

These are pretty durable and can be reused. Otherwise, toss them in your compost pile when you're done.

Herb Strings and Bundles

Made similarly to herb pendulums, herb strings and bundles have diverse magical applications. Smaller versions are good additions to key chains for car keys or to rearview mirrors, where they release their scents to refresh an area and promote your magical aims. Larger versions can become household ornaments for walls, doorways, or windows. They can also be part of handfasting rituals (tying the hands together), house blessings (placed decoratively in a kitchen), and rites of passage (as a pathway to cross over).

For herbal strings, your components need to be secured to long strands of ribbon, thread, or cord. Fruit rinds work well on the strings since they are easily dried and threaded. Between each herb or rind add other embellishments like silk flowers. This makes the finished strand more ornate.

Herbal bundles should be made from already dried herbs. Arrange these as you would bouquets of flowers, only upside down. At the top of the bundle, crisscross your chosen ribbons or yarn to firmly secure the sheaf together. If you are planning to use thee as incense do not add any other ornamentation. Simply bless the item and keep it safe.

Alternatively, if the bundle is to be purely decorative, also affix flowers, bows, and other flourishes at the top or at the ends of the ribbons. At the back of the fixture, make a small loop out of either hanger wire or the ribbon itself, for fastening to a wall. Choose your ornamentation so it mirrors your spell. For Air magic, for example, add feathers, waxed leaves, and a small dab of almond oil.

INCENSE

Incense is effective as a meditative tool and a spell component because it releases its energy to the winds to augment your efforts. It is simple to prepare at home using dried herbs, dried flower petals, spices, and wood shavings or powders. Look at your spell and consider which components would be best. If you can match either the total number of ingredients or their color to the spell's purpose after you have considered their natural magical sympathies, so much the better. Just take care not to use too many ingredients. This can produce an incense that is too strong or unpleasant smelling.

I recommend a base of dried wood—approximately one-third of your mixture—as it will readily burn and ignite your other constituents. Herbs and flowers should be finely ground or powdered for even burning. Since you are not including any chemical additives, this type of incense will not ignite by itself. It requires a fire source, such as charcoal. Make as much or as little incense as you think you need. Keep the excess stored in an airtight container, properly labeled, for future magical rites.

For concentrated aromas, add small amounts of essential oil to the powdered base. This mixture should be allowed to dry completely before you store it, otherwise mold can develop. Drying is best accomplished on a wooden board. Cover the mixture with a cake pan to keep out any dust. Leave this to set for at least twenty-four hours. Be sure the powder is dry before transferring it to a container. Here are two sample recipes:

Blessing or Creativity

- 1 teaspoon lavender
- 1 teaspoon rosemary
- ¼ cup orange rind, powdered
- 1 teaspoon geranium petals, dried
- ½ cup powdered wood

Perspective

- 1 teaspoon anise flowers
- 1 teaspoon thyme
- ¼ cup lemon rind, powdered
- dried 1 teaspoon angelica
- ½ cup powdered wood

For all powdered incense, be sure to have a sturdy, fireproof burner that distributes heat evenly. In the center of this container, surround the charcoal with sand or dirt. Light the charcoal carefully—it sparks and pops a bit as it ignites. When the charcoal glows throughout, sprinkle your herbs on top. Scatter only a little at a time on the embers so you don't accidentally extinguish the coals. Once a pleasing level of aroma has been reached in the room, let the incense burn itself out.

Masks

Masks are employed most commonly for imitative magic. For a time, masks allow us to symbolically become a person, situation, problem, or animal. This mimicry helps direct and channel our magical energy.

Masks work best when made from very sturdy material or heavy cardboard that has been decorated in accord with the goal. Simple masks may cover only the eyes, thus hinting at the theme of your magic. More elaborate full-face masks can also be created. For the latter, use a thinner cardboard or try papier-mâché to match facial contours more closely.

For the paper or cardboard mask, begin by cutting your form and making spaces for any combination of eyes, nose, and mouth.

Shape these openings to match the type of mask you are creating. For example, a cat mask would have almond-shaped eyes. Use your knowledge of symbolism to visually empower your creation.

Next, add fake fur, crystals, leaves, flowers, beads, or whatever external decorations you can think of to amplify the impact. Finally, add a piece of string or elastic to each side so you can secure it over your face.

NUT CONTAINERS

Nutshells, especially walnut and coconut shells, make excellent components for magic because you can symbolically seal your magic within them. To use nut hulls for this purpose, break them dry before filling. Seal your other components inside using a little glue. External decorations such as ribbons can also be added. The only time the shell should be opened in the future is to release the magical energy it contains. Otherwise, it may be buried (to drive away sickness or evil), carried (for protection), or kept somewhere safe until needed.

OILS AND SOLUTIONS

Oils and solutions have several functions for spellcraft including anointing, scenting, and flavoring. In all three instances, the fundamental components of the concoction should be in harmony with your magical goals.

To prepare an herbal oil, first gather your herbs, preferably fresh ones, a dark bottle with a secure cap, and good quality oil. If the oil is to be used in cooking spells, use olive oil. Oils that will be used for external application can be of your own choosing, but consider trying almond oil for wonderful, aromatic results.

In a nonaluminum pan, warm the oil with the herbs over a low flame. Do not allow this to boil or scorch as that ruins the scent or flavor of your oil. Allow the whole mixture to cool, then place it in the dark bottle. I usually leave the herbs intermixed so the scent continues to improve with aging. In this form, the bottle can be placed in sunlight or moonlight to charge the preparation. Just take care not to leave the bottles too long in the sun. Some oils go rancid. Label and use as intended.

Solutions are weak teas that have the extra benefit of carrying only minute flavors for cooking spells, and mild aromas for those with allergies. The basic recipe is to soak 4 ounces of herbs in 8 ounces of water for two weeks (shake daily). If you find this is too strong for your personal taste, dilute it further after straining. Refrigerate for longevity.

For quicker preparation, warm the herbs and water together over a low flame until the water smells heady. Let this simmer down to about half the original volume, then cool and strain. This yields a stronger solution that can be diluted. Store in a cool, dark area or refrigerate.

POMANDERS

Citrus fruits are the base for this bit of enchanted decoration. Begin with a lemon, orange, grapefruit, or lime, and poke holes in the rind using a thin metal rod or toothpick. Place the holes so that they form a pleasing magical pattern around the whole fruit. Choose the pattern and the base fruit to match the objective of your spell.

Push whole cloves (allspice beads or other small round seeds can also be used) into the openings. Sprinkle the entire creation with orris root powder. Finally, secure a ribbon around the fruit for hanging in an area where you can enjoy its fragrant magic. Add essential oil as desired to refresh the scent. Pomander

POPPET OR FIGURINES

Cut a human outline with rounded edges from two pieces of fabric with their right sides together. The choice of fabric is purely personal. If the poppet is for yourself, fabric snipped from some of your old clothing is recommended.

Sew most of the poppet together, with the right side of the fabric still facing inward. Leave one area at the head unstitched.

Turn the poppet right side out, fill it, and then sew up the final hole. Add button eyes and other decorative items to personalize the finished figurine. Please remember that one should refrain from making poppets of other people without permission. This is a courtesy, and it shows respect for another's free will.

You can vary this pattern by substituting a glove for the poppet form (see also how to make favors under "Quests"). While this doesn't look like a person when it's completed, the glove poppet is marvelously quick and easy to make when time is essential.

The best type of glove is an old-fashioned, formal one that reaches just past your wrist (elbow-length gloves require a lot of stuffing). The fabric in these has a weave tight enough to contain fine herbs, but still release their scent. All but one of your seams is already sewn for you, so you can just tie the open end together like a sachet.

For outdoor use, a gardening glove filled with garlic and marigolds is a neat alternative that also repels bugs.

POUCHES

Pouches make nice protective coverings for amulets, power animal figurines, crystals, and the like. They can also become reusable sachets since they do not get permanently closed and can be manufactured from washable materials.

You begin your pattern using two five-byseven-inch pieces of fabric with like sides together. Sew the sides and bottom together, leaving about ⅔ inch at the top to add a channel for your drawstring. Fold this over ¼ inch at the top edge and press with an iron. Then fold the entire section downward. Stitch this in place, leaving the ends open so you can pull your cord through.

The drawstring can be made from sturdy yarn, ribbon, or a leather thong. Knot the ends of the drawstring, adding a large knot or bead to keep it from pulling out easily. Remember to choose your colors and fabric patterns so they match the intended magical use of the pouch. For example, use white for cleansing or protection, green for healing pouches, and red for energy.

PUZZLES

While we can't make puzzles quite as neatly as commercial manufac-
turers can, puzzles prepared from sturdy cardboard make wonderful
spell components for magic pertaining to connections, relationships,
and alliances.

To your next gathering, take a large piece of cardboard along with
paints, crayons, markers, and colored pencils. Place the cardboard
in the center of your sacred space. Have each person in turn help
decorate the board using emblems or patterns that symbolize their
role in that group.

Once the pattern is completed, each person cuts off a piece of the
whole and becomes responsible both for taking care of this token
and bringing it to meetings. Each time the group assembles, the
pieces get placed back into their original form to empower that
group's unity.

Alternatives here that provide a much more finished look are to
buy a commercial puzzle without a picture or to paint the picture
white. Then, either each person can choose their piece and decorate
it, or a full magical picture may be created and the pieces distributed
among your group.

ROBES

A sheet robe is very easy to construct with or without a sewing
machine. If you want the robe to be colored, simply dye the material
before cutting and sewing.

Begin by folding a sheet in half. Hold it up to yourself in this
form to be certain it is both wide enough and long enough for
your robe. If not, obtain a larger sheet. Flat king- and queen-sized
ones work very well.

Next, lay the folded sheet on the floor and place a long-sleeved
shirt that fits you well at the center top of the fabric. Using this as
your pattern, cut around the shirt. Leave 1–2 inches at each side
for seams. Do not cut along the bottom of the shin. Next, turn
the fabric inside out so you can hem the sleeves and put seams
along each side. Since you did not cut the bottom of the sheet,
the selvage edge of the sheet will not have to be hemmed; it is

already a finished edge. Also, turn the neckline under twice and secure it by hand or machine so it won't unravel. Finally, add silver trim for lunar festivals, a gold belt for solar observances, or other ornamentation as desired.

Sachets, Portable Charms, and Herb Pillows

Sachets may be handsewn or bundled. To start your sewn sachet, place two pieces of fabric (any size) with their right sides together. Sew three sides together, leaving one end open. Turn the open-ended pouch inside out so the seam is internal, then stuff it with herbal components. For example, a love sachet might include lavender, rose, and almond scent to encourage peace, love, and happiness, respectively.

Finish the final side by folding under each edge ¼inch and using a looping stitch with appropriately colored thread. For our love sachet, red or purple would be a good choice. Decorate the outside using fabric paint, beads, buttons, or appliques in various magical patterns to accentuate your goals.

Larger versions of this sachet, measuring twelve inches by twelve inches and upward, become herb pillows for dreams, sleep, and visionary magic. For a pillow, add a little lace to the edges as decoration, and use good quality, soft cloth that will be comfortable in bed or on other furniture.

The bundled version of the sachet/portable charm affords more flexibility in your magical goals. You can use any number of fabric pieces from one to eight. Consider matching the number of swatches symbolically to your magical goal.

The sachet made from one piece of cloth should measure at least five inches square to allow enough room for filling. This only needs a little ribbon to tie it together. Trim any excess fabric off the top. If the ribbon is long enough, secure feathers, shells, or other decorations to the ends for additional symbolism.

Make a sachet of multiple fabric pieces similarly, but instead lay out your fabric like a star. Since the fabric will overlap, use slightly thinner, rectangular pieces. Bundle these together in the same manner as the single-sheet sachet, using thread, ribbon, or yarn.

Spell Boxes

I originally discovered this idea in Marina Medici's book, *Good Magic (Medici 78)*. Find a special box to use only for spell work. To begin, look for something simple that you can decorate with personal symbols by carving or painting. Then, fill the box with herbs and crystals that mirror your spell's intention. In the center of the herbs place a piece of paper that details your desire.

To accent the magic further, place the box on your altar and surround it with appropriate colored candles and other sympathetic objects for a specific period of time. During this time, repeat your verbal components or affirmations. Leave the request in the box until it manifests. Afterward, you may retain the herbs for similar spells or burn them as incense.

Wands

Wands act like pointers to guide and direct your energy. To make one from wood or metal is not as difficult as you might initially think. One advantage to using metal is that you don't have to clean away any bark. In this case, find metal tubing of a comfortable size at your hardware store. Secure a crystal to one end and cover the other with fabric, leather, or other material for a grip. From here, you can get as elaborate as you like in detailing your wand, even to the point of engraving runes in the metal with etching tools.

For wood, I suggest soaking or sanding off the bark, as it has a tendency to fall away after a while. Once the branch is cleared, use a craft knife to carve out small holes for various crystals or herbs you want to affix. Unless you want to, you do not have to place a stone at either end since most branches have at least one natural point. A handgrip is still recommended.

Consider choosing your metals, wood base, crystals, and decorations so they all combine to accentuate the type of spell for which you are creating the wand.

If the wand is to be all-purpose, it is nice to feature each of the elements in the finished wand, with the base being of one element and the decorative items taking care of the other three. For example, to a wand made of willow wood (for Water), fire agate and cat's-eye could be affixed for Fire and Earth, respectively. As a finishing touch, feathers could be hung from the handle to represent Air. This way, no matter what kind of magic you are working, at least one aspect of your wand will respond to that energy.

WIND CHIMES

Depending on their construction, wind chimes can inspire a variety of magical energies throughout your home. To create simple chimes, you need either a square or a circle of wood. Depending on how you plan to hang the chime, drill holes either all around the outside of the base or on just one side. Through these holes, insert sturdy strings. Next, using knots, to the strings attach stones, nuts, ceramic tiles, small bottles, nutshell charms, beads, small metal tubes, pieces of wood, feathers, bells, seashells, or other appropriate components. Make sure to tie the objects together closely so they will strike other sections of the chime when the wind blows.

If the strings are suspended around the full circumference of the base, you will also need a central clapper. Make this from another piece of wood or plastic. Wood is more natural, but plastic will endure the elements better and may be taken from your recycling bin!

As with all magical tools, the decorative items you choose for your chime should reflect its intended use. They should also be durable enough to withstand weather changes and blustery winds. Place the chime where the appropriate winds will reach it.

If a part of your chime gets broken, be certain to replace it, blessing the whole collection again before remounting.

WOVEN MATS

Weaving together strips of paper or fabric is an effective method for working magic related to forming connections and networks. This technique visually intertwines your spell with the base medium to increase sympathetic energy. Weavings can also function as knots do: each time a strand is unwoven, it releases the energy it contains.

To make such an object, think back to your days at summer camp when you may have made potholders by moving circles of fabric together in an over-under pattern. If you want fancier ideas, check beginner's books on macramé and woven wall hangings. If the mat represents a group of people, it is best to have each person pick their own material to represent their spirit. This way the finished product blends unity from diversity quite literally, giving greater potency to the magic.

WREATHS

Wreaths can be made in many sizes, shapes, and materials. Everything from fabric tubes to young branches can become a foundation. To this base add silk flowers, herbs, feathers, ribbons, bows, and assorted charms to support your magical intentions.

For fabric cube wreaths, gently stuff three long pieces of cloth with pliable herbs or commercial cotton stuffing so that they are not stiff but rounded out. Braid these pieces together, then connect the two ends into a circle. Any frills you wish to add should be sewn on so you don't run the risk of losing important parts over time.

Alternatively, when using grapevines or thin rose branches, soak the wood first so it becomes pliable, then fashion it into the wreath configuration. Wear gardener's gloves when doing this so you don't get poked and scratched.

The nice part about simple circular wreaths is that the emblem itself is one of unending motion. This naturally helps keep the energy of your magic moving! Affix other components to the wooden wreath using fine wire or even thread. Always work around your wreath in a clockwise manner so that the power placed there is positive and life-affirming. Soak the wood first so it becomes pliable, then fashion it into the wreath configuration. Wear gardener's gloves.

BIBLIOGRAPHY

Alexander, Marc. *British Folklore*. Crescent Books, 1982.

Baer, Randall N., and Vicki V. Baer. *The Crystal Connection*. San Francisco: Harper& Row, 1986.

Banis, Victor. *Charms, Spells & Curses for the Millions*. Sherbourne Press, 1970.

Baroja, Julio Caro *The World of Witches*. Weidenfeld & Nicolson, 1964.

Bartlett, John. *Familiar Quotations*. Little, Brown & Co., 1938.

Becker, Howard, and Barnes, Harry Elmer. *Social Thought from Lore to Science*. Dover Publications, 1960.

Beyerl, Paul. *Master Book of Herbalism*. Phoenix Publishing, 1984.

Black, William George. *Folk Medicine*. Bun Franklin Co., 1883.

Bravo, Brett. *Crystal Healing Secrets*. Warner Books, 1988.

Broth, Patricia, and Don Broth. *Food in Antiquity*. Frederick A. Praeger, 1969.

Brown, Peter. *The World of Late Antiquity*. Thames & Hudson, 1971.

Browne, Lewis. *The Believing World*. Macmillan Company, 1959.

Bouland, Margaret. *Old Wives' Lore for Gardeners*. Farrar, Straus & Giroux, 1976.

Budge, E. A. Wallis. *Amulets & Talismans*. University Books, 1968.

Burland, C. A. *The Magical Arts*. Arthur Barker, 1966.

Carroll, David. *The Magic Makers*. Arbor House, 1974.

Cavendish, Richard. *A History of Magic*. Taplinger Publishing, 1977.

Cavendish, Richard, ed. *Man, Myth and Magic*. Purnell, 1972.

Clark, Linda A. *The Ancient Art of Color Therapy*. Devin Adair Co., 1975.

Clarkson, Rosetta. *Green Enchantment.* Macmillian Publishing, 1940.

Complete Book of Fortune. Crescent Books, 1936.

Conway, D. J. *Ancient Shining Ones.* Llewellyn Publications, 1993.

Cooper, J. C. *Symbolic and Mythological Animals.* Aquarian Press, 1992.

Cristiani, R. S. *Treatise on Perfumery.* Baird & Co., 1877.

Crowley, Brian, and Esther Crowley. *Words of Power.* Llewellyn Publications, 1991.

Cunningham, Lady Sara. *Magical Virtues of Candles, Herbs, Incense and Perfume.* Aleph Books, 1979.

Cunningham, Scott. *Encyclopedia of Magical Herbs.* Llewellyn Publications, 1988.

Cunningham, Scott. *The Magic in Food.* Llewellyn Publications, 1991.

Davison, Michael Worth, ed. *Everyday Life Through the Ages.* Reader's Digest Association Limited, 1992.

Drury, Neville. *Dictionary of Mysticism and the Occult.* Harper & Row, 1985.

Edwards, Tryon. *New Dictionary of Thoughts.* Standard Book Company, 1936.

Farrar, Janet, and Stewart Farrar. *Spells and How They Work.* Phoenix Publishing, 1990.

—. *The Witches' God.* Phoenix Publishing, 1989.

—. *The Witches' Goddess.* Phoenix Publishing, 1987.

Felding, William J. *Strange Superstitions and Magical Practices.* Paperback Library, 1968.

Finley, J. *Sorcery.* Routledge and Kegan, 1985.

Forbes, T. Rogers. *The Midwife and the Witch.* Yale University Press, 1966.

Frazer, Sir James George. *The Golden Bough.* Macmillan, 1922.

Gordon, Lesley. *Green Magic.* Viking Press, 1977.

Graves, Robert. *The Greek Myths.* Penguin Publishing, 1983.

Gregor, Arthur S. *Amulets, Talismans, and Fetishes.* Scribner's, 1975.

Haggard, Howard. *Mystery, Magic, and Medicine.* Doubleday and Co., 1933.

Hall, Manly. *Secret Teachings of All Ages.* Philosophical Research Society, 1977.

Harlan, William. *Illustrated History of Eating and Drinking Through the Ages.* American Heritage Publishers, 1968.

Hendricks, Rhonda. *Mythologies of the World.* McGraw-Hill, 1979.

Hume, Paul. *The Grimoire.* FASA Corporation, 1992.

Kieckhefer, Richard. *Magic in the Middle Ages.* Cambridge University Press, 1989.

Kunz, G. Frederick. *Curious Lore of Precious Stones.* Dover Publications, 1971.

Laver, James. *Costume.* Jr. Heritage Books, 1956.

Leach, Maria, ed. Standard Dictionary of Folklore, Mythology and Legend. *Funk & Wagnalls, 1972.*

Leek, Sybil. *Cast Your Own Spell.* Pinnacle, 1970.

Loewe, Michael, ed. *Oracles and Divination.* Shambhala Publishing, 1981.

Lorie, Peter. *Superstition.* Labyrinth Publishing, 1992.

Mariechild, Diane. *Mother Wit.* Crossing Press, 1988.

Medici, Marina. *Good Magic.* Macmillan, 1988.

Monaghan, Patricia. *The Book of Goddesses & Heroines.* Llewellyn Publications, 1981.

Morrison, Sarah. Modern *Witch's Spellbook.* Carol Communications, 1971–1986.

Murray, Keith. *Ancient Rites and Ceremonies.* Tudor Press, 1980.

Mystical Year. Mysteries of the Unknown series. Time-Life Books, 1992.

Oesterly, W. O. E. *The Sacred Dance.* Dance Horizons, 1923.

Opie, Iona, and Moira Tatem, eds. *Dictionary of Superstition.* Oxford University Press, 1989.

Ostrander, Sheila, and Lynn Schroeder. *Handbook of Psychic Discoveries.* Berkeley Medallion Books, 1974.

Paulsen, Kathryn. The Complete Book of Magic and Witchcraft. *Signet, 1971.*

—. *Witches, Potions and Spells.* Peter Pauper Press, 1971.

Riotte, Louise. *Sleeping with a Sunflower.* Garden Way Publishing, 1987.

Rodales' Complete Illustrated Encyclopedia of Herbs. *Rodale Publishing, 1987.*

Russell, J. B. *Witchcraft in the Middle Ages.* Cornell University Press, 1972.

Scott, Rev. J. Loughran. *Bulfinch's Age of Fable.* David McKay, 1898.

Sheen, Joanna. *Flower Crafts.* Salamander Bocks, 1992.

Shumaker, Wayne. *The Occult Sciences in the Renaissance.* University of California Press, 1972.

Singer, Charles. *From Magic to Science.* Dover, 1958.

Skinner, Charles M. Myths and Legends of Flowers, Trees, Fruits, and Plants. *Lippincott, 1925.*

Spence, Lewis. *Encyclopedia of the Occult.* Bracken Books, 1988.

Starhawk. *The Spiral Dance: A Rebirth of the Ancient Religion of the Great Goddess.* Harper & Row, 1979.

Tarostar. *Witch's Spellcraft.* International Imports, 1986.

Telesco, Patricia. *Folkways.* Llewellyn Publications, 1994.

—. *A Victorian Flower Oracle.* Llewellyn Publications, 1994.

Walker, Barbara. *Women's Dictionary of Symbols and Sacred Objects.* Harper & Row, 1988.

Whitlock, Ralph. *A Calendar of Country Customs.* B.T. Batsford, 1978.

Witches and Witchcraft. Mysteries of the Unknown series. Time-Life Books, 1991.

Wootton A. *Animal Folklore, Myth and Legend.* Blanford Press, 1986.

Zolar. Zolars' Encyclopedia of Ancient and Forbidden Knowledge. *Simon and Schuster, 1970.*

BIBLIOGRAPHY